Praise for *Sylvie*
also by Sharon Kreider

Readers are talking about ...

"This is a wonderful book that reminds us of what it truly means to be human, to feel grief, to have doubts, and to have hope despite it all."

"This is a must-read for parents of teens, particularly the parents of pre-teens and teenage girls."

"Sylvie's story captured my heart, was beautifully poetic, and hard to put down."

"Simultaneously heartwarming and heart-wrenching, this book takes the reader on an emotional journey that is not to be missed!"

"Page turner—best book I've read in a decade."

"I found Sylvie to be a gripping and necessary read."

"A sensitive and deep exploration of love and loss."

"Everyone should read this book."

"This book is a page-turner and heartbreaker. Wonderfully written and deep in meaning."

Wandering
...a long way past the past

Also by Sharon Kreider

Sylvie
A Women's Fiction Novel

Wandering
...a long way past the past

Sharon Kreider

Wandering
… a long way past the past
© 2022 by Sharon Kreider. All rights reserved.

This book is a memoir.
It reflects the author's present recollections of experiences over time. To protect the privacy of certain individuals, some names and characteristics have been changed, some events have been compressed, as well as altering a few distinguishing details. The conversations in the book all come from the author's recollections, though they are not written to represent word-for-word transcripts. Rather, the author has retold them in a way that evokes the feeling and meaning of what was said.

All rights reserved, including the right to reproduce
this book or portions thereof in any form whatsoever.

Book Consultant: Judith Briles, The Book Shepherd
Editors: Barb Wilson, Peggie Ireland
Map illustrator: Natalie Aline Kreider
Author photo: Janel Gion
Cover, Interior Design, and eBook conversion:
Rebecca Finkel, F+P Graphic Design, FPGD.com

Books may be purchased in quantity by contacting
Gray Wolf Books | www.graywolfbooks.com

Library of Congress Control Number: 2022909102
hard cover: 978-1-7372393-3-8
softcover: 978-1-7372393-4-5
eBook: 978-1-7372393-5-2
audiobook: 978-1-7372393-6-9

Memoir | Travel | India | Life
First Edition
Printed in the USA

For Rea, Peter, and Natalie

Author's Note

What am I doing?
Where am I going?
Who am I?

Carrying a small backpack filled with minimal trekking gear and one change of clothes, I hopped on a plane from my native Canada to England and started my overland solo adventure from Europe to Asia—eager for a fresh start, a new beginning. The year was 1976 and I was 22.

I toured the best places in Britain—the Lakes District; Scotland; Wales; followed by a bus ride through France, Germany, and Yugoslavia, heading to Greece. After visiting the Greek Islands, I procured a sailboat ride to Turkey and began the journey to Nepal via Iran, Afghanistan, Pakistan, and India.

Once in Nepal, I obtained two trekking visas: one to the Mount Everest base camp via Sir Edmund Hillary's original route and the other for Muktinath in eastern Nepal. With my visas in hand, I hiked into the Himalayas without a plan, a good map, or knowledge about the terrain.

Traveling through the Middle East and Asia prior to the age of the internet or cellphones, the rise in tourism, and the wars of recent years, was nothing short of magical. The world felt vast and mysterious as if secrets were hidden in the landscape. Most everywhere I went, I got lost and often had to rely on the kindness of strangers to progress from one place to the other.

On several occasions, especially in uncharted territory such as Iran prior to the overthrow of the Pahlavi Dynasty, I had to examine my belief system and ask myself fundamental questions: What am I doing? Where am I going? Who am I?

The opportunities seemed as endless as counting stars on a clear night.

At the risk of sounding cliché, I yearned to truly live my life—and the story you are about to read did transform me in almost every way. My sense of smell deepened from all the different pungent, aromatic, and flavorful spices and foods I ate, many for the first time. I listened to Bollywood tunes blasting from Middle Eastern lorries and the soulful sound of Ravi Shankar's sitar in Varanasi. Learning new languages provided another challenge, and a profound affair altered just about everything I thought I knew about love, forcing me to discover how to be freer than I had ever been in my life.

At the beginning of my adventure, I knew little about the history of the countries I was about to visit. Nor did I realize how much those experiences would alter my view of the world—so much so that I ended up living in India from the summer of 1977 until the early autumn of 1979.

I have tried to recreate events, locales, and conversations from my memories of them. To protect privacy, I have changed the names of certain individuals and some identifying characteristics and details, such as places of residence. The conversations in this memoir all come from my best recollection, though they are not written to represent word-for-word transcripts. Rather, I have retold them in a way that evokes the feeling and meaning of what was said, the essence of those conversations.

I've longed to write this memoir for many years, especially with the continued unrest in many of the countries I visited. The world seems much more fragile now.

I don't have many pictures of that time since it was difficult to travel with the bulky camera equipment and vinyl film of the 1970s.

There is one photo of me, taken in 1978, from an ashram in Kashmir, sitting cross-legged on a woven straw mat, my long hair whipping off my face from a light breeze, and my eyes full of wonder. This is me ... this was me.

Nepal
and surrounding territories

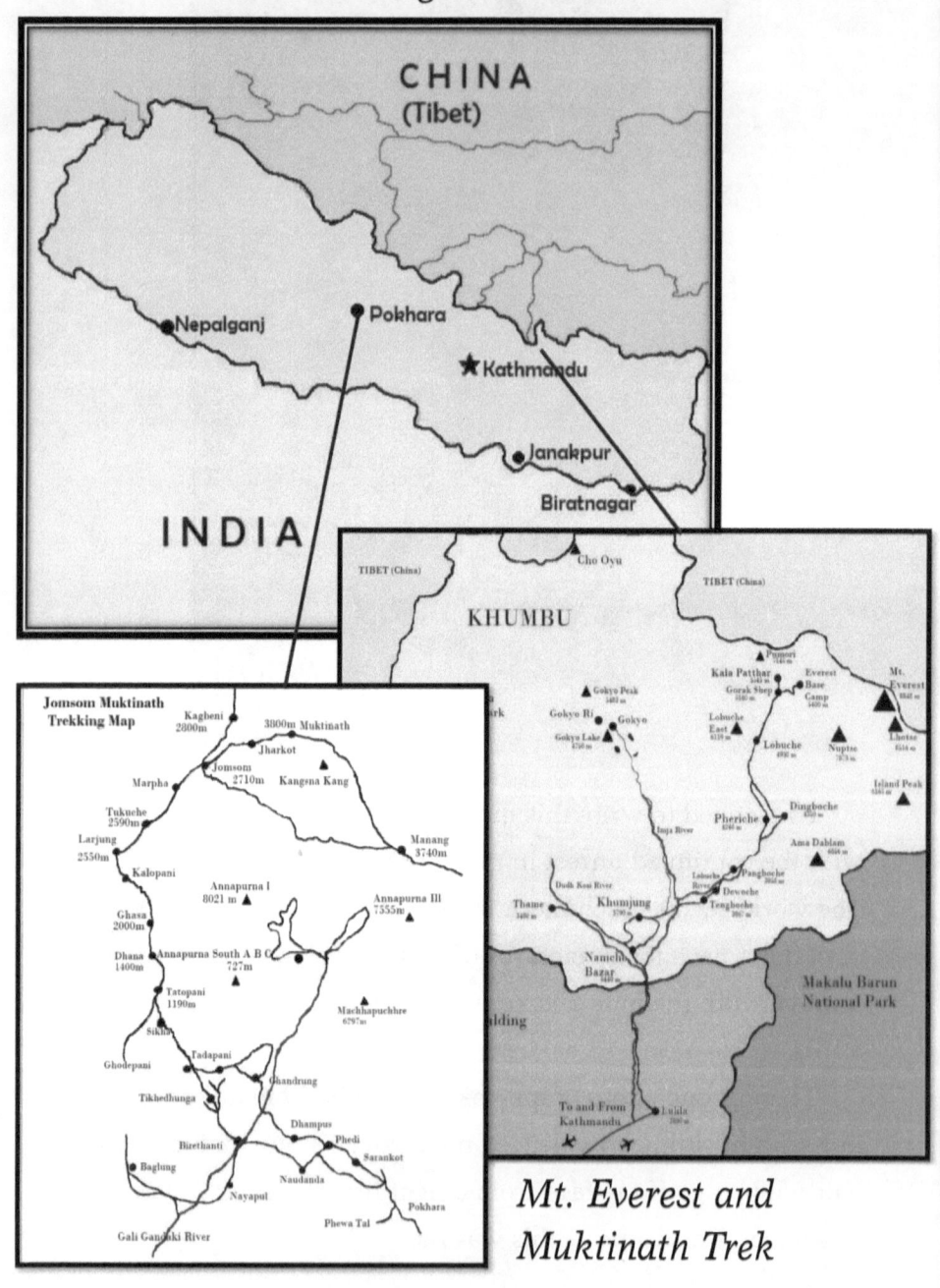

Mt. Everest and Muktinath Trek

1

Nepal – April 1977

*At the time, it never occurred to me it might
be wise to at least be a little afraid.*

Perspiration pooled underneath my shirt as I watched Nepalese villagers working in the lime-green rice paddies and golden barley fields; women in flowing ruby-colored dresses tending the young pastures while the men worked tirelessly alongside them with their hoes. Behind them, the sapphire sky was filled with billowing clouds looking like giant cotton balls.

The bus I chose to travel on, crammed with Indian and Nepalese people and a few chickens, made its steady upward grind on a narrow dirt road. Glassless windows let in the warm morning light and a constant stream of dust. Tattered seats revealed the rusted springs underneath, and pieces of the ceiling paint fell into the crowded aisles.

Every once in a while, children would sneak a peek at me, the "Ma'am Sahib," giggle, and then turn back to converse with their families in their native Nepali, their voices soft and rhythmic.

After four months, traversing the land between the British Isles and India, I was finally in Nepal and ready to do the Mount Everest base camp trek.

In the early evening, I arrived at the Katmandu bus station, a soiled patch of barren earth. Passengers got off the bus and collected their belongings, the late daylight filtering through the haze of kicked-up dirt.

I went up to a tin hut, which served as the bus depot ticket station, and tried to sound confident. "Excuse me, do you speak English?"

The vendor in his threadbare jacket, jet-black hair combed back in the style of the nineteen-fifties, shook his head from side to side–a typical Indian motion meant to imply, *of course, of course*. "Yes, yes, Ma'am Sahib, what is it you need?"

> I picked the cleanest doorway with no litter out front.

I let out a sigh. "Oh, good, you speak English. Do you know where I can spend the night?

"Oh, yes, yes, Ma'am Sahib. Freak Street for you." He snapped his fingers, and a bicycle rickshaw driver pedaled toward me.

"Ma'am Sahib, Ma'am Sahib," he yelled. "I take you hotel, yes. Best ride here. Best driver, yes. Especially best, Ma'am Sahib."

In the 1970s, most Westerners visiting Katmandu stayed on Freak Street, an area where young people from all over the world congregated for the beauty and peace of Nepal, trying to find Nirvana in Buddhism or Hinduism, and for others, in drugs.

With makeshift hotels on either side, Freak Street could barely accommodate a car. People, rickshaws, cows, dogs, chickens, pigeons, monkeys, and tons of finely powdered dust filled the thoroughfare. The small inns were so squished next to each other, it was hard to distinguish when one lodge ended and the other began. Some entrances were as small as a doorframe.

Most displayed a clutter of hand-painted signs written in Nepali and broken English. "Hotel Annapurna," "Hotel Yak," or "Hotel Karma." "Best place," "Cheap," "No bedbugs." I picked the cleanest doorway with no litter out front.

A thin Nepalese man wearing a long shirt tended the undersized desk. "Welcome, Ma'am Sahib. You share room?"

"No. I'm alone. Just a single room, thank you."

He stared. "Ma'am Sahib alone? No family? No friends?"

I shook my head. "No. I'm by myself."

"Mmmmm. No good Ma'am Sahib by her lonesome."

He showed me a tiny area on the second floor with a cot and an open, screenless window with heavy wooden shutters. I didn't think the shutters would do anything to muffle the sound of the street noises, conversations from the next room, or merchants shouting outside.

I paid for the hotel room, dropped my backpack off at my room, and went out to find something to eat. There were several small restaurants near the hotel, but I ended up buying *chapattis* and rice from a street peddler, preferring to stand and watch the sky turn from light orange to bluish purple with one or two twinkling stars.

When I headed back to the hotel, I paused to admire the quaint city: terra-cotta sculptures; red shrines, golden *stupas*, monastic courtyards, and exquisite stone statuettes; old buildings with carved images of gods and goddesses and sunken waterspouts; a trader making chai over a pail of crimson charcoal; dogs eating the day's scraps; chanting from a nearby temple; a family carrying their children on their backs.

It felt as if I had stepped back in time.

The next morning, I waited in line for several hours at the Nepal Tourist Bureau, a small primitive structure, for my turn to apply for a trekking permit into roadless Nepal. I listened to a group of scientists and climbers, trying to gather information for my trek as questions swirled in my mind.

Would I meet any of these people later? Would the original route to Mount Everest base camp be a wise choice? Would I see any other trekkers during the first week of travel through the jungle?

"Next." A small Nepalese man motioned for me to come up to his booth. "Your group?"

"No, I do not have a group."

"Sherpa?"

"No, I'm doing this on my own."

His eyes widened. "Porter?"

"No. I have everything I need in my pack. I plan on taking rupees to pay for shelter and food at teahouses, or maybe stay with families."

At the time, it never occurred to me it might be wise to at least be a little afraid.

After all, I had been traveling alone for six months. During that time, I had survived an uprising in Iran, an attack from a Bulgarian truck driver, heatstroke on the road to Syria, and was almost robbed at an Afghani border crossing.

He put down his pen and opened his mouth as if to say something, then picked up a metal stamp pad and embossed my permit. "You pay sixty-four rupees," he said and shook his head.

I counted out the blue and pink rupee notes. "Ten, twenty... sixty-four," placing them in a neat pile on the counter and I picked up my six-week permit.

The man mumbled, "Lonesome no good."

I compiled a list of things to do before leaving Katmandu: buy peanut butter and a pair of used wool socks from the expedition store near Freak Street; find a tailor in the central market to repair my jacket; go to the bank and get one hundred and fifty American dollars converted into one-dollar-equivalent rupee notes.

At the time, one American dollar was worth about eight rupees, and teahouses on the trek charged only a few rupees for a simple room and local food—maybe fifty cents a day. Basic food items consisted of rice, whole wheat *chapattis*, curried lentils, spinach or potatoes, and an abundant supply of tea. Cheese and yoghurt were luxuries.

Katmandu, the capital of Nepal, at an elevation of forty-six hundred feet, was surrounded by the tallest mountains in the world. The two-thousand-year-old nerve center sat in a large bowl-shaped valley and supported a flourishing Hindu and Buddhist society. Most of the people spoke Nepali, but English could also be heard in the marketplace.

A small outdoor store owned by two American men nestled among the local vendors. This store sold imported groceries: packages of freeze-dried foods; cans of fruit; condensed milk; and tins of peanut butter, as well as a wide variety of used expedition equipment and hardware. I bought a small can of peanut butter and a used pair of wool socks for the same price as a three-night stay in Katmandu.

"Yah, yah, we flyin' to Lukla, then hiking—ah—Thyangboche," said someone in a small group of European men. I guessed them to be from Switzerland.

"We're taking the bus to Pokhara and then doing the Annapurna Sanctuary," asserted two Americans.

"I'm hoping to catch up with two of me mates near Ama Dablam," uttered an Australian man. A woman looked at me but said nothing.

I decided to join in on the conversation. "I'm doing the Mount Everest trek starting southwest of Jiri, the original starting point. You know, where Hillary started his trek before the road extended farther north."

"Well, I think it's a lot of unnecessary hiking if you ask me. Why walk those extra weeks when a sixty-dollar plane ride can land you within two days of Namche Bazaar? Useless if you ask me," said one of the American men as he easily slipped his large backpack over his muscular frame.

> Our styles couldn't be more different.

"I want to see it. I think it'll be fun to be in an area where foreigners have not been for a while. Maybe I'll catch a glimpse of Nepal before tourism arrived." I was thrilled to be going into a part of the country where people grew their own food without modern machinery, did not drive cars or watch television, or even listen to the radio.

He smirked. "Suit yourself."

I watched him saunter out the door. Our styles couldn't be more different.

Next morning, en route at last, I swayed in my seat as the rudimentary bus, overflowing with mostly native peoples, heaved its way up the valley and then zigzagged higher into the foothills before disgorging all of us on the side of the road.

Chaos ensued, with families and porters fighting to claim their luggage or merchandise. Men shouted, women consoled crying children, a few boys peed in the nearby bushes, chickens clucked, goats bayed, and dogs barked. Then the bus driver waved, turned the bus around, kicked up a cloud of dirt, and headed back to Katmandu.

Porters and families put their hefty loads into oversized baskets and lifted them onto their backs with an attached strap stretching underneath the basket and continuing over the crown of their heads. Much of their cargo weighed at least eighty or a hundred pounds. Barefooted, some porters didn't even use the basket; they simply manipulated the strap to rest huge boxes of commodities on their backs.

Self-consciously, I slipped on my twenty-pound pack and followed them in my snug hiking boots.

It didn't take long before we reached a precipitous, north-western-facing hill, and the crowd thinned into a lengthy line. Wide enough for one person, the trail went straight uphill—no switchbacks, just steep, rocky terrain.

Feeling a little panicked, I checked the small handwritten map given to me at the permit station. *Is this it?*

Struggling to find Nepali words to ask if I was on the right trail, I asked a porter who passed me: "Janu? Namche Bazaar?"

"Ho. Thada. Namche." He pointed to the top of the hill and asked a few other questions I could not understand.

I replied with the one Nepali word I knew to mean *thank you*, "Dhanyabad," and paused for a moment. *Wow, this is tough.*

> **My stomach felt hard and hot like a brick in the sun.**

The steep incline left me fighting for breath. I fell behind quickly.

After a vertical, thousand-foot climb to a ridge, followed by a two-mile walk along a slender footpath, I saw my first destination spot in the distance and stopped to rest, quickly realizing all the people from the bus were long gone. I had tried to keep pace with the Sherpas and porters, but they zoomed up the slope, as if they were long-distance runners.

The sun, an orange ball, slipped behind a jade-green hillside.

As I approached a picturesque settlement of thatched homes on a knoll above terraced paddies, about a dozen or more dogs started to yelp and bark wildly before they formed a pack and came running straight toward me.

They rapidly made a circle around my body, showing their teeth, their backs raised for an attack, growling and howling like feral creatures ready for battle. One of the dogs started to nip at my boots. Terrified, my whole body went rigid, and my stomach felt hard and hot like a brick in the sun.

Suddenly, a silver-and-black dog jumped as high as my throat, and my heart picked up speed. Disoriented, I looked around, gauging if I could back away or escape.

Then, in my peripheral vision, I saw an older man, who I assumed to be the village elder, emerge from a very small hut. He waved and started walking, trailing several children behind him. When he was about twenty feet away, his mouth broke into a huge smile, and my breath released slowly like a deflating balloon.

The dogs raced to their village leader and proudly trotted back with him. Their snarls diminished to high-pitched yaps as if they were trying to convince their master, "She is not one of us. Don't let her in."

> I thought I was going to pass out.

When the distance between us closed, he extended his hand. His wrinkled eyes sparkled in the fading light, and his skin color was brown and leathery from years in the sun.

I extended my hand, eager to cement our camaraderie and quiet the dogs.

The moment I touched the elder's hand, two of the larger dogs ran behind me and bit into my calves with such viciousness, they tore through my pants and into the skin, leaving four enormous, deep puncture wounds. My chest tightened as if I couldn't get enough oxygen, and my fingers went numb. I thought I was going to pass out.

Time suspended for a moment, and then, everything seemed to move in slow motion.

The elder, along with several other village men who seemed to appear out of nowhere, ordered the dogs away and apologized in their native tongue—or at least they acted contritely. The dogs retreated to their respective homes, occasionally looking back at me as if to say, "remember who's boss."

The chief began to shout commands. Two village men grabbed my arms and helped me walk into their community.

Dazed, I felt no pain as I limped through their village before we stopped at a small shelter with a straw roof. An older woman, stooped over a walking stick, emerged through a doorway covered with a muddy blanket. The village elder spoke to her.

She had long, white braids pinned to the top of her head and a smile that creased across her robust face; the glisten in her eyes resembling a clear morning after a rain. A woven plum-colored jacket fit snugly around her slight frame, and a russet-colored skirt covered her felt boots. She said a few more words to the head villager, took my hand, and led me into her simple home.

I couldn't take my eyes off her.

Squinting in the dim light, I laid down on a wool blanket. The woman lit a few candles and busied herself for several minutes boiling water. When the water was hot, she gestured for me to remove my pants and lie face down. Chanting, she placed hot cloths on my wounds and washed the damaged skin. Every time she touched my skin, I flinched.

After that, she rubbed a lime-colored ointment all over my lower legs, placing a little bit extra on the open areas, which felt cool and comforting. She ended by wrapping my calves in clean strips of white cotton.

By candlelight, I watched her make tea and bake flatbread on her primitive stove. We didn't speak.

She put an ashen powder in my tea and said something that I thought meant, "drink it all."

I don't remember much after that because I fell asleep.

The next morning, I woke to the sun streaming through the doorway. I looked around and saw no one, only dust mites dancing in the golden light.

How long had I slept?

Blood had dried through the cloth bandages. When I unraveled the cotton bands, my calves looked like a patchwork of blue, green, and black. The adrenaline rush that overrode the pain the night before had since passed, and now my legs howled in a chorus of complaints. My head throbbed. I felt confused and insecure.

What to do? Go back to Katmandu? What if I had rabies? What if the punctures got infected? Do I need stitches?

As I mulled over these thoughts, the medicine woman came in. She touched my calves and nodded. I got lost in her eyes for a moment when she touched my face, her caress velvety smooth, and swallowed the lump in my throat. As I drank tea, she methodically reapplied the ointment and new strips of fabric.

My heart sunk at the thought of turning back. It was only day two.

I just couldn't let this stand in the way of my dreams, so I decided not to listen to the *what-ifs* and packed up.

When I emerged from the hut, a woman from the village offered me a mango and two warm *chapattis* wrapped in a clean rag. The young boy, who I assumed was her son, handed me a walking stick.

I looked at these gentle people and placed my hands in the prayer position. "Namaste. Namaste. Dhanyabad."

> **Feeling like a six year old, I burst into tears.**

Grandmother watched me leave the village and waved every time I turned to look back. When the trail came to a bend, and I could no longer see the community, I stopped, folded my arms under my breasts, and looked at what lay ahead. Miles of heavily vegetated hills undulated sharply and incessantly to meet snowcapped peaks in the distance.

That seems a long way.

I sat on a rock outcropping and closed my eyes. My legs hurt. My shoulders ached from carrying a twenty-pound pack. The hip belt dug into my low back. I doubted my ability to go another step.

Feeling like a six year old, I burst into tears.

In the weeks to come, I would learn that the long route into the Himalayas consisted of countless ridges and passes—an extensive skyward journey into a magnificent, massive mountain system; ascending one day to a high ridge or pass only to descend into a valley the next day with a fast river flowing at the bottom.

Crossing these rivers was sometimes challenging, as there was usually nothing more than narrow, unsteady bridges made of wood and woven fiber strung from a tree on one side of the river to another tree on the opposite shore.

I often felt a little like a character out of *Lord of the Rings*, except I was alone, not with a band of friends.

2

Canada – 1959

I pushed those memories so deep
inside my consciousness that they got
all twisted up with my nightmares.

One of my earliest memories was sitting on a man's lap with his hand down my white underpants. He touched my private parts and stuck his finger inside of me. I didn't want him to do that, and when I tried to squirm away, he held me tighter.

"*Ssshhh.* Stay still," he whispered in my ear.

We sat in a rocking chair on an open verandah facing a street. I watched a car drive by, wishing I could be in that car.

When the man had had his way with me, he stopped and put me down. "Just don't stand there; pull up your panties."

I glanced down at my underwear around my ankles and quickly lifted them up under my dress. I was four years old.

I never could put a face on that man.

When I look back on my early childhood, the only memories I recall are of me crying. Standing on a bridge with tissue stuffed in my pockets, my father said, "Smile."

I just kept sobbing.

In the summer of 1959, just before I turned six, a woman with red hair and red lipstick, dressed in a purple outfit with matching high heels, took my hand and said, "Let's go for a walk."

We strolled down a street, past the house with the white wraparound porch and the house with the blooming rose bushes. Confused, I asked. "Are you really my mother?"

The woman stopped walking and slowly bent her knees until her bottom touched the heel of her shoes. Her eyes glistened with moisture. "Of course, I'm your mother. Don't you remember?" She smoothed my wild hair and shook her head.

I didn't remember; it'd been so long. I had been living in what my father called "a boarding house," which sounded better than an orphanage or a foster home.

My father alleged, "I didn't have time to take care of you. I had to work, and I needed to hang out with my buddies. You know, get a beer or two."

I whimpered and whined a lot in the orphan home. The beds seemed like cradles for giants. I had difficulty climbing into the bunk bed assigned to me, and when I finally did settle in, I was afraid to get up in the middle of the night to pee. What if I couldn't get back into bed? I'd have to sleep on the cold floor, which happened sometimes.

> **I didn't have time to take care of you.**

The outhouse was in the back of the farmhouse. It smelled like rotten garbage and was so dark I couldn't tell what might be prowling in the nearby thickets.

One time, an older boy locked me in the outhouse. I blubbered, "Let me out! Let me out!" He laughed, "Crybaby, crybaby, misses her daddy."

I wept and screamed until an older kid came out to use the latrine. "What are you doing here?" he asked.

I didn't answer and ran back to the dorm as fast as my little legs could go.

When I asked my father why he didn't come to the home very often to see me, he stated, "I couldn't stand coming to see you because you'd bawl your eyes out all the time. Thought it was better just to leave you there."

Things must have gotten worse for me at the boarding house because he ended up calling my mother. "Jeannine, I can't do this anymore. Please come and get her as soon as you can."

Wearing her lovely purple outfit, my mother took a train south to Toronto and went straight to my dad's place. Once there, she marched in and announced, "She is going to live with me from now on."

My father yelled at my mother. She shouted some obscenity back.

When they stopped arguing, my mother found my small, dilapidated suitcase and began stuffing my meager belongings into it, all the while muttering to herself, "What? The lock on this thing doesn't even work."

My best assumption was that bad things happened in the orphan home, but I could never be sure. I pushed those memories so deep inside my consciousness that they got all twisted up with my nightmares.

That same day, we got on a train and traveled to a small mining town in northern Quebec. I couldn't stop ogling this woman. I still didn't believe she was my mother. And I watched her every move—the way she ate her food or crossed her legs or talked to me.

"I'm sorry about your father." She blew her nose. "I still can't believe he didn't enroll you in school."

My stepdad, Noel, and my two-year-old brother, Tony, met us at the station. Noel roughly pushed me into their beat-up truck. Tony cried all the way back home, a trailer located off a narrow dirt road with a tool shed out back. A clothesline drooping with hanging laundry swayed in the breeze.

A week later, my mother enrolled me in a Catholic elementary school. They changed my last name. I spoke in one-word answers, shook my head, or nodded whenever my mother talked to me.

First grade reminded me of the orphanage: lots of kids yelling on the playground; all the students crammed together at long tables in the cafeteria; having to raise my hand to ask to go to the restroom.

I became increasingly nervous about going outside for recess, afraid I might get stuck out there and not know how to get back into the school. Summoning up my bravery, I asked Sister Frances, "Oh, my tummy hurts. Can I stay in here with you?"

> **Her hand felt like sunshine when I placed my tiny hand in hers.**

She let me clean the blackboards and shake out the felt erasers, and encouraged me to catch up with the other kids because I had missed kindergarten. She even hugged me when I wept for no rational reason.

I loved her traditional dress: the long robes swishing together when she walked; the clink of the rosary around her neck; the spotless white-and-black wimple. Her eyes sparkled when she saw me each morning, and her hand felt like sunshine when I placed my tiny hand in hers.

One day I stayed after school to help clean the classroom. Sister Frances sang, *"Dominque, nique, nique...nique, nique, nique, nique."* I sang along in my high-pitched voice.

Halfway through the second song, my mother came into the classroom. "What are you doing here? It's almost *four o'clock!*" She stared at Sister Frances and pressed her lips into a thin line.

I knew that look. *Watch out, Sister Frances! You'll have to kneel in the corner!*

Without saying a word to Sister Frances, my mother yanked my hand and dragged me out of the school.

When we were home, she shouted, "Off to your room! Come out when you are ready to apologize."

I couldn't stay after school anymore, but I still loved Sister Frances, who continued to shower kindness all year long and looked out for me throughout my unruly elementary school years. This kind woman placed a card on my desk with the inscription *Never give up*, winked when I passed her in the school hallway, listened to my silly stories, and forgave my neediness.

She knew a childish game of patty-cake or singing a silly song healed—not kneeling in a closet.

3

Nepal – April 1977

What to do? Share or not to share?

As I trekked into the steep Himalayan foothills, soft countryside scenes greeted me at every turn: yellow and pink lilies, billowy white clouds, gushing streams, bits of color here and there like splattered paint on an artist's canvas.

Nepali families worked in green terraced hills. When I entered their small communities, local villagers burst into grins, reminding me of school children meeting a new teacher for the first time.

I felt vulnerable after the dog attack and frequently thought about my mother. This surprised me, considering we'd never been close. The walking stick provided critical comfort, and for the most part, dogs stayed away. Nonetheless, my bones always went soft on me whenever I met a strange mongrel.

In those first few days and weeks on the trek, I noticed how everything in Nepali society revolved around the core value of caring for each member of the tribe. This was such a contrast from the emotionally distant family I grew up in, where children had to behave and be quiet.

I watched as Nepali families showered their children with hugs and smiles. Relatives shared food and chores and worked together as they lugged as much water from the wells as they could carry, sometimes singing and chanting while precariously balancing jugs on the top of their heads. They then took delight in distributing what they had with one another.

Toddlers and schoolchildren appeared happy, running around playing games, laughing, skipping, and humming singsong rhymes. It reminded me of my childhood jingles: *not too big, not too small, just the size of Montreal*. Their mirth oozed a satisfaction I rarely felt as a child.

After several days into my journey, I stopped at a small thriving community of ten thatch roofed homes when the sun in the western sky produced long shadows. My boarding home for the evening had a separate guest room with polished wood floors and a covered deck overlooking the valley. Mountain rhododendrons in crimson bloom circled the perimeter, the smell intoxicating the air with sweet-scented breezes.

The lively mother of the house, wearing a long skirt covered with a garnet-colored apron, offered a basin of warm water for washing up. Drawing a tattered cloth closed around the bed area for privacy, I undressed and took a sponge bath using a rag and a tiny piece of white soap laying in the bottom of a porcelain bowl.

> The blue-black bruising had subsided to a golden color.

I eyed the cotton bandages around my calves and tried to convince myself not to worry about infection—or worse, rabies. The once-white material, now gray, was frayed and knotted in places. I took my time unraveling the plain strips and could hardly believe it when I saw that the blue-black bruising had subsided to a golden color. Even the puncture wounds had entirely closed.

When I pressed down on the fading bruise, the skin felt supple and young—no pain or sensitivity. Flexing my calves showed no sign of tightness or unevenness, and it looked as if I would not have any scarring. *Amazing.*

I dressed in a clean pair of jeans, now faded to a stone-washed blue, and a checkered cotton shirt made silky-smooth from many hand washings. Leaving the drawstring pants and top soaking in the same water I used for a sponge bath, I opted to rinse them out later.

When I pulled the curtain back, the late afternoon light flickered on the hand-hewn floorboards and warmed the soles of my feet. Refreshed and relaxed, I looked at my pack on the bed and remembered what was inside.

To celebrate the miraculous recovery of my wounds, I decided to open my one can of peanut butter and eat a spoonful. If I ate a tablespoon every few days, it could last until I reached base camp to give my body that much-needed extra boost of energy.

Digging around in the bottom of my pack, I found the can tucked efficiently away under my only other pair of socks and a jacket. The peanut butter tin had a resealable top with a piece of aluminum foil to guarantee freshness. This foil cover ripped off easily by pulling an attached tab. *Swoosh!* Underneath the foil lid, the peanut oil floated on top, revealing creamy nuts underneath and a rich aroma smelling like home.

Could I eat just one spoonful?

Where did these children come from?

Suddenly, two precious brown eyes gazed into my own. The house mother's five-year-old daughter then stared at the peanut butter. Her dark hair in two braids, tied with golden ribbons, swung gently from side to side.

How did she get here so fast? I didn't hear a sound.

"Kannus, ke?" she asked.

I caught the word *what* and maybe *eat*.

Surely, she wouldn't want some of my prized peanut butter. Maybe I should put it away.

She opened her mouth, revealing two missing front teeth.

A warmth radiated across my chest, and I took out my spoon from the pack's side pocket and gave her a dollop.

When I looked down to scoop up a larger serving for myself, there were three other pairs of sweet eyes watching me.

Where did these children come from? That took, what, four seconds for them to get here? What to do? Share or not to share?

And then, there were four more children. Within about twenty seconds, I went from being alone, with thoughts of satisfying my hunger for protein (or maybe just for comfort), to contemplating allocating several teaspoons worth of beloved peanut butter among eight children.

I observed their eyes glued to the can of peanut butter. *Will they ever get the chance to taste this Canadian staple?* This experience might be a culinary apex in their lives.

Of course, I needed to share.

No sooner had one of the children swallowed her ration, giggling, and chewing slowly when several more children arrived. The entire settlement's children must've been in my room, and if any more came, I would have nothing left.

"Tapaiko naam ke ho?" a small, barefooted boy asked. *What is your name?*

"Ma'am Sahib." The native people had difficulty pronouncing "Sharon," so I stuck to what was simple.

Another girl, around seven years old, whispered, "Dhanyabad," peanut oil dripping down her chin.

"Ramro, ramro!" cried two little three-year-old girls. *Good, good!*

I dished out more servings, laughing when their eyes lit up like fireflies at their first taste of this gastronomic pleasure. Within minutes, the feast had ended.

"Namaste, namaste," they yelled, leaving my room to play outside.

Alone, I looked at the empty can of peanut butter. Not a smudge was left; it was completely licked clean.

I walked out onto the terrace and watched them play a game using a stick and a ball made from odd pieces of material. They danced, shouted, and sometimes waved.

Chuckling, I yelled out, "Namaste!"

The sun ducked behind the foothills, casting silhouette shadows of the children's fun on the grass. A hummingbird buzzed by on its way to the cherry flowers surrounding the house.

The children went to their homes not long after that, skipping and whistling. My host family called me for dinner, and we sat cross-legged on straw mats as earthen clay pots of rice and lentils were passed around. Silence filled the room, and we ate carefully with our right hands, our left hands tucked neatly behind us.

In Nepal and other Asian countries at the time, there was no toilet paper. Instead, the left hand was used for cleaning oneself with water and soap. The right hand was used for eating. It was polite to always place the left hand behind you when consuming food with the local people—something I had learned while traveling in the Middle East.

The house mother's daughter reached over and squeezed my right hand just before I could scoop out a rice portion. She took the ladle, measured a hefty serving, and placed it in my bowl.

I glanced at this family, so relaxed and at ease with one another, tenderly sharing a meal, and swallowed. Their palpable warmheartedness filled my heart while my eyes threatened to leak a flood of emotion, my feelings spilling over like a garden hose left running, trickling everywhere.

Canada – 1960

*At that moment, she seemed like an angel, her
face as smooth as my new lilac blouse.*

The summer between my first and second school year, my biological father, who went by the nickname "Babe," came to visit and asked my mom if I could spend a few weeks with my paternal grandmother, Katherine. My mom agreed, and my dad and I took a train from the northern Quebec town where I lived with my mother to Toronto. It took a long time.

When the train attendant came around with the food cart, I got an orange and a carton of chocolate milk.

My dad laughed at my choices. "I missed you. You're growing up. You look good. It's for the best you know that you live with your mom now. She knows how to take care of you."

I wanted to say, "I miss you so much," but the words felt like sandpaper in my mouth, and my throat hurt. Instead, I yawned and fell asleep.

My grandmother lived in a slightly shabby pale, gray-colored Victorian house on a quiet street. Large trees shaded the open balcony, and the wisteria vines held a hint of the perfume my mother sometimes wore.

Grandmother Katherine hugged me tightly. "Ah, Chere-une... You grow much." Her French accent made her English words sound funny. She had a full head of black curly hair that framed her benevolent face. I looked into her cobalt eyes and saw my reflection.

We climbed the squeaky stairs to a small attic room. The room had a twin bed covered with a handmade quilt, matching curtains, and a soft pink rug. The clean window above the bed let in a stream of lemon-colored light.

I hugged my grandma's tiny frame. "*Merci*, thank you." A special room just for me.

That summer was one of my happiest childhood memories. Grandma, an exceptional seamstress, made me all new clothes. I'd go with her to the fabric store, and she'd say, "Pick what you want, Chere-une."

I spent what felt like hours touching the material: soft silks in powder blue and lavender; crisp cottons in pink and sea green. We looked at several sewing patterns. "Look, Grandma. Isn't this pretty?"

Always quick to agree, she'd reply, "*Oui, oui*. Yes, yes, much beautiful," her eyes mirroring the afternoon light.

> **I touched her warm cheek.**

One day, I came into the house to get a drink of water after playing outside with a neighborhood girl. My grandmother had her head in her hands; her low sobs seemed to fill the living room.

"Grandma, are you okay?"

She looked up. "*Oui*, yes, I okay," and gathered me in her arms, holding me tight. "Sometimes it's good to cry."

I touched her warm cheek. At that moment, she seemed like an angel, her face as smooth as my new lilac blouse.

I took my time packing my suitcase with all the new clothes Grandma had made: a dress with white bows, a cream-colored pair of pedal pushers with plaid cuffs and a matching top, navy shorts, and a hand-knit yellow cardigan. I especially loved the supple lilac blouse and placed it carefully on top.

On the train ride back, I cried into my pillow and wasn't hungry when the food cart came around. My throat felt tight and sore.

When my mom opened my suitcase, she exclaimed, "What's this? What did your grandma do with all the clothes I bought you? What? Does she think I can't sew?" She squashed her lips together and stared at the floor.

Later, at the dinner table, I couldn't eat. My mother continued to fume.

"Eat your dinner. If you can't eat the food that we work so hard to provide, you can go to your room, young lady."

I left the table, brushed my teeth, snuggled into my blanket, and wept until I fell asleep. The next day, when I wanted to put on my lilac blouse, I couldn't find it or any of the clothes Grandma had made.

> **The clothes Grandma had made suddenly disappeared.**

"Mom, where is the pink dress Grandma stitched for me?"

She crossed her arms and looked out the window. "Eat your breakfast, and then it's time for your chores."

The clothes Grandma had made suddenly disappeared, and I did not get to visit with her again.

5

Nepal – April 1977

Thoughts of the past faded, and a newfound pride soaked into my parched heart like a summer rain falling onto the earth, going everywhere at once.

In the 1970s, the trail to Mount Everest base camp began out of Jiri, a seven-hour bumpy bus ride from Katmandu. From there, it took about two or three weeks to get to Namche Bazaar. The route consisted of alternating ascents and descents from the foothills into the higher tundra ecosystem of the tall Himalayas.

Today, less than five percent take the Jiri route, and few, if any, get off the bus several miles south of Jiri, where I began my trek. Most take a plane to Lukla and make the one- to two-day hike to Namche Bazaar, where they can acclimatize before continuing to base camp or Gokyo Lakes.

I did not meet any other foreign trekkers during the first week or more of my journey. The trail I followed often intersected with another, and then another. At times, unsure of exactly where to go, I'd end up on the wrong path, ending up at a water hole or a pasture for yaks or water buffalo. Each time I got disoriented, a local resident generously pointed me in the right direction.

My body grew strong hiking on the steep terrain, and my lungs acclimatized well to the increase in altitude. I didn't miss Canada, my family, my ex-boyfriend Rick, or my Holland comrade from the Europe-to-India overland journey. I just put one foot in front of the other, rested when I needed to, or simply gazed up at the big Himalayan sky, hoping for good things.

When the trail I was on drew closer to the main Mount Everest track out of Jiri, I foolishly hiked well past the last village offering any sort of safe place to sleep. When twilight arrived, I found myself at the bottom of a gloomy ravine.

A small indigo river cascaded down the middle of a narrow valley, thick with foliage. The moist air quickly dampened my clothes. I studied the vertical slope on the other side of the river but could not see where the trail crested.

Should I go up and try to find shelter in the dark? Should I stop here?

The light faded from sundown to night in minutes while I was sitting on a soggy moss-covered rock, enveloping me in inky darkness. Suddenly, the thought of climbing at nighttime seemed crazy. I burrowed into my pack and found a three-inch white candle and a box of matches. Candlelight revealed the dim silhouette of a sultry forest.

I quickly went to work, putting up a makeshift cover using a blue plastic tarp and thirty feet of lightweight climbing rope. Then I scrambled into my feather sleeping bag and fell asleep to the sound of croaking frogs and noisy crickets.

> **I saw a tea shop looking like something out of a fairy tale.**

The next morning dawned clear and cold. I shook out the dew on the tarp, folded it into its tight roll, and splashed my face with handfuls of stream water. Tingling and wide awake, I started the climb. The river's roar dwindled to a distant gurgle, and my stomach growled when I stopped to catch my breath by a clump of barren gray rocks that provided a view of the northwestern valley ahead.

Clouds clung to the distant peaks in a peacock-blue sky, the morning mist suspended in the dells. Up a sharp embankment and around another corner, I saw a tea shop looking like something out of a fairy tale.

The small fire pit in the center of the shelter released a steady plume of smoke and loud hisses. Two Nepali men with wool hats pushed off their ears made chai on rustic gas stoves. A local woman, probably a wife of one of the Nepali men, kneaded dough for the *chapattis* while another woman effortlessly flipped the unleavened bread onto hot cast-iron plates.

The aromas of sweat, chai, bread, and hearing English words —*Hey, are you going up to Thangre Pass? This chai is great! Do you have any antibiotics with you?*—brought a smile to my face. I missed being with my own tribe.

One of the Nepali male cooks looked up and gestured for me to sit down cross-legged on the floor like everyone else. "Ma'am Sahib, sit, sit. Room plenty."

"Chai? *Chini?*" he said in a singsong voice, his head bobbing from side to side.

I slid off my pack and propped it against the last remaining seat, a rough spot on the uneven hand-planed floor. The hut had a sizeable northern opening offering exquisite views of majestic snowcapped peaks.

The Nepali man brought a cup of steaming tea. I thanked him and peered around at the other hikers in the hut.

"*Bonjour. D'ou es-tu venu?*" a striking man asked. His black hair fell to his shoulders, and several weeks' growth of beard gave him a disheveled look.

"*Je suis originaire de Canada,*" I replied with a distinctly Quebecois accent. "*Mon nomme est Sharon.*" My voice sounded strange to my ears. I hadn't had a conversation with anyone since Katmandu.

The man called France home. We talked for about an hour and drank several cups of tea while munching on at least a half-dozen sizzling *chapattis*. Before I wanted it to end, he lifted his pack. *"Je dois partir maintenant. Salut,"* he exclaimed. With a crooked grin, I invented my own story of needing to get going, too.

"*Bonne chance!*" He waved and turned toward the trail, going in the opposite direction.

Rejuvenated from the food and pleasant company, I slung on my rucksack and wandered down the trail, careful not to stumble on a few loosened rocks.

> **A newfound pride soaked into my parched heart.**

Soon the teahouse chatter and clank of dishes subsided, and the silence enveloped me. The air felt clean, and the panorama of imposing mountaintops glimmered in the distance.

Native words became more familiar, and the worry-free art of putting one foot in front of the other became a daily mantra. *Here and now, here and now, here and now.* A sense of calm slipped in.

I traversed mountain passes, trudged through thick forests, scrambled down barren inclines, and stopped at destination places for rest and food. After sunset, sleep came. Thoughts of the past faded, and a newfound pride soaked into my parched heart like a summer rain falling onto the earth, going everywhere at once.

At one mountain pass, I happened upon a wonderful teahouse and rented a small cabin overlooking the northern ridges. A steady drizzle fell when I arrived. Surrounded by five or six cabins, the teahouse resembled something you might find in Switzerland rather than Nepal. The main building had a large fireplace with a sturdy wood table next to it for trekkers to eat or play a game of chess.

When I first got to the teahouse, I noticed a weather-beaten Buddhist monastery built precariously on a rocky outcrop, slightly higher up from the teahouse area. Swirls of murky clouds played hide-and-seek around its edges. I wondered if tourists could visit this mysterious-looking place. I quickly found out.

"Ma'am Sahib, no allow," said the teahouse manager. He wore a long-sleeved cotton shirt and loose pants like pajamas. "Only Buddhist monks—sure, sure. No Ma'am Sahibs."

"Oh, I wasn't planning on going there," I lied.

He proceeded to show me where I would be staying. The little cabin had a rustic platform for sleeping and a substantial river rock fireplace. An enormous pile of chopped wood sat nearby. A window looked directly at the monastery. A rope clothesline hung between the fireplace and the bed.

For just a few rupees, I had the place all to myself. I could hardly believe my good fortune.

"Fast, dark. Shortly, eat," the tea manager said. He closed the cabin door with a loud clunk.

I took my feather sleeping bag out of its cocoon and let it rest across the polished wood. Then I made a pile of my soiled, stinky clothes. I decided it was time to wash everything and take a bath, which meant I needed to stay for two nights instead of one.

The rain fell steadily as I meandered to the main lodge, the early evening light giving way to blue-gray dusk. The heavy door groaned as I pushed against it, and the proprietor grinned when he saw me.

"Oh, Ma'am Sahib. Here food." He proudly gestured to a seat at the well-built table near the fireplace. On the table sat a warm loaf of whole wheat bread, butter, and a round of soft, creamy cheese.

A single candle burned on the table, and I ate in silence, savoring each bite.

"Ramro. Ramro, Ma'am Sahib?" he asked.

"Yes, yes, so good. Thank you," I replied as he positioned a steaming cup of sweet tea next to my plate. I watched the flickering flames of the fire, content and pleased to be warm as the rain continued to come down.

He placed a small white candle on the table, already lit. "Flame to walk Ma'am Sahib cabin."

I made hand motions for doing laundry. "Bucket for washing?"

"Oh, oh, yes, yes." He disappeared into the kitchen area and reemerged, carrying a metal pail.

"Water in well." He pointed to the back of the teahouse.

The well had an old-fashioned handle that lowered a bucket, tied to a rope, into the cold water below. It took several turns of this lever to fill the bucket. Doing laundry would take a while.

The rain continued to fall the next day. I spent the entire day doing laundry, boiling water repeatedly, and then hanging everything on the clothesline. The fire crackled and sizzled. It was still overcast when I left the cabin for dinner. When I entered the lodge, a small group of hikers—a man and two women—stood by the hearth.

"Why, hello there. The manager of this place said you are hiking to Mount Everest base camp?" the man asked. He had an English accent.

"Yes," I answered. "By myself."

"By yourself!" he cried out.

"Yep." *I am so tired of hearing that.*

"My name is Bob, and this is Karen and Heather." He put his arms around them like a protective bear. We shook hands all around. "We're also headed up to Mount Everest base camp. Our porters are sleeping in the caretaker rooms. Karen's husband is climbing Everest. Heather is Karen's sister. We're from New Zealand."

Oh, New Zealand, not England. I bit the inside of my cheek. "I don't have a porter. I'm just staying with the local peoples along the way."

"Really? Don't know how you can live on local food? We brought our own. Can't afford to get sick, you know..." He rambled on and on, a nonstop monologue, even as the teahouse manager set down our evening meal with some extra goodies: marmalade, salami, nuts, oranges, chocolate. "Please help yourself. We have plenty," Bob boasted.

I was so glad to be trekking alone.

As we ate and sipped tea, Bob rattled on about his mountaineering skills and the peaks he had "bagged." Karen spoke little, mostly wishing for a safe Mount Everest ascent for her husband. Heather buried herself in a book, perhaps tired of Bob's information overflow.

"Well, good night," I said. "Have a restful sleep and good luck on the rest of your trip. It's dark out there. You might want to ask for a candle."

"Oh, no need for that," he smirked, showing me his flashlight.

The rain stopped. A few stars shone through the clouds as I made my way back to the sanctuary of the silent cabin. I was so glad to be trekking alone.

The next morning dawned clear and cold, and a creamy haze filled the valley below. Karen, Bob, and Heather had left at dawn. The sun warmed my neck as I descended into the valley, stopping at a village tea shop a thousand feet below the pass. There I watched several craftsmen, using a primitive spinning wheel, make wooden containers; the pungent smell of the fresh wood permeating the air. I discovered porters carried these boxes in cumbersome burlap sacks to the Katmandu marketplace. I bargained for two small circular containers and stuffed them neatly in the corner of my pack.

Today, these urns sit on my dresser, holding a few cherished items: a *mala* from India, a key chain my late father-in-law gave me on my wedding day, coins from Nepal, and sand from the Ganges River.

For years, the rich, sweet smell instantly transported me back. However, their scent is now long gone. How I miss it.

6

Canada – 1963

*When he left, the click of the door
echoed off the living room wall,
followed by awkward taciturnity.*

On my bed lay a new outfit that looked quite modern and chic for a ten year old: a pleated green and black plaid skirt and matching vest with a crisp cotton shirt underneath, a velvet hair ribbon, soft socks, and a pair of shiny black Mary Jane shoes. I smiled and touched the woven fabric. A card with my name on it said: "To my favorite goddaughter, love, Uncle Eddie."

Great-uncle Eddie was my grandmother Katherine's younger brother who had lived most of his adult life overseas, working in foreign oil fields. I met him only once.

My mom came into my room. "Your godfather is here to see you. He's staying with Flo and will only be here for the evening. You're to have dinner with him in town. Better get washed up and wear your new outfit."

A slow tingle of excitement worked its way up from my belly, and I ran to my room to get ready. I brushed and brushed my wavy shoulder-length hair and stood on a stool to get a better look at my new outfit in our tiny bathroom mirror. My eyes glistened with anticipation.

A tall, angular man stood at our apartment front door. "Jeannine, nice to see you." He gave my mom a quick peck on the cheek. "And this must be Sharon." His gentle eyes held mine for a moment.

"I'm just taking her to the hotel restaurant. Shouldn't be too long. Thanks for letting me spend some time with her."

There were only two restaurants in our small town. The hotel restaurant stood beside a rowdy bar, and a Chinese restaurant sat next to the run-down, show-a-movie-once-a-month theater.

> Uncle Eddie, take me with you.

I slipped my hand into his calloused palm and waved goodbye to my mom. I had not eaten in a restaurant in years, and I had forgotten the last time I wore new clothes.

Uncle Eddie talked about his work and travels. "Saudi Arabia is very different from Canada... There are great expansive deserts, and the sand is honey-colored. I've been all over the Middle East and Asia...never got married, preferred the solitary life...strange to be here."

He looked down at his plate. "Maybe you'll travel, too, someday. It's worth seeing the world." He cleared his throat. "I'm sorry life has been difficult for you. Sorry, too, your dad doesn't see you often enough."

I squirmed in the booth. The red vinyl stuck to my thighs, and I hardly spoke, preferring to make little roads with my food. Words I wanted to say stuck in my chest, and the familiar lump lodged somewhere between my tongue and throat.

On the way back to the car, the rain fell and shimmered like silver cobwebs. I climbed into my seat. "Thank you for dinner."

"You're so welcome. Listen...uh...I don't know when I might be able to see you again, with my work and all." He gave my shoulder a tight squeeze.

My mother opened the front door. "Eddie, thanks for stopping by. I know this was way out of your way."

Uncle Eddie hugged us both. "Goodbye, you two."

When he left, the click of the door echoed off the living room wall, followed by awkward taciturnity.

Later, under the covers, I relived the evening. Uncle Eddie had kind eyes and dark hair speckled with gray, like a sparrow's egg I once found. He spoke softly, the opposite of my stepfather, Noel, and I cherished the tender way Uncle Eddie touched my shoulder. He took his time driving around the corners. When Noel drove the car, I'd be flung clear across the seat because we didn't wear seatbelts.

My chest hurt. I didn't want my mother to hear me cry.

Instead, I whispered: *Uncle Eddie, take me with you.*

7

Nepal – April 1977

I could hardly hear them over the singing and yelling, the noise such a contrast from the quiet monastery and solitary day of hiking.

As I hiked further north and deeper into the Khumbu Range, the ridges became sheer and precipitous, offering exquisite views: snowcapped mountain peaks, glaciers, clouds, and mist hanging close to the steep faces—the massive Himalayas towering over everything like kings governing the land.

The inhabitants of the villages began to change from the lowland Nepali people to the Sherpa community. Farms clung to the hillsides in patchwork precision; each terrace draped precariously against mountain walls where they grew millet, barley, and potatoes.

Some villages were used to Western trekkers, and the teahouse owners could speak a little English. Always up for a conversation, they wanted to hear all about North America or Europe. They seemed fascinated by the west and asked about American movie stars as if I should know them personally. "Oh, you from America, yes? You know *Godfather*?" They found it strange that I was traveling alone, but I found it even stranger that they knew Hollywood.

"Why Ma'am Sahib all by self?" they'd ask.

Replying "It's fun" or "It's just something I wanted to do" did not satisfy their curiosity. Women from their tribes did not venture out alone.

One time, at the bottom of a tight ravine, I crossed a river over a wobbly hand-built bridge and met an older European man hiking back to Jiri.

"Hi! Traveling up to Namche, are you?" he asked in a crisp Scottish accent.

"Yes, I'm going to Namche Bazaar. Then on to Mount Everest base camp with a side trip to Gokyo Lakes," I replied.

"I'm returning from a Tibetan Buddhist monastery." He pointed to a valley directly opposite from where I was going. "Beautiful place, about a half day's walk from here. The monastery has a cottage for visitors. The bungalow holds about six bunks—just plywood platforms, really—to throw down your sleeping bag or blankets. So peaceful there."

I looked at his serene face. "Sounds wonderful."

"Yes, you should go," he replied. "It'd be just a little bit out of your way."

I gazed at the valley. "Directly east from here? Is it marked?"

"No, there's not a sign." He unfolded a map.

Along with directions, he handed over his leftover antibiotics. "You never know when you might need them. Dysentery is horrible up in these hills."

I hadn't thought about getting sick and did not have an emergency kit. "Thanks." It amazes me still that I overlooked such an important necessity.

The man put on his pack and waved goodbye. In minutes, his form vanished into the lush forest. I turned onto the eastern path and walked until near sunset before arriving at the monastery.

Surrounded by large flowering trees, the small teahouse sat below the monastery and offered splendid views of the distant ridges and pristine peaks of the Sikkim Mountains. An aroma of frangipani lingered in the air, and I marveled at the peaceful scene.

I walked around to the back of the residence. There, a young long-haired Tibetan man dressed in western jeans and a T-shirt sat on the ground, stringing beads.

He looked up. "Oh, hello. Staying here for night?"

"Yes," I replied.

"The monks chanting soon. You won't meet them. So sorry."

Then, a humming began.

"Oh, that's all right," I squeaked, trying to hide my disappointment. "Do I just go down to the teahouse?"

"Yes, yes. You only person this night. Bring you chai and food later. A bowl for washing in main room. Latrine out back. Enjoy stay."

After washing up, I lay my sleeping bag down on the irregular sleeping mat, unfurled the hanging mosquito netting, and waited for the food to arrive. Minutes passed into an hour. I wondered if he had forgotten me.

Then, a humming began. The low voices, unbelievably deep, sounded like the growl of a wild bull and gradually changed to a constant droning, the echo similar to a thousand bees buzzing around my head. Mesmerized, I closed my eyes and nodded off.

When I woke, a steaming cup of tea with a bowl of rice and lentils sat on the little table next to my bed.

I ate in solitude, lulled by the tranquility of the place, and wondered about the chanting. *What does it all mean exactly?*

A delicate drizzle fell, obscuring any views when I left early the next morning. Eager to make up those extra miles I needed to do that day in order to arrive at the next teahouse before dark, I walked without stopping much to rest.

After several steep climbs, I finally saw my destination spot: a shallow valley with a fast river running through the basin.

When I got closer, I could see that the thatched roofed mud homes were perched on either side of the river and the village, home to about thirty families, had well-organized millet- and rice-terraced fields.

Children played games in an open area, a rugged dirt patch with tufts of grass swaying in the wind. Women danced, waved, and shouted, "Namaste, namaste." A small herd of goats bleated.

In the teahouse, several native people were standing around, drinking *rakshi*, an alcoholic beverage distilled from millet, laughing, shouting, and hooting. I looked around. Three Europeans sat at a corner table. My smile broadened.

"Hi!" I said, perhaps a little too enthusiastically.

"Hello! Please join us!" said a tall dark-haired man. "My name Jens and this my friend Marcel. We from Switzerland." Marcel's blue eyes sparkled above his wide grin. He made room for me to sit. I could hardly hear them over the singing and yelling, the noise such a contrast from the quiet monastery and solitary day of hiking.

A woman with long hair reached across to shake my hand before Jens could introduce her. "I'm so glad to see another white woman on this trek!" she shouted. "My name is Susanna, from Australia."

Susanna, also traveling alone on the hike to Mount Everest base camp, had arrived just an hour before me. It didn't take long for the two of us to become friends. Jens ordered us a round of *rakshi*, which tasted like turpentine. I asked for chai instead.

We talked late into the night. I learned Jens and Marcel were hoping to climb Ama Dablam, a mountain southwest of Mount Everest. From time to time, the village celebration became contagious, and we would unite in some singing. Our feeble attempt to sound out a few syllables had me laughing until my sides ached.

The next day, we decided to trek together to at least Namche Bazaar. Some of the high passes were absorbed in fog, and the vapor clung to our clothes. We watched a barefoot Sherpa with a hundred-pound cargo on his back pass us. "Namaste, namaste!" he exclaimed. Then he resumed his chanting, akin to someone strolling in the park whistling a tune.

Susanna, a few yards behind me, called out. "Can you believe that? How can they do that? I can barely catch my breath."

"Hey, girls!" Marcel yelled from farther up the trail. "I have the best Swiss chocolate. Want some? Just two more miles before we come to evening place. Come on!"

After a few climbs, we passed Lukla, and the number of foreign climbers, hikers, and tourists increased, as did opportunities for chai, food, and conversation. We stopped in beautiful places to admire the view, comment on our good fortune, or share food.

Marcel, who had waited for us girls to catch up, said, "Only one day now before Namche." Jens, the strongest member of our group, frequently hiked ahead. By the time we meandered into the evening stopover, Jens—washed and changed—would say, "Chai waiting, you slowpokes. Let's eat." Even his cleaned laundry hung in the wind.

Ahh. That feels so much better.

The weather was often clear, with warm days and cool nights. When it did rain, the next day was usually sunny, and we could quickly dry out socks, boots, and clothing. Most teahouses now offered basins of warm water to take to our rooms for washing up.

"I need to shave," Susanna whispered when we got to our room one night. "I've got a razor. If you bring me water, I'll bring water for you and let you use my razor. It'll be fun," she said.

How could I refuse? We giggled like school children and made an improvised private area using our sleeping bags as a personal space for washing and shaving.

"Ahhh. That feels so much better," Susanna said, rubbing her soft legs and letting out a long sigh. We changed into our relatively clean clothing and went to join the boys.

Tomorrow we would arrive at Namche Bazaar.

8

Canada – 1964

*BAM! Wham! Heavy pounding
on the front door jolted me from sleep.*

When I turned eleven, the mining industry—which supported most of the town's population, including us—shut down some of their quarries. Many people lost their jobs, or their full-time employment suddenly became part-time.

Wages fell, and stores went out of business; fresh fruit and milk were scarce. My mom started baking her own bread, and we kids drank powdered skim milk.

My mom and stepdad, now with three children of their own, argued often. My stepdad stayed away at the bar. When he drank, he told funny stories and sang his favorite Johnny Cash songs as well as other country western tunes. Sometimes I'd sing along. But that stopped when he started coming home muttering under his breath and sleeping on the couch.

One night my mom said, "You need to babysit. Your dad and I are going out. Lock the door."

I fell asleep on the couch and woke when I heard my mom come in. She sobbed and talked to herself.

"What's wrong, Mom?"

"Nothing." Her eyes appeared damp and overly bright. "Listen. I need you to lock the door. Use the top bolt. Lock the windows, too." She mumbled something I couldn't understand. "I'll close the curtains."

I did as she asked and went to bed after my mom turned off the lights.

BAM! Wham! Heavy pounding on the front door jolted me from sleep.

"*Marde! Tabernacle!*" My stepfather's swearing filled the apartment. Somehow, foul words in French sounded scarier.

I got up to let him in, afraid it would make him angrier if I didn't, but my mother stopped me.

"No! Leave the door locked" Her voice, a high-pitched cackle resounded off the wall. She tightened her robe and swept a shaky hand across her forehead, seemingly distant, almost as if she had gone entirely inside herself.

My stepfather kept hammering his fists on the door until the frame buckled. *Crack!* The glass from a picture on the living-room wall shattered when it hit the floor with a thunderous crash.

I watched my mom walk tentatively down our narrow hallway from my bedroom door. Then, I followed her into the living room. Her hands shook as she unlocked the deadbolt.

Bam! My stepfather stormed past her into the apartment. The veins on his face swelled as he shouted and started throwing things: my mother's nice glasses exploded against the wall, a ceramic figurine lay strewn in a thousand pieces across the brown rug. My stepfather broke everything in sight.

My mother put her hands over her ears and yelled, "Stop! Calm down! Stop!" and took a step toward him, trying to grab his arm before he picked up our old black-and-white television.

Too late.

He hurled the television into the air and let it drop onto the floor. A large fissure started to form and grow into countless, tiny tentacles like a mythical, writhing sea creature. Then, my stepfather turned to my mother, who had reared back, grabbed her auburn hair, and yanked her like a ragdoll to the floor. His wide eyes showed the whites, and spittle began to build up in the corners of his mouth.

"Bitch! Whore!" His nostrils flared.

Frozen with fear and horror, I watched as my mother's husband proceeded to beat her until I saw splattered blood and broken teeth.

I felt something tug at my nightgown. Two heavy tears rolled down my little brother's cheek. "Hey, don't watch this," reaching for his hand and leading him to the littler kids' room. "Stay here, and don't open the door until I tell you."

> Everything seemed unreal as if I was watching a strange horror movie.

His crying intensified. "Don't leave me..."

I didn't know what to do—stay with my brothers and sister or go to help my mom.

Should I call the police?

My head felt hot, and I tasted something metallic in my mouth. I closed the bedroom door—the wails of the kids almost as loud as the living room monstrosity.

Pretending to be brave, I went back.

My stepfather dragged my mom into the kitchen. I followed him. He opened the knife drawer.

I screamed. "Stop! What are you doing?"

My mom choked out, "Sharon, get out of here!"

My stepfather slammed the kitchen drawer and pummeled her with his fists like an enraged boxer.

I don't remember too much after that. Time slowed. Everything seemed unreal as if I was watching a strange horror movie.

Police came. Two policemen wrestled Noel to the floor and handcuffed him. It wasn't easy. He howled like a wild beast. One of the officers touched my mom's arms.

A minute or two later, another officer arrived. He said, "Let's get you and your siblings out of here. Can you show me where they are?"

We left the apartment from my bedroom window because of the chaos in the living room. One officer lifted us up and through the opened window. Another caught us and gently placed us on the ground.

The bitter cold cut through my cotton nightgown, and piercing pain in my foot revealed an embedded shard of glass. I didn't say anything to the policeman. The pain seemed trivial in comparison.

A sergeant took us to a friend's house. When we got there, it seemed everyone we knew was there. I felt small and ashamed, knowing they knew our secrets.

Later, my mom joined us. She stood burying her face in her hands, but I could see the swollen purple marks between her trembling fingers as she rocked back and forth on her heels, not responding to anyone or anything.

I didn't sleep that night and stared into the darkness, trying to still my beating heart, searching for a safe place.

The next day, volunteers came to the apartment and helped clean up the destruction.

We didn't see my stepfather for many weeks, and when I asked where he was, my mom said, "He is in the hospital and will not be released for a while."

Almost certainly he went to jail. When he returned, he had two bandages around his wrists and slept on the sofa for a long time.

We did not have enough to eat, and I learned to stay out of his way.

9

Nepal – May 1977

Friendship...what a gift.

"Ah, what a view," remarked Jens as he topped the rim of the Sun Kosi Gorge, overlooking Namche Bazaar, a small, horseshoe-shaped terraced community resembling a Greek theater. At twelve thousand feet, the settlement in 1977 had just a few shops, homes, and trading posts.

Standing near the edge of the trail, I followed Jens's finger as he pointed to the mountains around us. The cobalt sky seemed to go on forever. The white glaciers cascaded like melted ice cream on the sheer gray mountain rock.

"Stunning," was all I could manage to utter.

Marcel came up behind us. "Hey, let's find place to stay. Then take look around," he said. "I'm starving." Marcel's sunny disposition also included eating well.

I shot him a quick glance, admiring his fortitude. "Sounds good."

Jens found us a small inn perched right in the middle of Namche Bazaar, a rustic hotel made of stone and timber with a large coed dormitory room. Ten cots surrounded an old-fashioned wood-burning stove. The owners, a kind Sherpa family, lived in a room adjacent to our shelter, which included a separate kitchen nestled close to the hillside.

"Guess what, you guys?" Jens said with a grin. "Inn has shower out back. It costs few rupees more. I said we'd take it."

Susanna and I sighed with pleasure at the thought of a shower. The elder daughter, maybe twelve years old, proudly showed us the bathing arrangements. Three light plywood boards encased the shower stall; a cotton cloth draped over a length of frayed climbing rope served as the door and several river rocks, pieced together like a puzzle, made up the floor. Overhead, a large metal tub with a galvanized shower head sticking out the bottom sat precariously on a boulder.

> I can still feel the joy of that shower.

I looked at Susanna. "You go first."

She tipped her head to one side as if unsure of what to make of my generosity. "Ahhh, thanks."

Her five-minute shower felt like an hour. Humming a popular song, she meandered into the room with her hair tied up in a towel.

"Wow! I feel reborn." Her skin glowed pink and radiant. "Hey, you should know the daughter has to run back and forth to the kitchen to keep refilling the tub with hot water. It might take a bit, but well worth it."

The cold rocks hurt my feet, and I shivered while waiting for the first hot water to trickle down. *Goosshh...* A layer of dirt washed over the rock bottom. Steam rose as I lathered every inch of my body and waist-length hair. To this day, I can still feel the joy of that shower and how I wanted it to last forever.

Susanna and I asked for more hot water to wash undies, socks, and a shirt each. Afterward, we hung our clean laundry in the wind like prayer flags, then we went to find the guys. We found them walking on a path that surrounded the hotel.

"Girls, Mama Sherpa making us pancakes!" exclaimed Marcel. "Jens offered our jam to go with it."

Susanna and I looked at each other. "Pancakes?" we said.

"Yah, Yah. Sherpa family make this specialty for climbers. Good, no?" Marcel said, his eyes beaming. "Let's go back to room and wait. It's getting cold." The horizon had turned a ginger color.

We gathered around the woodstove, warming our toes and hands. I made room for Marcel. "There's space here."

Marcel scooted right next to me. "Ah, that feels good."

I wasn't sure if he meant the heat from the stove or sitting next to me. A rich aroma of cooking oil and batter emanated from the back kitchen, reminding me of breakfasts back home. My mouth watered, remembering the juicy smell of the homemade donuts my mom used to make.

Shortly after, the elder daughter walked in with four tin plates stacked with large, inch-thick pancakes and Jen's strawberry jam on the side. Except for an occasional snap from the fire, the room was silent as we savored each bite.

> **Does life get much better than this?**

"Church should be like this," whispered Susanna when we snuggled into our sleeping bags later that night. "This was the best day of my trek so far. Thank you, my friend." She reached over and squeezed my hand.

A sand-dry lump caught in my throat.

Friendship...what a gift.

Bright sunshine filled the room when I opened my eyes the following morning. The sound of children screaming with glee wafted through the open window. Jens' and Marcel's sleeping bags were neatly folded over the cots with their packs and equipment strewn about on one end.

I nudged Susanna. "What do you think is going on?" She rubbed her eyes and yawned, slinking farther down into her warm nest.

The cold, crisp air stung my nose and confirmed a nagging thought that I needed a few pieces of warmer clothing for the next part of the trek. Namche Bazaar's temperatures were fifty degrees in the daytime and around thirty at night. The higher camps would only be colder.

A shop not far from the inn served steaming cups of sweet or butter tea. Inside, I asked the owner, who spoke some broken English, "What's all the yelling about?"

"Ma'am Sahib. Special day. Hillary here." He poured a scalding cup of sweet tea.

"Really?" I asked doubtfully. "You mean Sir Edmund Hillary is in Namche Bazaar?"

"Ah, yes, Ma'am Sahib. He come see school. Also meet daughter." His head bobbed from side to side. "Daughter now base camp."

While I sipped my tea and pondered this new information, Marcel and Jens sauntered in. "Hey," I said to them. "Guess what?"

Jens nodded. "Edmund Hillary is here. Yes, we had tea here a bit earlier and heard."

"Should we go get Susanna and go over there?" I asked, pointing to the place where a large group of children had gathered.

"Yah, yah," Marcel and Jens said together.

A large crowd assembled outside the cottage diagonally across from our hotel. Children jumped up and down, tugging at Hillary's hands and clothing as he made his way through the village. His large frame loomed over them, and his genuine smile radiated warmth and tenderness.

The small pathway around the community filled with villagers, all of them wanting to catch some of the excitement of seeing Sir Hillary. We hopped off the path, up onto a narrow ledge, and watched as Sir Hillary made his way closer to where we were.

We bowed when he looked up at us. "Where are you off to?" Sir Edmund shouted.

"Mount Everest!" Susanna and I yelled.

"Ama Dablam," bellowed Jens and Marcel.

"Great stuff! My daughter Sarah is up at base camp. There is a New Zealand team climbing Mount Everest right now. Best of luck," he hollered.

"Wow," sighed Susanna. "I can't believe it! Seeing Hillary... does life get much better than this?" She pulled me into a big bear hug, her joy spilling into me like a contagious virus.

"I'm going to need some warmer clothing," I said to my new-found friends while we walked around the village. "I didn't bring a hat or gloves," I added. "What if we stayed another day and browsed the shops here, see what might be available?"

For such a small place, Namche seemed to sell everything: discarded climbing equipment, gifts from former expeditions, chai, soap, and staples such as rice, butter, or cloth. Sparkles of light resembling tiny diamonds reflected off the snow, making me wish for a pair of sunglasses—which I did not find.

Susanna rummaged through a bin containing scraps of western mountaineering paraphernalia and pulled out a teal coat. "Look, a down coat," she exclaimed. It had a small tear on the sleeve but otherwise looked to be in good condition. "You want it?"

"*Kati?*" I asked the trader. He wore fleece-like pants and a wraparound knee-length coat with a sleeved shirt. His long hair was braided into a tightly woven plait.

"Eight rupees," he replied. His English was clear and distinct as if he'd been doing business with foreigners for a while.

I added a Sherpa hat, some older European mitts, and a slightly shabby pair of wool socks to my bill, crossing my fingers they would keep me warm at higher altitudes and bad weather.

Arriving back at the inn, four western men stood around the woodstove warming their hands. Wearing denim and wool coats, they did not appear to be the climbing sort. The tallest one in the group said they flew to Lukla and planned to see Thyangboche. The other three greeted us and were impressed when Jens told them he and Marcel would be climbing Ama Dablam and that Susanna and I were headed up to Mount Everest base camp.

One of the men stood rolling a cigarette. His bloodshot eyes drooped, and he hummed a familiar rock song. Not thrilled with the prospect of sharing the dormitory with this guy, I rolled my eyes at Susanna. "Loser," I whispered.

After a dinner of pancakes, chatting about the trek, and the obligatory small talk, one of the men started to roll a "ciggy."

"Best Thailand pot. Fabulous high." He sighed and took a gigantic puff, his chest swelling under the pressure of holding in so much smoke, and then passed it to Marcel. "Here, try some."

Everyone in the group took big inhalations of the rapidly vanishing reefer. When my turn came, I just held it between my thumb and index finger. I looked at the joint as if it could tell me what to do.

"Hurry up. Take a hit," one of the men urged.

Out of embarrassment and fear of not fitting in, I took a whopping inhalation, pretending to be an expert pot smoker, which I wasn't. As I tried not to cough, my mind took me back to high school when my best friend's boyfriend criticized me for not doing drugs or having sex.

"You're such a strait-laced goody two-shoes," he'd say. He told me all the coolest kids smoked dope and loved sex. "Man, you're such a loser. I don't know why Julie hangs out with you." I never knew how to tell him I was scared. Even after Julie dumped our friendship, I still couldn't find the words.

"You ever do drugs, and I'll beat you until you are black and blue," my stepfather would roar. "If I catch you with those drug users, I'll chain you to your bedroom door."

I knew he would.

When Susanna passed me the cannabis cigarette again, I passed it on. "I'm good." I'd already started to feel strange. Distances appeared peculiar, and within minutes my sense of orientation went askew. Shapes and shadows around the room looked creepy and unnatural. A slow quiver of fear worked its way up my spine.

For most of the night, waiting for the affects of the best Thailand pot to leave, I lay petrified in my sleeping bag. Childhood memories drifted in and out of my consciousness. An aching sense of sorrow expanded in my chest. At the time, I did not have the emotional maturity to process those painful memories, and it would not be the last time I'd experience debilitating sensations of the real me buried within snowdrifts of hurt.

"Did you have any weird experience with the pot last night?" I whispered to Susanna over chai the next morning.

She smiled. "Nah! It was great getting stoned. Top stuff." She paused. "Hey, you don't look so good. Anything wrong?"

> **I kept my thoughts behind closed doors.**

"Well, I guess the finest didn't sit right with me. I've been paranoid shitless ever since." I had hoped talking about it would help.

"Everything will be okay," she replied. "Let's get something to eat. We should leave in an hour if we want to make Thyangboche today. I'm so excited to see that place."

Perhaps a sensitivity to drugs, the high altitude, or marijuana laced with a hallucinogen had caused my dramatic reaction. Either way, it took several days to feel *normal* again.

I'd wake in the middle of the night, my heart slamming against my chest, a feeling of thick, suffocating mud in my gut. I kept my thoughts behind closed doors.

Outside, the morning sun tiptoed over the horizon, spilling an orange cream color on the ice floes. A few birds perched on a branch of subalpine fir and chirped as we passed.

The four of us hiked down a steep incline and crossed an unsteady suspension bridge. The river roared below, drowning out any attempt at conversation. Rhododendron and magnolia forests covered the hillside.

"Magnificent," I shouted over the sounds from the raging river below. "The blossoms are huge." Blooming flowers, like giant red ribbon bows, dotted the trees, scenting the air with fresh fragrance. A faint breeze blew in from the river and swept away the mist and clouds.

Susanna nodded in agreement. "Thyangboche shouldn't be much farther." She suggested we spend the night and take in "this beautiful place."

Located on a hummock at the confluence of two rivers, Thyangboche, home to the largest Buddhist monastery in the area, boasted panoramic views of some of the highest Himalayan peaks, including Everest and Ama Dablam. In 1977, it was the quintessential medieval monastery with exquisite wall paintings depicting Tibetan Buddhist Bodhisattva art. It did not take much to convince me to stay a while.

Susanna's soft brown eyes lit up. "Oh, look! They even serve tea and rice. Oh, my gosh, the view is incredible." Soaring glacier-filled white mountains contrasted against a steel-blue sky with an occasional white cloud resting on some of the peaks.

Monks, wearing traditional Tibetan Buddhist clothing, greeted us when we entered the little tea shop. "Ma'am Sahib, tea?" asked a monk. His red and orange robes rustled in the wind. "Stay here, no?"

"Yes, to both!" said Susanna. "Boys, we're staying here tonight."

Jens wanted to continue to Periche. "Better for us get used to altitude there. Chance see Ama Dablam soon."

Marcel turned to face Susanna and me. "Okay, enjoy your stay. We'll see you in Periche." Within minutes, he and Jens were on their way up the trail.

Susanna yelled, "See you tomorrow night!" We walked back to the lodge, spending the late afternoon drinking tea and watching the sunset, a thin line of coral pink turning purple and then black.

In the late afternoon, we reached Periche, a small farming village located at over fourteen thousand feet. In 1977, the settlement consisted of just a few huts where villagers cultivated buckwheat and potatoes while others shepherded the yaks used for transporting supplies to base camp expeditions. Many of the village men served as guides or porters.

"Girls, tired, no?" hooted Marcel from the doorstep of a stone shelter. He wore a bandana around his blond curls, and his lips glistened from a white cream. *"Rakshi?"* He held up a clay mug, saluting our arrival.

The sun's bright and dazzling reflection bounced off the snow, blinding me a bit. When I entered the hut through a small doorway, it took a few moments for my eyes to adjust to the dim interior. Inside, a local family and several porters flashed friendly smiles.

Jens, Marcel, and a few natives sat comfortably on fur rugs surrounding a small fire pit. Yak dung burned fast and hot. A woman offered us a cup of *rakshi*. Susanna gulped down the astringent liquor and was on her second cup before I took my first sip.

"Chai?" I asked sheepishly, not wanting to offend their hospitality.

The *rakshi* kept everyone in good spirits. Laughter mixed tenderly with the chime of yak bells. Quickly, the cold evening turned frosty, and we climbed into our sleeping bags. All of us, including the locals, shared the same space on the animal-skin rugs.

A silver mist cloaked the peaks the next morning, and sunshine glowed gold along the horizon, shifting into rosy pinks and a striking, fiery orange.

Susanna sighed. "Guess this is the end of the road for you, me, Marcel, and Jens." I knew she would miss the guys who were preparing to leave. Susanna suggested we stay at Periche for another day and spend a few hours hiking with Marcel and Jens.

"Okay," Jens answered when we proposed our idea. He didn't seem to care one way or another. "We leave soon, so be ready."

After a simple breakfast of *tsampa*, ground barley made into dumplings, and butter tea, Susanna and I followed Marcel and Jens on a small trail. We carried boiled potatoes wrapped in paper with a bit of salt for lunch.

Dominating the eastern horizon, Ama Dablam—translated as "mother's necklace"—had long ridges that resembled the arms of a mother protecting her child, a beautiful, magnificent mountain. I marveled at anyone who could climb it.

"How are you going to ascend that?" I asked Marcel.

"Southwest ridge," he replied. He stopped and showed us their prospective route on a map. "Maybe we make it. Maybe no." Marcel didn't seem to mind if they didn't get too far.

Sweet and simple, our lunch ended quickly. Jens was eager to make camp as close to the mountain as possible.

"Have fun, girls," Marcel said. "Maybe see you in Katmandu after trek, no?"

I would miss his sheepish grin. They put on their heavy packs and walked toward the picturesque mountain. We watched them for a bit; their silhouettes draped in soft blond hues.

The afternoon sun formed long shadows on our path as

9 Nepal – May 1977

Susanna and I hiked back to Periche. "Do you think we'll ever see them again?" I asked.

"I hope so," she said. We didn't say much as we retraced our steps back to home—in this case, a stone-and-mud shelter in the middle of paradise.

I never saw Marcel and Jens again.

10

Canada – 1964

*I found a spot in the woods near our home
and daydreamed about a girl who gets rescued
by her real father.*

My mother came into my room. "Your father is here. He's staying at Flo's, and you can go over there after your chores."

I rushed through my household tasks and ran the two blocks to my mom's best friend's house. As soon as I saw him, I literally sprinted into his arms and gave him a big hug. "I missed you!" I tried not to cry, but I did.

Wiping away my tears, he said, "Hey, no need to cry." He wore nice slacks and a silk shirt. His aftershave smelled nice, too. Noel, my stepdad, wore work overalls and rough cotton T-shirts. "How are you?"

"I'm good," I lied, "and happy you're here. I've been waiting and waiting and waiting for you." I tried not to sound too bitter or upset that he had not visited in so long. "Where have you been?"

"Oh, I've been traveling and dating someone. I went to see my sister, Toni, in California. You know, the last time I was here, you cried so much I thought staying away would be better for you."

Really? I told myself not to shed tears anymore on his visit. I promised to put a smile on my face and enjoy every single minute. He only stayed the weekend, leaving on Sunday night.

I didn't weep when he left. But that night, I couldn't help it and ended up sobbing for hours in my room.

> Maybe he shouldn't see her.

My mother opened my bedroom door. "Hey, that's plenty of crying, already. Come into the kitchen, and I'll fix you some toast and tea." My mother let out a big puff of air as if she had had it with me. "Go to the bathroom. Wipe your face, for God's sake."

I sat at the kitchen table in the dark and tried to eat the now-cold toast and tea. I felt like a lonely audience to my stepfather, who read the paper and talked to my mom in the living room.

"Maybe he shouldn't see her," Noel said. "She gets so bloody upset every time he sends a gift or calls. He can't waltz into town and expect us to cater to him while he's here. He's a selfish bum if you ask me."

My mother nodded.

What? I'm sitting right here. They can't do that, can they? And he's not a bum!

The next day, my mom said, "I think your father should stop visiting until you are older; when you can handle it better. You cried most of the night and your face...all swollen up." She shook her head. "Besides, your home is with us now, and your stepfather provides for you. Your father never sends any child support. I'm done with him."

I'm not! I munched on my cereal.

Later, I found a spot in the woods near our home and daydreamed about a girl who gets rescued by her real father.

That evening, my mom stood in my bedroom doorframe. "Your dad and I are going out. You need to babysit your brothers and sisters. I'm leaving a load of laundry for you to fold and no watching any television until your homework is done." She folded her arms across her chest. "Now, go wash up for dinner."

I folded my arms across my chest and glared at her.

11

Nepal – May 1977

Walking beside these blue giants
made my insides ache.

Susanna was quieter than usual. We ate a simple dinner and then climbed into our sleeping bags. The Sherpas' soft and rhythmic singsong voices caressed my nerves as the wind howled and beat against the stone hut, the whistling sounding eerily human. Not wanting to think about the possible approaching storm, I slipped deeper into my warm cocoon and fell asleep.

Thick and unremitting, snow fell when we left the quiet protection of the isolated community. Although primitive, it seemed like a luxury hotel compared to the scene outside. Snow came down quickly in thick sheets that stuck to our clothes and seeped into our mittens, the cold air piercing through my down coat.

I pulled my wool hat down over my forehead and began the ascent to our next stop, about four miles away. The sound of yak bells and the occasional porter passing us with supplies for base camp kept us on the trail.

Susanna wheezed and coughed. "This is rough. I can hardly catch my breath with the wind, snow, and altitude. You know, we'll have to keep going until we reach the next settlement. There's no place to stop. Just put one foot in front of the other, I guess."

Winded, I replied, "This is a pretty steep section. Maybe it will level out once we crest the ridge."

After days and days of brilliant sunshine, warmth, and ease, we both felt out of practice, forgetting how to hike in bad weather. My feet hurt, and I missed Marcel's encouraging voice. I struggled with the thought that life might be just a series of losses.

On the last vertical incline, the snow lessened before we reached our overnight stop, and we spotted a group of seven or eight people descending toward us. One of them said, "I can't wait to get to Pangboche. Let's get these porters and yaks down quickly."

When we stopped to let the procession pass, a woman asked us, "Heading up to base camp?" She had a crisp English accent.

Susanna paused and answered, "Yes. We've come from Periche and have spent the day hiking through this mush. How much longer before we reach Lobuche?"

"Just over this and then a short hike. Hope you have a splendid time and the weather improves. I'm joining my father in Khumjung. Nice meeting you." She beamed and seemed to skip down the trail.

"She can do that because she has no pack," smirked Susanna. "She has five porters to carry her stuff!"

I stopped for a moment. "Hey...you don't think that's Sarah, Sir Edmund Hillary's daughter?"

Susanna angled her head to the side. "Probably."

We burst out laughing.

Lobuche, at a little over sixteen thousand feet, was a small settlement in 1977 of just one tiny cabin; a place to stay out of the wind and cold situated near the foot of the Khumbu Glacier, about eight or nine miles from base camp. Inside, the walls were made of mud and stone. In the front entryway, a crude coat rack held felt coats that smelled like wet dogs.

We huddled around a primitive fire pit and drank butter tea. Despite the all-day exertion, I didn't have much appetite.

The ruddy glow of the Sherpa people's cheeks shone in the firelight, and I marveled at their cheerful disposition; how they bowed to each other, showing respect and humility, always saying "namaste, namaste" with such kindness. They kept asking if we were all right, if we needed anything, and were quick to fill our cups with more tea. I especially appreciated how they sat comfortably in the silence, simply watching the fire, or listening to the wind. It seemed refreshingly different.

> I'm wearing every piece of warm clothing I have, and I'm still shivering.

Most of the native people I had come across on this trek were poor but seemed far happier than anyone I knew back home.

A little morning sunshine streamed in from the open doorway. The snowstorm had passed. We drank a cup of lukewarm tea and ate a meager serving of rice before setting out for the final hike to the Khumbu Glacier. The sun didn't stay out for long as low clouds quickly moved in, and light snow began to fall, obstructing views of the mountain peaks.

By late afternoon, we made our way to Gorak Shep, roughly translated as "steps to heaven." It was another primitive destination spot at almost seventeen thousand feet and the final stop before reaching base camp.

Susanna sniffled. "God, it's cold. I'm wearing every piece of warm clothing I have, and I'm still shivering. Let's check out this hotel if you can call it that."

Our lodging turned out to be a rough shelter, made from the surrounding rock, and just big enough to house a few trekkers and porters. In the middle of the one room, yak dung burned in the dominant fire pit. Around the depression, animal furs lay scattered on the stone floor.

A Sherpa, stationed cross-legged on the cold rocks, made tea for the six people spending the night. He used an old gas stove, possibly a leftover gift from a former Everest expedition, to heat a large aluminum pot full of snow.

> Was there such a thing as a Himalayan gossip train?

Later, when it had melted enough, we drank a cup of chai. I appreciated the sweet liquid and sipped it reverently.

Someone from outside the hut began shouting. "Hey, Pasang, I heard there are two young women spending the night here."

Pasang, our Sherpa tea maker, looked up and grinned. "Oh, Keeeittt yah, in here. Chai making now." His English sounded slightly off as if he'd just learned the words. I bit the inside of my cheek to keep from laughing.

Keith—or Keeeittt—had several weeks' growth of facial hair, and he wore a light coat. His face split into a huge smile. "Not often we see two women hiking up to base camp. We couldn't pass up the opportunity to share in some female company."

His accent sounded like Susanna's. I didn't know how he knew we were at Gorak Shep. Maybe, a porter told him—or was there such a thing as a Himalayan gossip train? The thought made me chuckle.

We sat on the tiny porch overlooking the Khumbu Glacier and talked about the trek. Keith and his New Zealand friends were climbing Mount Everest and had been at base camp for a few weeks, building camps up the mountain. He talked about the possibility of summiting Mount Everest.

"Follow our porters and yaks through the Khumbu tomorrow. The route is safe. When you get to base camp, I'll make you tea and take you up Kala Patthar, where you can get an excellent view of the entire Mount Everest area. I'll bring binoculars so you can see our Camp II and III."

11 Nepal – May 1977

He pulled on his fur cap and left. The sky, a deep bronze color, profiled the Himalayan range, a jagged line of blue-black, pink, and lavender.

The Khumbu Glacier, with its enormous towers of ice or seracs, ranging in size from cars to large houses, paved the way to Everest base camp. Since the glacier and icefall were constantly shifting, some seracs happened to be precariously on their sides, like wooden blocks tipped on their ends, ready to topple down.

Walking beside these blue giants made my insides ache. The deafening cracks of this frozen world ricocheted in the distance, and an avalanche boomed above us. This was the highest elevation I had ever reached. Although seasoned by hiking and climbing in the Canadian Rockies every summer since I was eighteen, this proved far more difficult.

Keith told us temperatures on Everest often fell below zero, and wind gusts could exceed one hundred and twenty miles per hour. The icefall above base camp, an immensely unstable moving sea, sent large ice blocks down onto the glacier. I was grateful for the porter and yaks in front of us, who were bringing supplies to the climbing teams at base camp.

My toes stung from the Siberian air, even though I had slept with my leather hiking boots on inside my sleeping bag. In fact, I had on everything I wore the evening before: wool hat, fleece mittens, socks, and pants.

I stopped. "I can't catch my breath. The altitude must be getting to me. Let's stop for a moment."

Susanna was reluctant to leave the porters but agreed. We stopped under a mammoth ice block, transfixed by the robin's egg-blue color. "This is so utterly unreal. How can I ever explain this to anyone?" She let out a long sigh.

Neither of us had cameras. Most of the trekkers I met did not carry the heavy, cumbersome camera equipment of the 1970s.

The collapse of another avalanche echoed off the ice walls, and the grind of the glacier moaned below. The bitter air seeped into my down jacket. Suddenly, things began to appear dreamlike, soft, and elusive. "Okay, enough rest," I said, "it's time to catch up with the porters."

I inhaled and made a conscious effort to breathe fully, knowing my brain lacked oxygen.

It did not take long to catch up with a porter and his yak. The yak's long fur was covered in icicles, and she plodded slowly with her head down, laden and top-heavy with supply boxes. It was hard not to feel sympathy for the animal.

Before long, base camp loomed in front of us.

Susanna lifted an eyebrow and whispered, "Wow, it's tiny. I always thought base camp would be this huge establishment."

Indeed, it was small. At the time, there was only enough space for the three expeditions climbing Everest that spring. Several red, green, and blue tents huddled together to form a community of self-confident climbers, all sharing a common goal—to stand on the top of the highest mountain in the world.

Rainbow-colored prayer flags quivered in the wind, fragile and alien in the snow and ice. Porters huddled around a propane stove, making tea. One person hung his laundry over a do-it-yourself clothesline. The sun peeked out from behind white billowing clouds. The morning air was cold, crisp and clear.

> **Camp II looked like an ant against the fathomless topography.**

Arriving at such a long-desired goal felt anticlimactic, ordinary. I had only seen a few older black-and-white photos of base camp but thought it would be ostentatious. Instead, *simple* was the best word to describe it.

I watched Keith gingerly walking toward us, carrying two cups of tea in small tin cups. "After you finish, I'll take you up Kala Patthar so you can see Camp II and Camp III. You get a great view of the whole Everest range from up there." He pointed west to a giant hill looming over base camp. Kala Patthar, at 18,209 feet, provided the best views of the Mount Everest massif areas (Mount Everest is part of a massif together with Mount Lhotse and Mount Nuptse. A mountain can have several peaks, but the highest point is called the summit.) The hike also did not require a climbing permit. It seemed easy enough.

Once we started, I found it difficult to ascend this relatively undemanding rise, often stopping to catch my breath. Even without the packs we left at base camp, it seemed to take a long time.

One step, take a breath, two steps, rest.

On top, a silver mist cloaked some of the peaks, and sunlight bathed the surrounding area of Kala Patthar in liquid gold. Majestic mountain peak after mountain peak came into view. It was the most beautiful sight I had ever witnessed.

Keith passed the binoculars and pointed. "See up there, just past the icefall? You can locate one of our camps."

When I peered through his binoculars, I couldn't believe it. The steep Khumbu icefall was nothing more than a dangerous sea of chopped ice. Camp II looked like an ant against the fathomless topography.

Who would want to climb that?

The entire landscape seemed ominous—surely a place for gods, but not humans. I took a moment to look in all directions and silently said a prayer. I don't know who I was praying to, having abandoned my Catholic upbringing, but paying homage to something felt appropriate: the kindness of the New Zealand team, Susanna's company, the grandeur.

When we got back to base camp, I gave Keith a quick hug. "Thank you for the tea and taking us up Kala Patthar. Hope all goes well for your climb. Stay safe up there."

He looked around at two of his teammates, who had suddenly appeared. His cheeks reddened. "Uhhh, nice meeting you two. Good luck on the way down. Shouldn't take you too long." He zipped up his coat, pulled down his hat, and gave us a little wave. "See ya."

Keith went from super-friendly one minute to quiet and embarrassed the next. I watched him head toward his tent and fraternity, wondering if I said or did anything wrong. Maybe I shouldn't have hugged him in front of his colleagues.

I wasn't quite up to speed on high Himalayan etiquette.

Later, I learned that the New Zealand team did not reach the summit that spring. Many teams did not, due in part, to a particularly stormy season. I didn't see Bob or Karen from the Swiss-like cabins earlier in the trek and forgot to ask Keith about them. I speculated they might have stayed in one of the nicer chalets in Namche or had taken a side trip.

Susanna and I caught up with two porters heading back to Periche. A light wind kicked up swirls of snow that stung my face. "I think we should keep hiking past Gorak Shep and go down as far as possible before nightfall. I can't wait to see some green."

Susanna cupped her hands under her armpits, and her breath vaporized into a white mist. "Let's go. I'm freezing."

The journey back to living things took less than half the time of our ascent. When we got to the junction of the trail where one path went to Namche and the other to Gokyo Lakes, Susanna took off her pack and motioned for me to do the same.

She took out a small plastic bag that held a piece of chocolate from Jens, broke it in two, and gave me the larger piece. "Here's to our successful trek to Mount Everest base camp," she said.

She eyed the valley that I would begin to ascend. "Are you sure you want to go up there?" Her dark brown eyes held a glimmer of sadness. "I don't know how you can keep trudging up these mountains. I'm filthy, stinky, and so done with walking every day, sleeping on the ground, eating sandy rice and yucky tea. I want clean clothes, real food—to lounge on the streets of Katmandu. We could fly out of Lukla. Besides, my boyfriend, Lou, will be meeting me there. I want you to meet him."

I declined to follow her, explaining that I might never get back here and tried to reassure her. "I'll see you soon. Just wait and see."

Susanna squeezed my hand and smiled. "I'll miss you."

"I'll miss you, too," I told her. "But I just gotta see those lakes. They're apparently holy. Maybe some of it will rub off on me." We laughed. "See you in Katmandu."

I watched as she headed up the incline. Just before she was about to enter a dense undergrowth area, she turned and waved goodbye again. I waved back and then turned north.

A few white clouds skimmed quickly across the sky, and I almost said, "Hey, Susanna, look at that," before remembering she wasn't there.

The stars shone like brilliant diamonds on a bed of black velvet.

So many stars...

I buttoned up my down coat and went back into the shelter, glad to get out of the wind but missing the fresh air and the beautiful quiet of the night.

After hiking through the afternoon and early evening, I found the destination stop—another rock hut. This time, a single Sherpa woman managed the outpost, making tea and food for two Hindu pilgrims and myself. The Hindu men treated the woman poorly, seeing her as nothing more than a servant.

They shouted out orders to her. "Chai, chai!" And after the woman rushed to get them their tea, they started to complain, saying, "This tea is not hot enough."

After she placed a plate of potatoes and barley in front of them, one said, "You call this food?"

Appalled by their lack of respect, I made a point to roll my eyes when one of them pushed his plate away. She giggled, grateful for the commiseration.

But they wouldn't shut up and talked late into the night. I thought they could have at least whispered.

The next morning, I began the ascent to the Gokyo Lakes region, leaving early to avoid hiking with the men. The ultramarine sky sparkled against the patina surfaces of the mountains. A few birds tweeted from the lower-lying bushes.

Otherwise, silence.

At the end of the hike, an ice crest sat elegantly between two giant Himalayan mountains, both over twenty-six thousand feet. The sun disappeared behind a bank of clouds, but not before I had the chance to drink in the spectacular views, perhaps the finest scenery on earth. Bright green lakes nestled in the alpine tundra with tufts of lemon-colored and sugary-pink flowers swaying in the breeze. This land, not visited much by trekkers in 1977, had a sense of calm and serenity. I sat on the alpine floor for a while, wrapped in quiet, before hiking into camp.

> I wondered if a camera could ever adequately capture such beauty.

The world's highest freshwater lake system, Gokyo Lakes, consisted of six main lakes fed from glaciers and underground seepage. The lakes, considered sacred by Hindus and Buddhists, dwelled in the valley directly west of the Mount Everest region, exactly one mountain range over.

One puny cabana sat on the northeast side of Thonak, the largest lake. A solitary Sherpa woman ran this destination stop while also shepherding a group of yaks. Inside the hut, a fire burned in the middle of the room. Yak skins covered the mud floor, and she chuckled when I entered.

"*Pocha?*" the Sherpa woman asked.

I gladly accepted a steaming cup of salty tea and two small boiled potatoes. The yak furs smelled funky, and the door was nothing more than a blanket nailed to a post beam. While the walls were thick and sturdy, the shack had a low ceiling and no windows. A small Buddha statue sat in a corner on a woven ruby-colored blanket, a tiny bowl of alpine flowers at his feet.

Just before dark, the same two Hindu men bolted in. *Oh, darn.* They shouted orders to the Sherpa woman and vaingloriously talked late into the night.

I tossed and turned in my sleeping bag. Lucky for me, the men left at sunrise the following day.

After a breakfast of boiled potatoes and tea, I spent the day exploring the lakes. The spongy tundra made for easy walking. The sun warmed my back, and by midmorning, I found a little beach on the western side of the lake. I sat cross-legged on the polished stones, took out my journal, and wrote. For lunch, I ate two more boiled potatoes and a drink of glacier water.

Later, I climbed up a rim to get acquainted with the area. The Himalayas towered in every direction: massive cerulean glaciers falling from ancient mountain peaks, rolling jade tundra, blooming delicate flowers, a never-ending sky, and water too blue for words. I wondered if a camera could ever adequately capture such beauty. My feelings bounced between enjoying the solitude one minute and wishing for someone to share the memories with the next.

Before the sun set behind the western peaks, I sauntered back to the hut. The Sherpa woman had already made a fire and handed me a serving of boiled potatoes and a clay cup of murky tea. I looked at the potatoes and stifled a sigh. We ate in quietness, just the two of us.

She smiled, but it was a sad smile. I wondered if her life was difficult in this beautiful but unforgiving land. She bobbed her head in a little nod, and we proceeded to our respective sleeping places. When I went out to pee, the sky was the color of bruised plums, the air hushed and still.

The cold morning air tingled against my face like the prick of tiny needles. "Namaste, namaste." I gratefully took the potatoes, wrapped in paper, from the Sherpa woman.

Oh boy, potatoes for lunch.

I wondered if I could eat them, but I did. After all, it was all she had. After the trek, it would be a long time before I could eat boiled potatoes.

I still don't care for them much.

12

Canada – 1966

I counted the days until I turned eighteen.

One summer, while visiting my step-grandfather, Pepere, I noticed an old framed black-and-white photograph placed among other family photos. In it, a full-blooded Iroquois woman in full traditional dress sat on a chair.

"That's your great-grandmother," Pepere said. A white man in a suit stood rigidly behind her.

My mother had once told me, "Your stepfather can't drink whiskey because of his Indian blood. That's what makes him violent."

So, when I saw that picture, I thought it must be true. Maybe he should just drink beer.

At church, I prayed for my stepfather: "Please, drink only beer."

My stepfather had four sisters and three brothers. His mother died before I entered his life. He grew up on a farm and was used to hard physical labor so working in the mines suited him well—a man's world.

Five mornings a week, he drove his truck ten miles to a uranium mine, deep in the muskeg country of northern Canada. My mom made his lunch, neatly packed into a metal lunchbox with an olive-green thermos filled with hot tea.

For most of the year, he'd come home after work and drink his beer at the head of the dining room table, surveying us kids while we ate our dinner in silence. If we talked or fooled around, he'd hit us with the long-handled wooden spoon he kept close by.

The mines shut down three weeks a year. Everyone took vacation then. My family headed to the bush to camp by a pristine lake, canoe, fish, and eat by the campfire. Sometimes relatives or friends joined us for a few days.

> My hate grew black and caustic, biting at the edges of my psyche.

Usually, it was a happy time until my stepfather drank whiskey and beer together and got angry, shouting swear words at the trees. Then, we'd all try to keep out of his way—hiding in the bush, taking the canoe out on the lake, or waiting for him to fall asleep.

One time I didn't get out of his way fast enough, and he kicked me hard in the back. I dropped to the ground and covered my face. He kicked again, this time to the chest, knocking the wind out of me. It hurt something fierce, and I cried for a long time.

Later, my mom said, "He didn't mean it."

That night I slept outside the tent, the haunting call of a loon in rhythm with my internal sobs. My hate grew black and caustic, biting at the edges of my psyche.

I counted the days until I turned eighteen. Five years seemed a long time. I wondered how to survive the misery or who I could talk to. But I couldn't find answers then. I didn't trust adults, and I certainly wouldn't tell my friends.

My shame burned like the embers in the fire.

13

Nepal – May 1977

Holy shit!
My mouth hung open for a few seconds.

The uneventful walk back to Namche Bazaar passed quickly. The cornflower-blue sky peeked through a thick layer of white clouds. Each day got a little warmer.

I passed the time in reflection about all my experiences on the trek thus far: getting to know the benevolent people of the Himalayan hills; making new friends with Marcel, Jens, and Susanna; walking in such a dazzling landscape.

Before long, I found the same inn I had stayed at with my friends just a few weeks prior and I asked for the ten-rupee shower...ten minutes of luxury.

"Ma'am Sahib, water hot for you now, come." The owner gestured for me to follow her to the crude shower.

"Thank you." I closed the thick cotton curtain around me. When I took my clothes off, I noticed something moving along the inseam of my brown Afghani top. Closer inspection revealed several pregnant lice, thick and yellow with eggs, glued to the strings of my top.

Holy shit! My mouth hung open for a few seconds.
What to do?

Since I only had one clean change of clothing, I washed everything in the hot water and used every second of the ten minutes to cover the whole lot in soap. I'd rinse it all out later. I worried about possible lice in my hair.

The lice situation made it an easy decision to get to Lukla as fast as I could and wait for the next flight to Katmandu. I overheard another trekker in Namche say that flights were dependent on weather and whether or not a tourist group was coming in.

The trekker said, "Hey, I knew one guy who waited a week at Lukla to get out."

I hoped a plane would arrive in a day or two. I could get to Lukla in one long hiking day and then hopefully catch a flight out with the next incoming tourist group. Funny, I didn't think of myself as a tourist anymore, with five weeks of Himalayan hiking under my belt. I felt more like a local.

Lukla used to be a small settlement of villagers tending goat and sheep herds. Then in 1977, a small airstrip was built with a very short and steep landing field. A relatively modern lodge was added to offer tourists western-style meals and trail supplies.

Private parties landed irregularly, and trekkers caught on to the opportunity of a return flight to Katmandu rather than hike back the way they came. Nowadays, twin-engine planes make frequent daylight flights between Lukla and Katmandu, and the once-quiet village, now filled with tourist lodges and shops, has replaced the goats and sheep.

An American couple, Mike and Elise, also waited for air travel to Katmandu the afternoon I arrived at sleepy Lukla. The man had black dreadlocks, and his bloodshot eyes sagged slightly. "Hey, man, we've been waiting for two days now," he told me. "The weather sucks, raining every day and too socked in for any plane to land. Hope it clears soon because I can't wait much longer."

I agreed. "I want to get out, too. A friend is expecting me in Katmandu." I didn't mention my new role as hostess for baby lice. "Can we set up camp near the airstrip? What about food?"

"You can put your sleeping bag over there." He pointed to a small shed at the end of the runway. "The new lodge serves local fare—the usual chai, rice, and *chapattis* for a few rupees more than Namche, but you get to sit inside out of the rain. The owners want us to stay at the inn overnight, but it's too expensive."

Indeed, it was pricey, and I began to worry about having enough money to pay for the flight if I had to wait much longer.

The noise grew louder and more intense.

It rained for two days. Low-lying clouds swirled around the village like ghosts. Camped outside, under a tarp, I found a paperback novel in the lodge and spent my time reading or watching the rain turn the world into a blue-green kaleidoscope.

The third morning dawned bright and sunny. I put everything in my bag, hoping to hear the plane. Soon, Mike and Elise appeared, and we sat on our packs. The sky became our movie theater. We would think we heard a motor and say: "Hey, did you hear that?"

We waited all morning. Then, about midafternoon, I thought I heard a dull whirring. "I think that's a plane."

Elise and Mike looked at the sky. The noise grew louder and more intense. "It is! It is! Look!" We craned our necks like three little ducks on an otherwise empty field.

Hovering over the hillside crest, a small twin-engine plane began its descent onto the short airfield. I held my breath as I watched the plane try to come to a halt. I was sure it would fly off the cliff.

The plane squealed and then jolted to a stop, seemingly inches away from sliding down a rock face. I lifted my shoulders and scrunched my eyes as the wheels grated against the ground. Then, the door opened, and four well-groomed men jumped off the plane. When they approached us, I noticed one of them smelled of a cologne whose name I once knew but had now forgotten. They laughed and joked in their language. I couldn't tell where they were from. Germany maybe? They didn't pay any attention to us.

I turned to look at the plane. The pilot waved and motioned for us to climb aboard. The plane engine deafened any attempt at conversation.

"Strap yourselves in... Rupees... Off in a few!" the pilot yelled at the top of his lungs. I thought he looked handsome in a rugged American-west way, with shoulder-length sandy hair, his lean frame fitting easily in the cockpit. "Ready! Here we go!"

The red-and-white plane was much tinier than I guessed it would be, more toy flier instead of a four-passenger aircraft. The seats were not soft but sturdy and rough. The tight seatbelts pinched my shoulders. I was a little nervous about how quickly things were unfolding. A moment ago, I was trekking in the hills.

The plane lifted quickly, and I marveled at the Himalayan topography, mountain after mountain after mountain, like giant waves on a sea with the undulating lush green hills seemingly in prostration before kings. The entire countryside looked like a painting against a vibrant blue sky and an egg-yolk sun.

The silence felt manageable. Words did not.

Turbulence and the constant air pressure shifts caused the ride to feel like a roller coaster. The loud drumbeat of the motors shook everything inside the cabin. My teeth chattered, and the relentless ring in my ears left me feeling nauseated.

I said an inaudible goodbye to the Himalayas as we began our descent into Katmandu. An hour plane ride covered my five-week journey. My dream expedition was now over...in the past. Melancholy seeped into my skin.

The landing turned out to be far less bumpy than I had anticipated. With just a few jerks and a rough bounce, the plane set down on the Katmandu runway. We hopped off the plane onto the airfield and walked toward a miniature air controller station.

Elise and Mike waved goodbye and found a bicycle rickshaw into the city.

I turned to the pilot. "Thanks for the safe trip," and shook his hand before he quickly spun around and ran back to his aircraft.

13 Nepal – May 1977

My clothes stuck to my skin in the soggy, heavy air. Within seconds, perspiration pooled under my armpits and dripped off my chin. My ears ached with a continued droning sound. I squirmed uncomfortably in the lower elevation temperature and watched the pilot lift off into the sky, wanting to go with him, already missing wide-open spaces, the quiet, people not moving very fast, and little to no mechanical noise.

A man on his rickshaw waved to me. "Ma'am Sahib, Freak Street?"

Susanna would be there. My spirits lifted. "Yes, yes."

I passed a tall Sikh man with a brown turban on his head, two women in crimson saris, naked children running in the streets, groups of porters, Sherpas, Tibetan refugees, western hippies, climbers, diplomats, and even a young woman in high heels. The market smells of burning oil, freshly baked bread, flowers, and the sweet odor of cut mango and papaya, including a symphony of sound—temple bells, the pounding of hammers, people shouting, dogs barking—overwhelmed my senses. What a change from the soft hushes of the Himalayan hills. The sun, a brilliant roasting ball in the sky, felt unbearably hot.

"So sorry, Ma'am Sahib. No room here." This became the response from anyone I tried to speak to about finding a place to stay. It was the peak tourist season in Katmandu. I couldn't believe how much things had changed.

I walked back to the first hotel I had stayed at several weeks ago and inquired again. "I could share a room if necessary."

"Ma'am Sahib. Maybe...have one room with lady." He looked apprehensive.

"Oh, okay. No problem." Fearful I'd be sleeping in the street if I didn't, I booked the room.

The room contained two single beds with mosquito netting draped over them. On one of the beds, my roommate was curled into herself like a rolypoly bug, the sheet tangled among her limbs. I decided to shower and soak my lice-ridden clothes in a bucket. When I got out of the shower, my roommate was still sleeping. I thought it strange she should be sleeping during the day but didn't think much about it at the time.

I left to find food and ask if anyone had seen or knew Susanna.

A European man overheard my conversation with the hotel manager. "I remember her. I think she left a few days ago." My insides tumbled, sorry that I had just missed her.

When I got back to the room, my roommate was in the shower. She came out wearing a sunflower-colored sarong tied around her torso. "Hi there," she said. "Staying in Kat long?" She lay on her bed and closed her eyes.

"I don't know. I wanted to meet my friend here, but it looks as if she might've left, and I don't know where to find her. Thought I'd check at the post office tomorrow. Maybe there's a letter. Just got back from trekking..." On and on went my monologue.

Suddenly, she sat up and rolled a piece of cloth around her arm. Then, using a propane lighter, she heated up a powdery white substance on a spoon. When it resembled water, she poured it into a needle, tapped the pointer a few times, and injected the clear liquid into her upper arm. She moaned, her eyes rolling back into her head.

> **Her sarong, dipped low in the back, revealed a tattoo, a black coiled snake.**

I glanced in the opposite direction, not sure what to say.

She let out a long sigh. "Oh, that's good." She laughed as if knowing I was shocked. "Don't mind me, sister. I'm up all night and sleep all day and won't bother you at all. See you in the morning." She went out the door with wet hair. Her sarong, dipped low in the back, revealed a tattoo, a black coiled snake.

I didn't know what to think. It was surreal after the trek. The overhead fan swooshed the muggy air round and round. I had never seen anyone shoot up before and only knew about drug addiction from the movies.

I kept thinking of my roommate's bruised arms and legs, her popped veins, and the dark circles under her eyes. It gave me the chills.

The following day, after waiting in line at the snail-paced post office, the clerk finally handed over two letters and a postcard from Susanna from my general delivery post office box. Susanna's card read:

> *"Dear Sharon, so much to tell you. I hope I can fit it in. Our plans have changed. It's unbearably hot here so we left, went to Rishikesh but couldn't enjoy it because of the weather. TOO HOT!! Lou flew out last night, and I'm leaving for Afghanistan and then Greece. Planning on meeting Lou in Vermont in August. Everything is great with us! I had my ears and nose pierced, and it didn't hurt. I'm wearing a ring in my nose until it heals, and then I'll get a diamond stud. I wish we could've spent more time together. I'm sorry we missed you in Kat. I'll send you a postcard from Pokhara with my new address. Are you still going to do that trek? Love you much, dear friend — Susanna."*

I still have that postcard with a picture of the Taj Mahal on the front. She wrote and sent the card from New Delhi.

I got another postcard from her sent to my old address in Canada later that year, which a friend kindly forwarded to me in India. Things did not work out with Lou after all in Vermont, and Susanna flew home to Australia. We lost touch after that.

Life was like that.

Great friends were made quickly, and then they were gone. Together we experienced a wonder of the world that was both extraordinary and ordinary. The people I met fed an emotional famine and nourished a lifetime of weepy poverty.

> Hot and smelly, Katmandu didn't seem fun anymore.

In fact, it has taken most of my adult life to fully integrate the richness of those experiences. The journey overland to India, the treks I did in Nepal, the people I met during that time are some of my fondest memories. I can easily lose track of time whenever something reminds me of those years: the smell of sandalwood, someone playing the sitar in a popular song, hiking in the mountains—nothing but the blue sky and my own heartbeat for company.

At the time, though, an internal transformation was underway. I smiled more and didn't think as much about the past or worry about the future. The inner barricade I usually kept high and strong started to crumble, exposing an ember of hope, shiny like tinfoil, sparkly like mini-fireworks. My awareness flourished, and I began to believe that everything might turn out all right after all.

Hot and smelly, Katmandu didn't seem fun anymore, and I also felt uneasy about sharing a room with a junkie. Every time she heated up the spoon, filled the needle with clear heroin, and swooned after she injected, my stomach flipped.

I worried her addiction might be contagious or that she could infect me somehow. The oppressive heat made it hard to sightsee during the day. I missed Susanna. After two days in Katmandu, I walked over to the trekking station.

"Trekking permit, please, for Muktinath."

I thought three weeks would be plenty of time to figure out what to do with the rest of my life.

14

Canada – 1967

The terror of not knowing what to expect grew,
and I began to hemorrhage despair
that oozed like black tar.

When I entered eighth grade, we moved from our flimsy apartment to a white bungalow with yellow trim on the other side of town. The backyard didn't have grass, only a lonely cement pad next to a small barren tree.

My mom put on her sunglasses. "It's a start. We can spend the summers fixing up the place, and your dad can finish the basement. Someday, you'll have your own room down there."

I helped her clean the house while my stepdad painted and tried to "pretty up" the exterior. The seven of us shared three tiny bedrooms. I could hear everything through the thin walls.

The mines started hiring full-time again, and my stepdad got his job back. Mom stocked the cupboards with bags of oatmeal, flour, and sugar. I loved opening the refrigerator and marveling at everything inside—butter, not margarine; real milk, not powdered skim milk; cheese; eggs.

That winter, we had a record cold spell. The temperatures dipped to negative forty-five and negative sixty, with days of deep snow and ice. Homemade bread and donuts became our normal. I didn't mind the freezing temperatures.

That year my responsibilities multiplied: taking care of my younger siblings, devoting all day Saturdays to cleaning, laundry, ironing, homework, and attending church on Sundays. If I was lucky, sometimes I got to watch a television show with popcorn.

For years when I went to church, I spent a lot of my time there praying for my stepdad and mom. I asked God, "Please help my parents to stop fighting and not to worry so much." I silently repeated those prayers over and over and over again, always hoping for things to change.

> **Anxiety swarmed my flesh like fire ants.**

They didn't, and I lost faith.

Every few months, my stepdad came home drunk.

My mom started nitpicking. "Where have you been? Why are you wasting our money? We need that money. Your breath smells."

Noel clenched his fists until the veins on his forehead stuck out. "I can do whatever I want with my money, you bitch! I work my tail off at that fuckin' mine. Don't tell ME what to do." He often beat her up, leaving appalling discolorations on her body.

She wore dark sunglasses to hide the bruises and covered the ugly contusions on her arms with makeup. Occasionally, she went with him to the bar and got drunk, too. They either came home fighting or went to the bedroom, their violent sex pounding against the paper-thin walls.

The terror of not knowing what to expect grew, and I began to hemorrhage despair that oozed like black tar. Anxiety swarmed my flesh like fire ants. I spent long hours before and after school practicing gymnastics, dreading going home, and started to plan how to leave everything I knew and never come back.

15

Nepal – June 1977

*I watched in horror as leech after leech
dropped, blood splattering on the rocks.*

I judged that the round-trip trek from Pokhara to Muktinath would take about three weeks. In the northwest corner of the Pokhara valley, the town of Pokhara was roughly one hundred and twenty miles west of Katmandu. Three out of the ten highest mountains in the world, situated thirty miles from the city's center, dominated the sky.

After an uncomfortable bus ride from Katmandu, I arrived in the sleepy village of Pokhara, which was nestled close to Lake Phewa. The village contained several low-lying lodges for trekkers doing the Annapurna circuit and pilgrims traveling to Muktinath.

The following day I packed up and left town, following the path that would lead me to my destination spots, enjoying the solitude and the quiet, my own thoughts for company.

The rain fell steadily as I made my way up to the teahouse. The air was still, like an indrawn breath. The warm, gentle droplets fell onto my shirt and jeans, into my socks, but I didn't mind. I welcomed the moisture.

Inside the teahouse, a few trekkers huddled around a central fire pit. The rectangular building looked as if it could house at least a dozen guests. After a brief exchange with the manager, I set my pack down on an empty cot and proceeded to take off my wet hiking boots and smelly wool socks. I noticed several black blobs on my feet.

"Oh, look at the leeches on you." A long-limbed man, closest to the hearth, peered at my feet. "Those buggers seem to get into everything, even through thick leather boots. Get close to the flames, and they'll drop off."

"Uh. Thanks." I hobbled over to a flat stone and hung my feet near the blaze. Then I watched in horror as leech after leech dropped, blood splattering on the rocks. I was fascinated when they sizzled in the heat, despite being grossed out by those parasites at the same time.

> Just what I need, more rain and more leeches.

The man inspected my feet. "Looks as if they've all fallen off. Hi, my name's Liam. Just returning from doing the Annapurna sanctuary. And you?"

"I'm hiking up to Muktinath." I shook his hand. "Name's Sharon."

Liam then offered a part of his clothesline to hang up my socks. "Thanks," I said. "I didn't realize there'd be so many leeches, and that they would be so persistent."

He picked up my foot. "Just gotta keep pickin' them off ya. Bloody nuisance. Weather should be turning rainy now that the monsoon has settled in."

Great, I thought. Just what I need, more rain and more leeches.

For the past two days, I had hiked through the undulating hills of the Pokhara area basin: meandering along gentle rivers, through settlements offering food or shelter, and climbing sharp inclines. Different groups trudged through this crowded pathway into the Annapurna range: porters bringing supplies to their villages, researchers, Peace Corps clusters, climbers, tourists, pilgrims, backpackers. The teahouses along the way were usually packed. English could be heard at every destination stop, and it was easy to find someone to hike with or share a meal or late-night tea by the fire.

I caught distant views of the Mustang area now and again, showing a desolate landscape, the air noticeably drier. Hiking eastern Nepal felt dramatically different than from around the Mount Everest massif. However, in Ghorepani that night, the lush pine and rhododendron forest was pleasant and refreshing.

The next morning, after a quick goodbye to Liam and the usual trekker talk of *nice meeting you, good luck on your return trip,* and *see you in Katmandu,* I made my way to Tatopani, which means *hot water*. The trail descended steeply to the Kali Gandaki River and onward to the hot springs. The rustic lodge near the undeveloped (at the time) Tatopani hot springs had several bunk rooms with varying accommodations.

My room had one twin mattress on the floor with a window. With my arms spread out, I could touch both plywood-thin walls. The couple in the next room sounded as if they were arguing, but they spoke a different language, so I couldn't really tell; their voices shrill one moment, subdued the next.

I opened my door and walked to the river, hoping to soak in one of the hot pools. The sun warmed my back as I stretched out against a big boulder and dangled my feet in the pool, testing to see how hot it was. The sound of a man and a woman bickering in that same foreign language drifted in from behind me. I turned and watched them meander through the river rocks, gingerly stepping on one stone at a time.

I waved. "Hi. Are you staying here?"

The man with shoulder-length blond hair was naked except for a pair of flip-flops on his feet. He spoke with a thick accent. "Yah. We spending few days here in Tatopani. Enjoy hot springs."

His face was covered in tattoos—black teardrops, the yin-yang symbol, and several other intricate markings around his eyes, forehead, and neck. The woman also had tattoos on her face, neck, and arms. They sat down next to me. I guessed them to be in their early forties. I tried not to gawk, but I was uncomfortable with their nakedness and especially the tattoos.

I didn't know what to say. I think my eyes were big and wide.

He smiled. "We get that stare a lot. My name is Philippe, and this is my wife, Ana. We were heroin addicts and did this at the height of our dependence. We've been sober for five years now."

"Oh. Sorry for staring. It's okay, doesn't bother me." But it did.

Nevertheless, their strange appearance and then candid forthcoming had me intrigued. We soaked in the pools, they naked, me with my clothes on. I listened to their story until the sun began to dip behind the horizon, turning the sky into beautiful brushstrokes of scarlet, sunflower, and amber.

Philippe pointed to the sky. "Beautiful, yes?"

"Yes. Sunsets in the Himalayas are really something. Must be the clouds."

Later we walked back to our paltry shelter. Philippe and Ana invited me to share dinner with them. "We brought extra," Ana said.

We talked long into the night. I found out they were from some island off of Spain and had lived most of their lives along the Spanish Riviera. I guessed they were trust fund babies living off some family fortune, but I don't know that for sure because I never had the courage to come right out and ask.

The next morning's sunlight danced on Philippe's corn silk hair. "We'll be in Pokhara for a few weeks. Come find us after the trek."

Although they were different from anyone I had hung out with before, I liked them. "Yes. I'll look you up. I should be back in about ten days or so."

Philippe grinned. "You know, a group of musicians—friends of mine—coming into Pokhara around the time you finish. Maybe hang out?"

My cheeks warmed. I'd never hung out with musicians before. "Okay. Sounds fun. I'll definitely ask around when I get back."

I thought about Philippe and Ana throughout the day, remembering pieces of their story: living the high life in Thailand and India, years of heroin addiction, the nightmare of getting clean. I appreciated their honesty.

The shimmering heat beat relentlessly against my back. Relief came only when I crossed an occasional stream or rested in the shade of rhododendron bushes. I tried wearing my flip-flops, too, just like Philippe and Ana, but within an hour, I had stubbed and cut my big toe badly enough to warrant putting the boots back on.

I'm such an idiot, I thought.

The mountains—Dhaulagiri and Annapurna—peeked out of the clouds, magnificent snowcapped summits against the crystal-clear blue sky. Along the riverbed, I stopped at a memorial for those killed trying to climb these mountains.

I gazed at the Kali Gandaki gorge in the distance, looking impossibly formidable—a profoundly deep and narrow canyon, snaking its way up to meet the snow and ice. I turned north into the wind.

After a night's rest in a small settlement, I hiked most of the next day and stopped in Marpha, a town with a strong Tibetan Buddhist presence. I found a place to stay with a family. A Tibetan monk lived there as well.

The home had three areas. The ground floor included a partial outdoor kitchen, a common area with a central courtyard, and a small room in the back. The second floor had a Buddhist shrine and meditation area at the top of the stairs. To the right was a guest bedroom. To the left was a separate quarter for the monk. Through an attic stepladder, the roof provided expansive views of the town, fields, and river. In the southwest corner sat an outhouse, exclusively for the monk. The rest of the family and guests had to use the latrines outside, away from the house.

While waiting for tea in the common area, the monk came in and seemed fascinated by my journey. He spoke English.

"You by lonesome? No family here? You Buddhist? Christian? You from where?" He broke out in a grin after each question.

> **"Man or woman is own master."**

I told him a bit. "...brought up in a French Catholic home and went to church every Sunday." I didn't tell him how hard it was to sit in the pews and that the incense made me sick because we were not allowed to eat breakfast before communion. Or that my mom made my brother and I walk the two miles to church, rain or shine—or that she and my stepfather never went. In church, my brother and I hit each other, and we didn't listen to the sermon. The priest often glared in our direction.

One day after school, that same priest was sitting at our kitchen table sipping a cup of tea when I walked in the front door. I eyed him suspiciously from under my long brown hair. When he left, I asked my mom, "So, what did he want?"

"Oh, nothing," she said, crossing her arms over her chest.

I raised my eyebrows. *Really?* The easily broken trust between my mother and I seemed to grow from tenuous to unstable.

"Why you by lonesome?" the monk asked.

I came out of my musing and shrugged. "Well..." wondering how much he'd understand. "Wanted to discover things on my own, I guess..."

15 Nepal – June 1977

After a moment or two of silence, the monk told me about his Buddhist faith. He believed anyone could become a Buddha and that each of us can attain realization by using our intelligence. "Man or woman is own master. No higher being sit in judgment of you."

"Thank you for telling me all that."

I thought about how to chart my own course, set sail to where I wanted to go. Not sure of the correct protocol, I bowed and went back to my room, deep in thought, and even tried to meditate. But really, I didn't know a thing about meditation.

At sunset, the monk began chanting, and the soothing hum of his voice lulled me to sleep.

In the middle of the night, I woke up with intense stomach pains and dashed for the outside latrine. Without electricity or candles, I quickly became disoriented, blackness staining everything.

On the street, I vomited, leaked out the other end, too, and sat down with my head between my knees, rocking back and forth, feeling sicker by the minute.

Then, I felt a hand on my shoulder. I looked up. It was the monk.

He took my arm. "Come. I help you back to house."

I puked along the way and then again in my room.

Each time, the monk cleaned up my mess and wiped my face. "Please, use my toilet."

Up and down the stairs throughout the night, I used his rooftop toilet or heaved my guts out on the way. The monk kept his vigilance, cleaning and chanting until the wee hours of the morning.

I fell asleep just as the sun peeked through the window.

The mother of the household held a cup of hot liquid to my lips. "Sun gone."

My newly washed, sun-dried clothes lay neatly folded on the blanket next to me, and the murmur of the monk's voice crooned like a never-ending river. Alternating between sleep and foggy awareness, I never recalled much except for a cool, wet cloth on my forehead.

I woke just as the sun's head emerged, sending tendrils of amber light across the clean floor. A bowl of warm water sat on a table next to the bed, and I felt light-headed when I stood to wash. In the bottom of my pack, I found the antibiotics given to me by the man on my Mount Everest trek and said a silent thanks.

> Did he do some Buddhist magic thing and take on my sickness?

Everyone in the household was eating breakfast when I entered the common area. "Oh, Ma'am Sahib better, no?" They motioned for me to sit and offered hot food and drink.

"Thank you for taking care of me—washing my clothes, bringing tea, cold cloths, and the monk." I searched for his face, but he was not with the family. "How do I thank him for doing all those, I mean, so much for me?" I didn't know how to tactfully say, "for cleaning up my puke and shit."

I continued, "Can I go see him and thank him?"

"No, no, Ma'am Sahib. No thank. Monk in room. You no disturb. He no allows."

A little girl tugged at my sleeve. "Monk sick."

What? Did I infect him? Did he do some Buddhist magic thing and take on my sickness? I didn't know what to think, but I wanted to sprint up those stairs and find out for myself.

After breakfast, I took my time folding things into my pack, one item at a time, cleaned my hairbrush, shook out the blue tarp, rewound the rope, and secured it into an almost-perfect knot, but there was still no sign of the monk.

My heart sank a little, feeling the need to at least thank him. My own mother never cared for me quite like the monk had.

15 Nepal – June 1977

I left the beautiful settlement of Marpha around midmorning, passing villagers working in terraced fields, their rhythmic singing in tandem with the swaying of their scythes. Golden sheaths of wheat and millet grew everywhere, and the mountain, Dhaulagiri, loomed like a peaceful god.

The wind blew bits of sand and river rock into my clothing and hair all day long.

In Jomsom, a Nepali armed officer checked my visa and permit. "You cannot go Mustang, understand? Only Muktinath." He handed back my documents.

In 1977, Mustang was forbidden territory, completely closed to all foreigners. Formerly known as the Kingdom of Lo, Mustang, a remote and isolated region of the Nepalese Himalayas, was restricted until 1992. In 2008, Mustang's status as a kingdom ended, and it became a republic of China. That once incredibly preserved Tibetan country...now long gone.

The town of Jomsom, primarily a government administrative center, was built close to the banks of the nearly quarter-mile-wide Kali Gandaki River. The unappealing gray plywood structures seemed depressing after lovely Marpha. I decided not to stay.

I walked east from Jomsom and began the three-thousand-foot climb to the small temple of Muktinath, passing through meadows of wildflowers on all sides. The sun had dropped behind a ridge, and a half-moon had begun to rise above the mountaintop when I entered the ancient hamlet. A few stars were already visible.

Accommodations were primitive: a stone hut with one open window and an earthen floor with a few canvas cots. A candle nestled in a clay dish burned bright, creating shadows on the dark walls. I crawled into my sleeping bag and listened to the wind.

The next day dawned cloudless and warm.

Muktinath, situated at the foot of the Thorong La mountain pass in the Annapurna ranges, looked as if it could be a small settlement out of the sixteenth century. The temple, built around a shrine dedicated to the five elements, had an outer courtyard featuring a hundred and eight minuscule fountains, all in the shape of a bull's face with each spouting water. The inside of the dark and foreboding temple felt a little surreal, like walking on to a movie set for a thousand years ago. Thick coats of dust snuggled in the corners.

The caretaker, a Buddhist nun, rose from her seat and moved toward the covered holy place, motioning for me to come closer. She lifted the heavy cloth, stiff with dirt. Inside, a water spring bubbled out of the earth and a natural gas flame burned above it. It looked just like my aunt's gas flame on her modern stove back home.

A Hindu man and his son came in and immediately kneeled on the ground next to me and paid their respect by offering incense and a garland of ginger flowers, their heads lowered in prayer.

I thanked the nun by bringing my hands into a prayer position and bowing slightly. Then I donated a few rupees for the temple and left. Outside, I gulped lungfuls of mountain air, glad to be out in the open, not feeling any connection to the place.

In the afternoon, I hiked around the tundra above Muktinath. The rock faces held massive clusters of snow and ice, and the wind blew across the peaks; plumes of pale flurry drifting to form cloud wisps, the collapse of avalanches echoing in the distance. A slight breeze came over the ridge, whipping my hair across my face and the delicate alpine flowers played do-si-do with each other.

Mesmerized by the beauty of the expansive Himalayan terrain, I hoped my memory would always remember the moment.

It has.

15 Nepal – June 1977

On my return to Jomsom, I met a boisterous group of people coming in from Mustang. They wore dark robes and were covered in dirt. Their skin looked like chocolate leather, and they spoke a dialect I had not yet heard. I moved off the trail to let them and their animals pass. They waved, laughed, and danced, seemingly without a care in the world.

Not long after, I encountered a trio of scientists studying the butterfly population. Intrigued by my solo traveling, they invited me to join them for lunch. Over bread, cheese, and cold water from a canteen, I learned a bit about their research as I watched a nectarine-colored butterfly zigzag through a nearby bush.

From then on, the trek went by quickly. I stopped in Marpha to try and speak with the Buddhist monk, but the house mother told me, "Oh, Ma'am Sahib. He no here. Left for Gompa. He meet teacher, past Mustang."

The monsoon crept into the hills like a ghost.

I let out a sigh. "Please, tell him thank you when you see him. His kindness meant a lot to me."

She bobbed her head from side to side. "Oh, yes."

I wasn't sure how much she understood.

I trudged through days of rain. Leeches seeped into my boots. A continual gray mist cloaked the peaks and valleys. The novelty of trekking in the Himalayas diminished, replaced by thoughts of a hot shower, clean laundry, and fresh food.

The five-week trek to Mount Everest and the three weeks to Muktinath were beginning to take a toll on my body. Traveling back to Pokhara, I noticed the villagers busy harvesting grain and working to get as much done as possible.

The monsoon crept into the hills like a ghost. A few clouds passed over the sun. I watched a leaf fall softly to the ground—restless, drifting, doomed.

16

Canada – 1967

*What I didn't realize was that the black,
sticky, corrosive memories would follow me
wherever I went.*

As a teenager, I tried not to sleep past my alarm. If I did, I paid.

My stepfather was strong. His muscles bulged under his white T-shirt. Years of hard physical labor had given him both stamina and rock-solid vigor. He laughed when I tried to fight him off. It seemed my pathetic attempts to ward off his advances aroused him.

He'd come to my room in the basement, located in the far northeastern corner next to the laundry room, the furnace, and my stepdad's work area. His workbench contained hundreds of tools and my Sleeping Beauty lunch box from first grade. A tall glass cabinet housed his six rifles for hunting big game.

Sometimes I would not know he was beside me until his calloused hand caressed my private areas. Then, I'd bolt awake, go rigid, and start fighting. "Stop it. Please, just stop," I'd beg.

"Whoa. Whoa," he whispered, "let's snuggle." His arm or leg wrapped tight around me so I couldn't move.

"Dad, don't do this." My heart was racing so hard I felt pain in my chest.

I guessed whenever he felt he'd been gone long enough to possibly cause my mother to ask what he was doing in my room, he'd jump up and say in a loud voice, "Okay, time to get up now." And wink at me, as if we were coconspirators in his play.

It was not play to me.

I tried to tell my mother. "Mom, Dad won't leave me alone." My neck, face, and ears felt impossibly hot.

"What do you mean? He's always got your best interests at heart. Stop whining. You're always selfish."

I retreated further into myself, foolishly pretending everything would be all right.

I joined the high school cheerleading team to get up early for practice and avoid any contact with my stepfather; became a member of the student council and stayed for their afterschool meetings; made friends with a popular crowd which got me invited to parties where I could spend time at their wealthier homes. Eventually, I even had a boyfriend who took me out on dates.

> One heartbeat at a time, I plotted to leave and never return.

When I graduated from high school, I weighed ninety-eight pounds and had developed a large spidery-red rash on either side of my spine.

The doctor said, "Looks as if you have shingles. Have you been under some kind of stress or something?"

I lied, "No. Must be all the extra physical stuff I'm doing—track and field, cheerleading competitions."

I woke in the middle of the night, my heart beating wildly; panic puddles under my armpits, dry mouth, cracked lips. One heartbeat at a time, I plotted to leave and never return.

What I didn't realize was that the black, sticky, corrosive memories would follow me wherever I went.

17

Nepal – June 1977

When I opened my eyes,
the sitar player glanced my way,
his warm smile as natural as rain.

When I got back to Pokhara, I busied myself with laundry and numerous showers to eliminate lice remnants, even finding a few eggs on some of my hair strands. In the sunlight, they were a deep ochre color.

One other thing I did, which I regretted later, was to pierce my ears and nose. In those days, it was rare to see a western woman or man pierce their nose, or have rings in odd places. I thought it would look cool, but I didn't know how to get that done, so I asked around.

A local villager insisted he did silver ring piercings. "No problem, Ma'am Sahib. Five rupees only for you." He brought me to his home, a small hovel on the outskirts of the town. His wife came out wearing a white and blue sari. Several grubby children played in the small courtyard.

"Ma'am Sahib, Ma'am Sahib, sit, sit." He went into his mud house and brought out small round metal rings, sharpened at one end. Without sterilizing anything, and before I could process what was going on, he punctured both ears and slid the rings in. Within seconds, he stabbed my nose and plopped in the nose ring.

"See, easy." He beamed and held out his hand for the five rupees.

My face throbbed and my ears hurt as I quickly gave him the money, wishing I could take back my steps. I can't remember if I walked or ran out of the filthy place, but I do remember his children trailing behind me, laughing and coaxing their friends to join them, their singsong voices seemingly full of ridicule.

When I got back to my hut, I closed the door and looked in the small dirty mirror. Swelling had begun around the rings, and my skin had turned a cherry color. The piercings in my ears were uneven, one slightly higher than the other. My mind raced in all directions as I chastised myself for my foolishness.

What was I thinking?

I stayed inside and stared at the floor until the sounds of the children faded into silence. By morning, my head still ached, but the puffiness had subsided, the skin around the piercings now rosy instead of beet-red.

Because I didn't want to run into any of those kids or their family again, I took a different route into the village for breakfast and happened to see Philippe, the naked man from Tatopani. He easily stood out among the locals with his wispy blond hair, wearing a mauve-striped sarong around his waist with no shirt, his black tattoos glimmering in the sun.

I waved, eager to get his attention. "Philippe!"

He looked up and deftly put a purchase of bananas in a cloth bag. "Hello, hello. You're back. Ana and I wondered if we would see you again." His accent emphasized the wrong syllables. "We're renting home not far from here. Tomorrow big party. Please come. Lots of food. Friends. Great music. Ana will be happy to see you." He jotted down directions on a small piece of paper. "Salut."

I watched him return to the marketplace and barter with a Nepalese woman, his confidence smooth as a placid lake. A bird flew above his head, the wings catching the early light.

17 Nepal – June 1977

From the reflection in the mirror, my new piercings looked obviously crude. For a moment, I wished for a drop of makeup to cover the still-pink skin. The copper luster from my long brown hair did little to boost my confidence. I pinched my cheeks and smoothed out the wrinkles in my ankle-length skirt.

The directions to Philippe's house were simple enough: down the main street, turn left at the intersection, then follow a small path to a two-story home with a wraparound verandah.

Perspiration had already begun to accumulate in my armpits as I pushed my way through boughs laden with summer blooms. Beautiful sounds filled the air—the exotic strum of a sitar, thumps of a drum keeping pace, rhythmic vibrations of a few instruments I could not name, laughter. Even a few birds seemed to sing along.

> I could only equate it to the first sounds of spring.

Several people smoked cigarettes on the porch. I caught a few different dialects: French, Spanish, Italian. A woman with flaxen dreadlocks past her waist nodded when I approached.

Even though I was feeling shy, my pulse unexpectedly tripled. "Hi, is this Philippe and Ana's house?"

"*Oui, oui,*" the woman said.

I switched to French, and we talked for a moment.

Growing up in a French-Canadian family, we conversed in both English and French, although I preferred English because of my hometown's prejudice toward French Canadians. I used to cringe when my stepfather spoke to my English-speaking friends because he didn't use the correct grammar: "Close the lights. Hey, make me two eggs, eh, side by each."

The smell of pot and brewing chai floated past my nose. Ten people surrounded the covered entrance. A dozen more sat on the rail, and several people came up from behind the house. This must be some group, I thought.

I heard someone shout, "They're starting!"

We all proceeded through a slender doorframe that opened to a sizeable room. Two overhead fans rotated above. Blankets and colorful cushions lay strewn across the uncluttered floor. Twenty people or more situated themselves near the front.

Philippe saw me and waved. I took a seat on a bolster, squished against the western wall. In front, woven mats and an amethyst-colored blanket covered a raised façade.

Four musicians came in from the back, dressed in flowing white cotton shirts that fell to their knees. One wore a black sarong tied with a big knot around his slim middle. The others sported white yogi pants. They looked lean and tanned. Each began to tune an instrument: a Spanish guitar, tabla drums, violin, and a cello. Then everything went still; only a cough or someone clearing their throat could be heard.

> I nervously gazed into Taj's molasses-colored eyes.

A slender man with dark olive skin and thick black hair past his shoulders walked in carrying a sitar. He sat in the middle of the musicians, conversed, and laughed. He placed one leg over the other and tapped his foot.

Next, the music began.

Exquisite sounds, different from anything I had ever heard —I could only equate it to the first sounds of spring, a bluebird song, the gentle patter of rain, the distant rumble of thunder, the mysterious resonance of ancient Asia, the chime of a bell, the violin, a baby's cry.

The off-tempo sound made my stomach drop and filled my head with images of a bygone era—women walking with bundles on their heads, children bathing in cool river pools, men hunting tigers with spears, snakes waiting in the grass.

I closed my eyes and drifted, each cord taking me on a journey. When I opened my eyes, the sitar player glanced my way, his warm smile as natural as rain.

Philippe introduced us. "This is Taj, my good friend from Majorca." He pointed to the group of musicians. "And that's his band. They here for vacation. After, they go Varanasi to study Indian music. He doesn't speak English."

I nervously gazed into Taj's molasses-colored eyes. Something passed between us, swift as an electric shock. My cheeks warmed, and I felt my heartbeat in my throat. "Nice to meet you."

A few people jostled around him, and even though I could not understand what they were saying, the body language was clear. They all loved him.

The next day, a petite Nepali girl delivered a note to my room. "Please come for dinner." It was signed *Philippe*.

When I left, a kaleidoscope of reds and pinks painted the sky. A soft breeze whispered through my long hair. The thought of seeing Taj again sent zigzag patterns of excitement through my veins. When I pushed the heavily-laden flowering branches back and entered the back lane, the familiar sound of music—sitars and tablas—ricocheted off the adjacent hedges.

Up ahead, I saw Ana sitting on the railing of her home. I waved.

Ana gestured back. "Hello. Glad you come."

I noticed the group of people bordering the deck: two of the musicians from last night, six people from the close group up front, and a small child.

Ana introduced the small crowd. "This is Roberto. Tabla player for Taj." She gestured to a nice-looking man. "Stephan plays violin." She continued to introduce the group. "Diana, Maria, Jon, Jose, Osamu." Each gave a slight nod. "And this is Domenico and his little daughter, Marcella."

I felt a little light-headed, trying to remember all their names. "Nice to meet all of you."

Ana grabbed my arm and said, "Come on. Dinner must be ready."

We made our way inside. Philippe and Taj sat on comfy cushions with Taj's sitar positioned between them. Taj looked up, and I took a large, savoring breath, forcing myself to remain calm. Incense burned slowly from a corner of the room.

Roberto and Stephan plopped down next to Taj and began a conversation in a language I did not know. Domenico and Marcella went into the kitchen with Ana. I tried to mix with the crowd and feigned interest when Jose asked me questions.

We situated ourselves on soft cushions around a circular table raised a foot off the floor with a tall candle burning in the middle. Two Nepali women served a feast of fluffy rice, curried vegetables, sizzling *chapattis*, cucumbers in yoghurt, and seasoned lentils. Stephan poured a wine of some kind he had brought from home; a sweet, thick liquid with a tangy smell.

Laughter filled the room. Taj's magnetic charisma sent sparks, like tiny firecrackers, trailing up my spine. I guessed him to be from Greece, Morocco, or even India, maybe still in his twenties.

In his broken English, Roberto asked, "So, Taj wants you to stay for music later."

I lifted my hand to cover my smile. "Oh, yes. I'll stay for sure." I felt my cheeks heat up, wondering if anyone could hear the thumping of my heart.

For the next several days, drawn to Taj like an ant to a sugar bowl, I accepted every invitation. I was lured into a world filled with music, laughter, and affluence: a boat ride on Lake Phewa; staying up late; eating rich food.

17 Nepal – June 1977

One night, Taj gently tickled my back and played with my hair. My eyes flickered with emotion. The cinnamon spice of his skin made me feel dizzy.

"Katmandu ke lie a kripaya."

Did he just ask me to come to Katmandu? Hell, yes, I thought.

I looked him right in the eye, nodded, and couldn't help but smile, my body infused with warmth.

He jumped up and shouted something to Roberto and Stephan. They whooped and hollered something back.

I became Taj's girl.

18

Canada – 1972

*I felt dizzy, as if my brain
had stopped working.*

Nightmares of large beds, outhouses, knives, a screaming woman, and an enormous crowd of people surrounding a table—their mouths open wide, emanating cigarette smoke—haunted me for years. I'd wake up in a sweat, my heart pounding ...*kaboom, kaboom*.

Just before leaving home at age eighteen, my mom finally confessed. Tears streamed down her face. "You know those nightmares you've been having all your life? Well, they are not nightmares. They are real."

She covered her face with her hands. "You see, when you were little and your father and I separated, I did not take you with me. I thought it would be better for you to stay with your dad and I could care for your brother, who was on the way. I didn't know he would give you up."

I was not crazy!

I felt dizzy, as if my brain had stopped working.

"Your father couldn't take care of you, so he placed you in a boarding house north of Toronto." My mother swallowed. "Well, it really was an orphanage of sorts."

I was three. The boarding house was actually a working farm where unwanted children were placed, a predecessor to our modern-day foster care system. After years of research, I discovered the place was shut down in the early 1960s by the provincial government.

"You stayed there off and on for about three years until your father and I decided it was best for you to live with me." She lowered her chin. "I'll never forgive him for placing you there."

I cried, too, but not because I was sad. The truth liberated me from my internal torment about those nightmares. *I was not crazy!*

I remember looking out the window. The moonlight danced on the driveway, the light touching the top of the small spruce tree we had planted when I was fourteen. I kept breathing through my nose and couldn't hear the rest of what my mother had to say, her words muffled as if I was wearing earmuffs.

A few months later, I boarded the Canadian Pacific Railway bound for Banff National Park. My friend Karen had been living in Banff for the past year and got me a job waitressing at a pancake house. I packed a duffle bag of things I thought I needed for the summer and vowed never to return.

In the last hours at home, before I got on that train, I hugged my brothers and sisters. I held my mom close. "Bye, Mom."

I waited for her to say something, hoping for a conversation or a few inspirational thoughts: *You can do it. Have a good summer. Be all you can be. Enjoy yourself.*

Instead, her stiff embrace said it all. Putting on her sunglasses, she said, "You'll never make it."

My vision blurred and a tightness spread through my chest.

My half-sister Robyn put her arms around my middle. "I'll miss you."

Robyn had a stable temperament rooted in the earth like a crimson plum tree: beautiful flowers in the spring, stoic in winter. As a child, she rarely complained and humbly accepted her status as the favored daughter, my stepfather's first child. He never hurt her, and she was never afraid of him. She enjoyed skipping on one leg and singing nursery rhymes. Her eyes moistened when her feelings went unchecked, but she never really cried.

Dissimilar from me, of course.

I opened my mouth to speak, pausing for a moment to collect my thoughts, trying not to let the worry for her future show. "Take good care of yourself," was all I could manage.

There were tears in my brother Tony's eyes when I left. His face looked soft and young, just like when I first got to really know him when I was in first grade...

A line of girls snaked down a stark hallway to the only restroom in the school. While I stood in line, I saw a young boy bundled up in his snowsuit on the outside of the school's doors. His face was squished against the glass, and his frozen breath made a halo around his head.

Tony?

I put my hand over my mouth, stopped, and looked up at Sister Frances. "I think that's my brother."

"My gosh. It must be negative twenty out there. What is he doing?" She ran to the door. Just then, the office secretary, another nun, her long black skirt swishing against her plump legs, barked out an order. "I'll let him in and find out why in the world would any mother not know her child is missing, and in this weather..." She shook her head.

Sister Frances knelt down on one knee and placed her hands on my shoulders. "Your brother, you say?"

All my failed relationships are because of Mom.

Would I get in trouble? I replied with a timid, "Yes."

My brother held the office secretary's hand and broke into a big grin when he saw me. "Rona," he said, skipping the *S* and the *h* and adding an *a*.

"What are you doing here?" I asked.

"I find you to play." His cheeks were bright red circles.

Embarrassed, I shrugged. What decent six year old plays with her two-year-old brother? Not me.

Tony let go of the office secretary's hand and wrapped his arms around me, hugging me as tightly as his pillowy snowsuit would let him. "Love you."

Ambushed, I choked back a sob and hugged him back. He came to the school because he couldn't find our mother. I never found out why.

Years later, he told me, "All my failed relationships are because of Mom."

A deep bronze color filled the sky when I boarded the train. The whole world smelled of wet leaves.

I swallowed a few times, the taste bitter like a mouthful of pennies.

India 1977 – 1979

19

Nepal and India – June-July 1977

*We arrived on the hot plains of India
in a blistering heat, which felt more like being
inside rather than outside of a simmering stew
that pulsed and moved.*

Taj rented a home on the outskirts of Katmandu for his band and us. A Nepali woman cooked two meals a day—breakfast, dinner, and of course, a large pot of fresh chai. Another woman cleaned the home and brought fresh flowers to our rooms. We stayed in Katmandu for two weeks.

Taj, Stephan, Roberto, and any number of fans filled his home. Stephan and Roberto spoke some broken English, and Taj spoke Spanish, Italian, Greek, and Hindustani.

Without the commonality of the English language for us to communicate with one another, I heavily relied on his body language: a slight turn of his head in my direction; a wink; his foot reaching for mine under the low table; his eyes. I scrutinized how he interacted with his friends, marveling at his grace, and swore his carefree laugh seemed to drift toward me like a cool breeze falling off the mountain.

Watching him play music became my favorite time of day. I appreciated how he set his sitar down after a recital or jam session—with the greatest of care, as if he were cradling a child. Then he'd lift his head and search for me. When his chocolate eyes found mine, my heart felt as if it just might beat out of my chest.

I loved his lips and the perfect row of white teeth underneath. Whenever he directed his gaze toward the bedroom, it made my insides quiver. I couldn't wait for his velvety warm touch. When we were alone, he'd affectionately touch my cheek, resting back against the soft cushions behind him, and stare more into me than at me.

> My fiery desire obliterated any other need.

Taj made love like the way he handled his sitar; tenderly, with just the right touch, smoothing his hand over the voluptuous base while his other hand tuned the strings, one by one. Then he'd stop, admire his instrument for a moment before the next round of tune-ups, adjusting all six strings until they were perfectly aligned, stroking them for an absolute precise, liquid honey sound: his graceful body supple and yielding like the softest leather.

I couldn't get enough. My fiery desire obliterated any other need.

In the mornings, he'd bring two cups of steaming chai into bed with us and stroke my arm. "Beautiful." His new English word.

No one had ever called me beautiful before.

One morning, in those first two weeks in Katmandu, I sat on a bridge overlooking a river, the sky a robin's-egg blue. The sun warmed my back, and the light glistened on the water; a child played in the water and laughed. A light current of air spilled into my eyes.

I thought about Taj's delicate fingers touching the inside of my thighs, his black hair entwined with mine, the gentle feel of his lips, the apple-pie scent of his skin, and my belly fluttered with promise; the past fading like a photo left in the sun.

The vivacious nature of this new lifestyle had an effervescence that drowned any common sense. Taj's aura simply dazzled me. He was different from anyone I had ever known.

At the end of the two-week stay in Katmandu, when he asked if I would consider coming to Varanasi, I quickly answered, "Yes, of course." If he had asked me to sign a contract, I probably would have.

His olive skin brushed against my English pink as he took a large gulp of some kind of wine, a gift from one of his fans, and then passed a hand-rolled cigarette to Stephan. "Good you come Varanasi." Taj's dark hair shone in the candlelight.

I was thrilled by the fact he was trying to learn English and breathed in his musky scent, wanting to crawl into his smile. "I'm looking forward to it, Taj. I want to see your Varanasi. Listen to you play and get to know Stephan and Roberto. Thank you for inviting me." I might have even batted my eyes.

Taj introduced me to other musicians in the area and showed me the correct protocol when entering Hindu and Buddhist temples. We went to out-of-the-way eateries where I tasted new foods, so hot and spicy my eyes watered; the strong incense burning the inside of my nose. Sometimes we took baths in the courtyard with all our clothes on and laughed until my sides ached. I fell hard.

Taj had a breathtaking elegance—bordering on magic—when it came to dealing with the people that encircled him. Once, when Stephan messed up a drumbeat, Taj embraced him in a big bear hug and whispered something in his ear. Stephan's eyes were moist, and his lip trembled.

Then, Taj gathered his band together and shouted in his own language, "Stephan, you beast. I love you!"

On the train to Varanasi, Taj rented a cabin that quickly filled with the band and their supporters. On the ride, some of his fans played music. Others shared food: ripe, buttery-orange mangoes, *chapattis* wrapped in cloth. We laughed, joked around, pointed at things through the open window—a herd of water buffalo, farmers tilling the land, a woman carrying a huge load on top of her head, children playing in the mud.

We arrived on the hot plains of India in a blistering heat, which felt more like being inside rather than outside of a simmering stew that pulsed and moved. People were everywhere: on top of train cars; camped by the railway tracks—a massive human sea dotted with elephants, camels, lively markets, colorful merchandise, saris, vibrant temples, painted cows, decorative trinkets hanging from every rickshaw, strewn litter, bits of dirt and dust all over the place.

The sound was intense, too: squeals and horns, distorted garble blaring from outdoor speakers, cowbells, chai *wallas* selling tea. My senses, already on overload, could hardly take in the spicy aromas from the vendor stalls cooking curries and sweets, along with the heady smell of incense and cow dung—including the sour taste of inadequate sanitation and feces.

Varanasi, extraordinary in her ordinariness, seeped into my pores and any connection to the modern world wandered away. I felt light and carefree and didn't give a damn about anything whatsoever, other than being swept into a whirlwind of living in the moment.

Believed to be about three thousand years old, Varanasi, situated on the sacred Ganges River, attracted thousands of pilgrims every year who primarily visited the many *ghats*—stairs—leading to the river embankments. While reciting supplications unique to their philosophies, the travelers entered the water with their clothes on and poured the trusted spiritual water over their heads.

19 Nepal and India – June-July 1977

When I was there, the old city quarters surrounding the *ghats* were filled with crowded, narrow, winding lanes supporting culturally diverse shops and temples. Many foreigners were eager to study in such an ageless place, especially musicians.

Taj and his band lived near the last *ghat* on the Ganges River, a two-story home with an open internal piazza. An older Indian woman dressed in a red sari opened the heavy house gate when she saw Taj.

Inside, large trees and flowering bushes surrounded a fountain; a wiry older man was bent over working in the circular gardens. Then, a young woman and her husband came out of the kitchen area and talked to Taj. Later, I learned these people were hired to cook, clean, and run errands for the band.

Taj showed me to my room on the second floor and left me alone to explore my new surroundings. A slight breeze came through the iron-barred window, and I could see two papaya trees. I closed the door, undressed, and washed, taking a moment to freshen up.

At dinner that evening, on that first day in Varanasi, Taj leaned over to Stephan and said in his language, "She should wear a sari. Best if we all wear traditional Indian clothing when we are in India. When I'm in Paris, I might wear a tie, but here, we need to blend well." He nodded, and Stephan translated.

A flush appeared on my face and neck. I smoothed my hands over my jeans. Desperately wanting to fit in, I whispered to Stephan, "Okay. But how?"

After dinner, Stephan introduced me to the woman in the red sari. "This is Amita. She can help find a tailor and get some fine Varanasi clothes made. Maybe even a sari. They're beautiful." He winked.

Amita, who spoke a little English, put her hands in the prayer position in front of her chest and bowed. "Oh, Ma'am Sahib. Go now, yes?" She seemed thrilled to get me out of my jeans and T-shirt.

I shook my head. "Not now. Tomorrow?"

She waggled her head back and forth. "Yes, yes. Morrow. Good."

> **Was I drunk with love or passion?**

Amita talked with her tailor in their native Hindustani. They clicked their tongues and spoke rapidly, taking measurements and pulling out yard after yard of fabric. One sari takes five yards of material, plus more for the cotton undergarment skirt and short blouse. The tight-fitting shirt leaves the midriff bare. I felt a bit like a movie star with all the attention. The tailor's assistant brought chai, and we sipped tea while the tailor worked.

While Amita preferred flashy reds and purples, I chose a delicate white color with a sugar-pink embroidered edge and a short-sleeved top to match the embroidery. It was the nicest thing I had bought myself in years.

A week later, Amita placed a beige-and-crimson sari on my bed with a pair of handmade leather sandals. She smiled. "Gift, Ma'am Sahib." *Taj*.

Taj's presents touched me every time: a dark red flower in a chai cup we shared; a scarf with gold thread he saw me admiring in the market; a toe ring scripted with the Sanskrit symbol meaning peace; and a small, intricately woven basket.

I gravitated to him more and more. Was I drunk with love or passion? I wasn't quite sure.

At dinner, Taj would wait until the band and I were all seated, the food hot and steaming before us. He'd lift his glass, his face radiant, and look at each of us. "Nothing is more important right now than all of you."

Stephan quickly whispered the translation in my ear. I thought we were special—our alliance strong and beautiful like sailing on a cobalt lake, the wind just right, puffing up the white sails.

Despite my worries, the holes in my ears and nose had healed well. In the market, I bought gold hoops for my ears and a small diamond stud for my nose. Taj preferred my hair free-flowing, not tied back in my usual braid, so I spent extra time brushing my hair, trying to emulate the women around me.

June floated into July. My skin bronzed. I listened to Taj and his band play. I waited for him at night. I lost direction. Although we had only been in Varanasi a month, it felt like years.

At breakfast one morning, in the middle of the monsoon, Taj announced, "I'm going to Rishikesh to meet a few friends just coming back from Europe and America. You should all come. Besides, I want to get away from the heat."

Of course, I had to wait until the cheering settled down and Stephan could translate.

I thought it would be nice if it could just be the two of us, but I knew better. Taj loved traveling with a group. In fact, I think he preferred a crowd.

I told Stephan to tell Taj, "Yeah, I'll go. Sounds fun," dropping my head to hide any sign of disappointment.

The streets and nearby areas of Rishikesh, noticeably cooler, was home to many different groups, native pilgrims, light-hearted foreigners, dedicated *sadhus*, wealthy Indian vacationers, commissioned artists. Rickshaw drivers wrangled for our rupees. Merchants shouted out incessantly: "Chaaaaaaiiiiiieeee!" or "Ma'am Sahib, you buy this, no?"

Rishikesh, located in the Himalayan foothills in northern India, was known as the gateway into the Himalayas for popular pilgrimages to Gangotri, Badrinath, and Kedarnath. The town also had many yoga centers. In 1969, the Beatles visited the Maharishi Yogi Ashram, now closed. They composed many of the songs on the *White Album* there.

I remembered those first days in Rishikesh five months earlier and I shook my head, hardly believing how different I felt—beautiful, strong, and part of something bigger, hoping never to see my ex-boyfriend Rick or have to face anything bad again.

Our rickshaw drivers pedaled quickly and efficiently dropped us off at a street on the western edge of Rishikesh. An Indian man with long gray hair opened a solid gate adorned with a big padlock.

Taj greeted him affectionately. They talked for a few minutes in Hindi, laughed, and then Taj motioned for us to follow. Like baby ducklings, we trotted behind. Several low-lying, rectangular-shaped structures surrounded a terrace filled with trees and bushes in bloom.

Stephan put his arm around me and said in a low voice, "They are not here yet. Taj thinks we should travel up to Badrinath for a few days while we wait for them to arrive."

At the time, I did not think to ask who *they* were.

We showed up at the depot before dawn. The bus, packed with people, snaked up the foothills on a skinny road meant for one vehicle at a time. Steep switchbacks cut into the hillsides like a Z. When one bus screamed around a tight bend, the other bus stopped and hugged the hillside. When this happened, the mud squished against the open window as the other bus inched its way past us.

Taj, Roberto, and Stephan laughed. I closed my eyes. The gas fumes chugged out of the rusty pipes, thick and black. It took all day. At rest stops, we drank tea, and I noticed the cooler air. The loamy smells of the plains were replaced by fresh evergreen. A wind fell off the mountains and I snuggled up to Taj.

In Badrinath, the clouds thickened and cloaked everything in a wintry mist. I could barely see more than fifteen feet in front of me.

Badrinath, located about one hundred and eighty-five miles north of Rishikesh and set on the banks of the Alaknanda River, drew devotees of all faiths and schools of Hindu thought. The fifty-foot tall Badrinath temple resembled a Buddhist *vihara* monastery. The Tapt Kund hot springs, situated just below the temple, where most pilgrims bathed in the year-round 113-degree water before visiting the temple, looked inviting.

Stephan whispered, "We're going to go to the hot baths first. Taj is freakin' freezing up here."

I looked at Taj. He wore sandals and traditional Indian clothing with a wool shawl draped around his shoulders, and his eyebrows were pulled close and down, creating a forehead crease.

I zipped up my down coat, smug in my mountain know-how. "I'll meet you after the baths," I told him.

The enclosed hot-spring bathhouses with soaking pools were separated by gender. All the women and children immersed themselves in hot water with their clothes on. Wrapped in a light sari, I sat in the heat and steam and closed my eyes. The thick fog made it hard to see. Some of the women talked in Hindu. Others washed their children. Some sang. I let my mind float in and out of a peaceful heaven. It was great to be away from the men.

However, I couldn't stop thinking about Taj. I'd never fallen for anybody quite the way I'd become obsessed with Taj, wanting to share all my hopes and dreams with him. I wondered when he'd realize just the two of us could be so much better.

Later, I found the guys up by the temple. They talked with a group of *sadhus*. I knew the sadhus were supposed to be holy men, but they looked like a bunch of unruly hoodlums to me.

Sadhus, abundant in both Rishikesh and Varanasi, were wandering monks dedicated to an ascetic way of life. They dressed in orange, red, or pink clothing to show their renunciation from the material world and dedication to spiritual practice. Some *sadhus* were nearly naked and wore their hair in thick dreadlocks. *Malas,* a type of rosary or prayer beads, hung around their necks. Stephan told me they usually engaged in a wide variety of religious practices, from extreme asceticism to maintaining a silent life or even continuous prayer and meditation. Some lived in temples or ashrams, others in remote mountain caves. Still others, I was informed, live in constant motion, traveling from one pilgrim spot to another, supported by donations from the community.

Many *sadhus* consumed different forms of cannabis. In 1977, many visiting foreigners showed a fascination toward the *sadhu* community, maybe because of the high quality of the hashish.

Taj paced back and forth and rubbed the back of his neck.

"Hey there, should we find something to eat?" My hands tingled as I zipped up my down coat.

Taj stopped his pacing, stared at the ground, and then turned to face a small group of *sadhus*.

Roberto's ears turned red.

Stephan seemed to share a conspiratorial glance with Taj. "Uh. Hmmm. We're going to get stoned with these guys."

Should I follow them? Was this a men's club only?

Silence.

Taj and an older *sadhu* led the way up several stairs onto a covered deck north of the main temple, where Hindu pilgrims gathered and slept. Some made chai or food on crude do-it-yourself coal stoves. I followed Taj, Roberto, Stephan, and a group of five *sadhus*.

They made a tight circle and then sat down on the cold concrete floor, clearly not making any room for me to squeeze next to Taj. One of the *sadhus* lit a bong with hash and passed it to Taj, who then passed it to the next person, around and around and around. They did not talk.

I sat on the outside and watched them get blurry-eyed, not really knowing what to do. So, I slipped into my sleeping bag, pulled a wool hat over my damp hair, and drifted to sleep. The soft murmurs and chants of the pilgrims were the last things I remembered of that evening.

The next morning, a rough shake on my shoulder woke me up. Nestled inside my down bag, insulated from the cold and whatever was going on around me, I reluctantly poked my head out and blinked at the morning light.

Taj.

"Come. Food."

Hey, he's learning more English. I smiled.

Taj's blank gaze felt icy and distant.

At the tea shop, Roberto and Stephan greeted us with large glasses of hot tea and sizzling *samosas*, a triangular fried bread stuffed with curried potatoes and vegetables. Taj barely spoke and kept tightening his blanket around his lean frame.

Stephan whispered, "We didn't sleep last night. Too cold. Taj is pretty miserable and wants to head back as soon as we can get on the next bus. He says he can do without Kedarnath and Gangotri."

I looked at my traveling companions dressed in light cotton, goose bumps on their legs, blue lips. In contrast, I wore a wool hat, down coat, and boots. After Nepal, I could have easily stayed on. However, I didn't think twice about going with Taj and the guys. Taj's aloofness didn't seem odd at the time. "Okay." My raw enthusiasm was spilling over, eager as a puppy waiting for the next ball to be thrown.

When we boarded a bus jammed with returning Hindu pilgrims, a constant drizzle obscured any view of the nearby Himalayan peaks. The air, damp and thick, crept into our clothing and a frosty wind tumbled off the high mountains. Taj lifted his knees and wrapped his blanket around himself, including his head, refusing to engage in any conversation. I tensed in the brittle silence.

Stephan and Roberto gave Taj a little round black ball about the size of a nickel. Then they gave me one. It felt soft and sticky.

I squished the ball between my fingers. "What is it?"

Stephan smiled. "Opium for the ride down."

Taj smiled—the first smile in twenty-four hours.

"Just swallow it whole." Stephan popped the opium ball into his mouth like popcorn.

I mimicked him, but the round, sticky globe adhered to the sides of my throat. I had to swallow several times to get it down. Not long after, I felt nauseous and vomited at the first rest stop. Afterward, I gagged and retched on every sharp hairpin turn. For most of the journey back, I laid my head in my arms, counting my breaths.

We arrived in Rishikesh in the late afternoon. The balmy summer sunlight danced on my skin. After the long ride and opium malaise, I agreed that walking would be better than trying to negotiate rickshaws.

Taj came alive. He told Stephan, "Let's get some curry, rice, and tea."

We found an open-air restaurant, enjoyed hot food and the warmth of the late-day sun.

Taj laughed, told the group he'd be back in a few minutes, and returned with garlands of flowers, like Hawaiian leis, and draped them around our necks. "For my friends."

When he sat down, he placed his foot over mine and pressed a small *mala* into my hand, resting his forehead against my shoulder for a moment. I breathed a whiff of his masculinity, hoping I could remember it forever.

We arrived back at the hotel just as the sun was setting, the sky turning pink, orange, and then dark blue.

I hugged Taj, Stephan, and Roberto. "I'm not feeling well. I think I'll go up to my room and call it a day. Enjoy the music." After a tepid shower, I curled under a silky blanket and fell asleep.

The following morning, bright sunshine streamed through an open window, the air hushed and calm. I dressed in a clean sari and stacked laundry in a corner. Outside, the sun climbed over the trees. A few birds cooed and sang from the high branches of a large *Bodhi* tree. The hotel owner sat on a bench and nodded when he saw me. He spoke some pidgin English.

"Morning. Where is everybody?" I asked.

He didn't respond right away. "Big party. Taj's friends arrive. They stay out late. Music at different place. No here."

"Oh, okay. I think I'll wander into town. Would you let them know where I am?"

He bobbed his head from side to side, and a slight sadness seemed to linger around the corner of his eyes. Later, when I left for the market, I searched for him, but he was no longer in sight.

I did not see Taj, Roberto, Stephan, or any of his band of followers that day.

The next morning, Stephan strolled into the hotel. I waved and walked over to his room.

"Hey. Where have you guys been?" I asked, trying not to let my desperation show. "I looked in the market for you and asked around. No one seemed to know where Taj was. I was worried." In fact, I was more than just worried. "Everything okay? Why didn't you leave a note or something?"

Stephan stared at the cement floor. "Hmmm. Uhh. We're heading back to Varanasi with Taj's friends from home. Taj will be back soon." He gathered up a thick blanket, carefully pleating the creases.

"Oh. Going back to Varanasi...Already?"

Stephan looked in my eyes and let out a groan.

"What?"

He shook his head, a visible color rising in his cheeks. "Nothing," as his eyes darted to a lizard crawling on the wall. "Just busy right now."

I swallowed a rising unease. "Okay. I'll leave you be. Have to do the laundry anyway." I managed a weak smile.

Stephan muttered, "Mmmm."

When I had rinsed and hung up my second-to-last piece of clothing, I heard Taj's laugh and glanced over at the main gate.

Taj came through the entrance, his washed dark hair coiling around his shoulders. An attractive woman held his arm. Her emerald sari glittered in the sunlight, and her thick hair cascaded in waves down her front. She whispered something in his ear, and he laughed again. They looked as if they were married. Taj's band and a few other people trotted in behind them.

My throat tightened.

I clenched my wet sari top in my hands. The woman waved at the group gathered in the courtyard. Everyone started talking at once. The different European dialects blended together to form a crescendo of sound. I caught a few words: party, music, food.

Taj avoided my gaze, but I watched his movements from where I stood—the breath he took, the hair that fell across his eyes, the finger that stroked her arm. My throat tightened. I picked up the empty laundry bucket and soap, searching for a way to flee as quickly as possible.

When I burst into my room, I closed the door and slid to the floor, my pulse pounding at my temples.

Complicated emotions choked me as if someone's thumb was pressed into the hollow of my heart. A dull pain spread across my chest, making the air feel thick, heavy, claustrophobic. I lay my head on my bent knees and sobbed.

19 Nepal and India – June–July 1977

How could I have been so naïve? What was I thinking?

I remembered Taj's words when we got back from Badrinath: *For my friends.* Was I just a friend, then? Someone to keep him warm until he was with the woman he loved. Was I just a convenience?

I'd hoped he'd be the one for me. That we'd fall madly in love and do a thousand adventures together; live happily ever after. I felt those expectations wash away like chalk marks in the rain. The whole thing hurt something fierce.

That night, alone in my room, I listened to the evocative sounds of the sitar. I fought for control; as if I couldn't get enough oxygen, my head full of conflicting thoughts.

In the early morning, when everyone had left or fallen asleep, I went outside. A pale moon dipped across one horizon as a thin sliver of bright gold popped up on the other.

When I left for tea, the sky was blood red.

I saw Stephan sitting by himself at a little table outside one of the teahouses we had visited earlier and sat down across from him. He didn't say anything at first.

"Karina and Taj have history." Stephan offered after we decided to have breakfast together. "They've known each other for a while. Taj has been waiting for her to arrive. She's here on a modeling project in Delhi and will be coming with us to Varanasi. It's hard to explain Taj's moods." Stephan would share a piece of information, twist up his mouth, hesitate for a few moments. "We're leaving tomorrow. Sorry." He squeezed my hand.

> **An uncomfortable hush landed between us.**

I offered a weak smile. "It's okay." We both knew it wasn't.

He pushed back his chair. "Have to go." Slowly lowering his chin to his chest, he continued, "Take care."

Later in the day, after I'd returned to my room, Taj knocked at the door. "You stay?"

"Yes, I'm staying in Rishikesh. It's better that way." I folded my arms across my chest, willing myself not to cry. I felt numb with defeat, my mouth gummy with saliva.

He lifted his face. "Okay. Maybe, you come Varanasi later? No?"

An uncomfortable hush landed between us. I watched the soft exhalation of his breath and a longing, pure and simple, spread through my bones. I resisted the urge to reach up and smooth his hair or trail my fingers down his strong cheekbones.

I tried to appear nonchalant, but I felt as bare as the yolk of an egg separated from its whole. We didn't touch.

I kept hoping he'd change his mind. I imagined his caramel eyes looking into mine while he whispered, "I'm sorry. I made a mistake. It's you I want." And then, I'd find careful words to say what was in my heart.

But that's not what happened. I shoved the pain down as far as possible, hoping the sting would lessen a bit.

That evening the stillness seemed oppressive. Images of our time together flashed through my head: his smile when we first met; sitting together on the train; laughing in the marketplace; sipping chai on a street corner. I touched the *mala* Taj bought me just a few days ago and twirled it around a few times.

I tried to be the strong, independent woman I knew that I was, trekking through the hills of Nepal, but I just couldn't seem to summon her to life. I felt more like a wilted, neglected houseplant.

Two days later, the hotel manager knocked on my door. I was still at the hotel Taj and all of us had rented when we first got to Rishikesh. "Ma'am Sahib. Rupees owe for room." He put a folded piece of paper in my hands and walked away.

I opened the bill and stared at the amount. Fear gripped the back of my neck, and I counted my breaths, chastising myself for not paying attention to the fact that the days of Taj paying for things were over. I went to talk to the manager, my fear and sadness rolling together like turbulent ocean waves. I had enough money to cover what I owed but I wouldn't be able to stay a day longer.

He listened. "Ma'am Sahib, ashram no far from here. Swami owns. He may have room for you. Cost very cheap."

An ashram was a spiritual hermitage for the study of yoga, music, or religious instruction. Often ashrams were located near natural surroundings, such as a forested area or in the mountains, to encourage devout learning and meditation.

The hotel manager accompanied me on our half-mile trek toward the Ganges River. The road narrowed, and large, lilac bushes grew wild on either side. A cow passed us on her way to find a handout. Two birds squawked high above in a huge guava tree.

The hotel manager cupped his hands around his mouth and called, "Swami-ji. Swami-ji."

A lean man with short white hair, dressed in an impeccable salmon-colored robe, peeked out from behind a grove of azaleas. Tiny wrinkles surrounded his kind eyes.

The hotel manager explained my situation. The swami glanced in my direction and looked at my flip-flops. He turned and spoke in surprisingly good English.

"Yes, I think I may have room for you. We study Vedanta. Up early for meditation or yoga. Rest of the day for you to spend in spiritual practice any way you choose. We have five Europeans here now. One is an artist from Denmark painting our Bodhi trees. Two are from France studying yoga at the Sivananda Ashram up on the hill. Another man from England is writing a book, and one more is learning our Ayurveda medicine. And you?"

> **I'm trying to decide right now.**

"Uh." *Suffering from heartbreak and serious immaturity?* "I'm trying to decide right now." *Best I could do.*

"Okay. Maybe I help."

The simple ashram contained a few thatched huts around a well and a flourishing garden. The swami's home stood at the front. Trees encircled the down-to-earth compound. A bathhouse and latrine bordered the back; roses and vines crawled up the concrete walls, moss gathered in the corners. Inside the only vacant hut, a spigot for water jutted out of the north wall, concrete floors, whitewashed walls, and a tin roof. Rustic indeed.

I let out a long breath. "Thank you for letting me stay here."

When I got back to the hotel, I noticed the door to my room was slightly ajar. When I pushed it open, I saw my things scattered across the bed, and a few things on the floor. My mouth got a little dry, and I began to take mental inventory.

Several belongings were missing: my backpack, hiking boots and wool socks, blue tarp and rope, the stainless-steel bowl from Greece, all my western clothing—and more importantly, my sleeping bag and space blanket and coat and some money were all gone. The Indian clothing and a few souvenirs, along with my journals and a few toiletries, were all that was left.

I felt as if someone had kicked me in the stomach. I wanted to scream and beat something senseless, at least throw a few books around. How could someone do that? Steal from me? Why? My weak heart tumbled. I bent my face to my knees and wept.

Later, I told the manager, "Someone stole all my stuff." My emotions threatened to bubble up again like warm milk on the stove.

He replied, "Did you lock your door?"

I couldn't remember.

"Sorry, Ma'am Sahib. These things happen in our India." He shrugged and looked away.

For the next few weeks, I went to the market to buy things for my new home: two bulky cotton blankets, a hand-sewn three-inch mattress pad, a fat straw mat, a charcoal-type stove, powdered milk, sugar, tea, and spices to make chai, two pots, and a large ceramic cup. The luxury of eating in restaurants, endless cups of chai in tea shops, and cozy inns were now a thing of the past.

I noticed how the local people made their food, and I tried to mimic them. The distractions helped. Thinking about Taj or the things I had lost brought on a sensation like razor blades cutting into my skin.

The only problem with the mud hut was the rats—big gray rodents with long, ugly tails. They'd run about the hut at night, looking for food scraps, and sometimes got tangled in my hair. One chewed the beads of my *mala*.

There were precisely nine rats. I know because I killed them all, one by one, by first capturing them in a live trap and then drowning them in a metal pail full of water.

Once their eerie sounds stopped, I would walk down a deserted path to the Ganges and throw their still carcasses into the thick greenery. I thought I'd gotten rid of them once and for all, but unfortunately, I couldn't eliminate their dying screeches from disturbing my sleep every now and again.

I kept small talk with the other ashram members to a minimum. "Hello. Nice day. Finished with your shower? Can I use that pail?"

The watercolorist from Denmark had thin ashen-pale hair tied back in a ponytail. Every morning at sunrise, he left for a secluded spot near the Ganges River and painted all day. At sunset, he'd saunter into the ashram, head down with his portfolio tucked under his arm, muttering a few obligatory hellos before closing his cabin door. The distinct smell of marijuana and smoke puffs seeping from under the door soon followed.

The French yoga couple were early risers. The woman, Denise, showed me how to keep my hair from getting lice. I brushed my hair upside down with strong, downward strokes. Then with a twisting motion, like wringing out clothes, I'd tie the hair into a tight knot on top of my head. Next, I used a scarf as a turban. For the next two years, I often used this hairstyle, which minimized issues with head lice.

The man from England was a recluse. I never saw him much.

The other man—the one studying medicine—only stayed for a short time. I hardly remember him.

The ashram, a place for seclusion and reflection, was often quiet, intensified by the fragile beauty of the monsoon. The rain washed away the filth, leaving streets clear of litter and refuse. The air smelled fresh with a hint of rose. At night, the bushes surrounding the ashram were filled with fireflies, a thousand tiny lights twinkling in the sky.

Some days the rain fell in sheets, keeping everyone inside. It matched my mood, gray and hazy. Depression crept into my sleep. Memories thrived like the thousands of mosquitoes buzzing around my head.

20

Canada – 1972

*I brought a hot cup of tea outside
the little cabin and watched the sun rise
over the mountaintop, a comfortable warmth
expanding across my chest.*

On my train journey to Banff National Park, I felt like a pioneer woman heading west instead of an inexperienced, seasonal, wannabe waitress. I spent most of my time in the viewing dome of the train, daydreaming, looking out the window at the passing landscape.

In the seat next to me, a couple in their early thirties ate vegetarian food. Occasionally the woman lovingly touched her partner's hand, seemingly happy and at ease with the world. I looked at the candy bar in my lap and my scruffy out-of-date running shoes and wished I could someday have good things in my life.

When I first saw the Canadian Rockies, I could hardly believe the beauty: bulbous white clouds drifting across a velvety blue sky; jagged granite peaks; deep green forested hills. During those first few days in Banff, I couldn't help but gawk at the surrounding landscape, goose bumps sliding along the back of my neck.

However, waitressing was not as pleasant. My feet and back hurt from carrying the heavy food trays, and the hectic pace tired me out. In short, I hated it. But being on my own, away from my family, was worth the hardship. Every morning, I brought a hot cup of tea outside the little cabin I shared with two other seasonal employees and watched the sun rise over the mountaintop, a comfortable warmth expanding across my chest.

Three months slipped by quickly. In August, I was back on the train headed for Toronto and college without nearly the monies I needed for my first semester. I secretly hoped to find my dad and ask him to help me out, even just a little bit.

I hadn't seen him in years—not since the time my mother came into my room and announced, "You're going to visit your father for a few weeks this summer. I think you're old enough to see him again. You and your brother will take the train and stay in Toronto for two weeks." Her face looked flushed and moist as if she'd been working out.

I ironed my clothes and placed them carefully in the worn-around-the-edges plaid suitcase, hoping to appear grown-up.

When our father picked us up at the train station, he said, "Look at you! All grown up. Your mom has done such a good job raising you." He'd put on weight, and his black hair showed some specks of gray.

> You screamed in your sleep. Do you do that a lot?

"Look at my new car. It's got a leather interior, so no shoes on it, okay? And don't eat in the car." He told my brother to sit upfront.

My father's apartment smelled of beer and urine, with empty pizza boxes on the floor and dirty laundry piled by the closet. He shrugged. "Sorry about the mess."

That night I had a familiar nightmare; someone chasing me into a dark room and locking me in. The following morning, my dad asked, "You screamed in your sleep. Do you do that a lot?"

"No. No. Of course not," I lied. "It's nothing."

My dad believed me, or he didn't really want to get into it. "We're going to a summer resort. Nice place. Swimming. Golf. Shops." Later, while he stuffed his clothes in a duffle, he said, "You'll love it there. I want you to meet my new girlfriend."

The new girlfriend, Mary, had a tight bikini on when we arrived. "Oh, you must be the darling little girl." She held a full martini in her hand and offered one to my dad. I thought her bikini seemed too small for her.

My dad put on his swim trunks and said, "I can't wait to hit the beach."

I wore an old-fashioned one-piece, and we spent the afternoon swimming and lying on the beach. Later, Mary and my dad drank martinis.

> The days in the city were filled with one disappointment after another.

Mary began to slur her words and whispered in my dad's ear, "Honey, let's go out tonight." Or, after basking in the sun for a while, she'd sit up and say, "Sweetie, put some oil on my back."

Over the course of our visit, my dad and Mary got drunk, and ignored me and my brother most of the time. They frequently argued.

Mary wailed, "Babe, I need you..." If he didn't pay attention to her, she'd add endearing words: "Darling, I can't wait for us to be alone."

More than once, he gritted his teeth and barked, "Leave me alone, for God's sake! Can't you see I got my kids with me?"

On our last night at the resort, I asked him if I could help make dinner. "I help Mom sometimes. I know how to cook."

He stirred the tomato sauce. "Okay, get me that large pot and fill it up with water."

I placed the pot in the kitchen sink and opened the cold-water faucet, filling it to just a couple of inches from the top. I tried to lift it, but it was simply too heavy, and the pot slipped out of my hands, spilling water everywhere. "Oh, no... Sorry."

"God damn it!" he yelled. "Get out of here. You've been in my way the whole friggin' time." His spit splattered on the counter.

I burst out crying. "I'll clean it up."

"Nah, get outta here. Can't stand it when you start your friggin' crying."

The days in the city were filled with one disappointment after another. My dad complained, "I'm not used to kids, y'know. Never really knew how to take care of you two anyway."

We were relieved when the day came for us to board the train and return home to my mother's house. My dad's hug felt awkward and stiff. He shook my little brother's hand.

Mary already had a few martinis and was a little unsteady in her high heels. "Take care, kid."

A fluttery feeling filled my stomach. "When will I see you?"

"Ah, don't know. We're headed to Las Vegas. Gotta travel for my work." He smoothed out his hair. "Ummm, you know..."

My father did not write or call or visit us again, and I gave up on my fantasy of him being the person who could solve all my problems.

However, on the train, after my summer in Banff, I felt energized and awake to new possibilities, believing my dad would surely want to see me.

Maybe he would rescue me after all.

India – September 1977

*Taj's abandonment had kicked up
a typhoon of emotions.*

At the end of August, I woke one night saturated in sweat. I had never experienced a fever that hot.

For many days, I burned, blistered, and sweltered inside and out while the monsoon raged on. September passed in a blur. Swami-ji placed cold cloths on my forehead. An Indian woman in a yellow sari draped a mosquito net around my sleeping pad. I experienced a sensation of floating above my bed and looking down at myself, hearing drops of rain on the tin roof, trying to sip from a cup filled with a hot, clear liquid while Swami-ji talked to a man in a white coat. I slept and slept and slept. I lost weight. I couldn't think.

One morning I opened my eyes and could lift my head. My heart felt like a small dead creature. Memories fluttered like dandelion wisps. The door to the hut was open, and a stream of light spilled onto the concrete floor.

Swami-ji came in with a hot cup of tea. "Oh, you're awake. We've been worried about you. Here, drink some of this." He touched my forehead. "Maybe the fever has passed?" He let out a loud breath.

I rose on my elbow and sipped the clear liquid. "What happened?"

"Doctor-ji thinks you had malaria."

Malaria, a mosquito-borne disease causing fever and headaches, similar to flu symptoms, flourished in monsoonal India. A cycle of coldness, followed by fever and sweating with nausea, could persist from eight to thirty days.

"Really?"

He nodded. "If you feel up to it, there is warm water in the shower this morning. No rain today and the sun already hot."

I caught a foul smell coming from my armpits. Indeed, it was time for a shower.

After Swami-ji left, I sat up. When the dizziness passed, I stood, made my way to the shower stall, and used up all the warm water, soaping, rinsing, lathering, and rinsing again. It seemed to take a vast amount of time to get dressed. The clean fabric rested comfortably against my skin.

When I got back to the hut, Swami-ji stood near the door. "My friend makes best South Indian food. Rich, creamy coffee, *ragi mudde*, and *masala dosa*. Come. My friend also has been worried about you, and he will be happy to feed you this day. You need to walk, get away from the ashram, yes." Sometimes Swami-ji talked like an English nobleman. "Here, take this." He held a walking stick in his hand.

Lemony sunshine glowed overhead, and the air smelled fresh and clean. Everything seemed doubly alive—or maybe I was glad to be so. The crickets and bees buzzed. Pigeons cooed. I breathed in the lush smells of late summer with renewed wonder and vowed to try and forget the past, appreciate the present moments more.

We walked slowly. Swami-ji pointed out things along the way.

"This is where the doctor lives. This is where Swami-ji Ramana lives. This is where I get my vegetables. Oh, you see this? This is one of the oldest trees in Rishikesh."

He proudly pointed to a gigantic tree, its roots a twisted and tangled web. A bird twittered from branch to branch, while a *sadhu* sat in perfect lotus position on the ground.

"He hasn't talked for twenty years," Swami-ji whispered. We continued on our walk until we got to his South Indian friend's shop.

> The buttery smooth liquid slid easily down my throat.

A small open deck, situated in front of a modest home with no sign out front, managed to hold three small tables with a variety of rickety chairs. A middle-aged man with a sizeable tummy waved to Swami-ji. "I see Ma'am Sahib better, no? Come, come. I make best *idlis* for you."

Tamil cuisine, a rich culinary fare from South India, consisted of a wide variety of delicious foods, including *idli sambar*, a steamed rice dumpling with spicy, full-flavored side dishes. Coffee was more common in South India, while chai was the preferred beverage of the north.

Swami-ji introduced him. "This is my good friend, Urdu. He is from Madras and makes the best food in Rishikesh."

"Hi, Urdu. Thank you. I can't wait to try this food Swami-ji has been raving about." A growl erupted from my empty stomach. I couldn't remember the last time I ate; a bite of *chapatti* two days ago?

Urdu brought two cups of rich coffee with thick cream and sugar.

The buttery smooth liquid slid easily down my throat. "Mmmmm."

Urdu formed balls of rice and then placed them in a steamer. My mouth began to salivate at the savory aroma.

The dumplings had a slightly tart taste. When dipped in the mustard-colored dahl, a sweet-spicy tang lingered. "This tastes wonderful, Urdu. Best meal I've had in a long time. Thank you."

Swami-ji chuckled. "Only meal you've had in a long time." He pointed to my arms.

I looked at my emaciated limbs, thin and withered. How much weight had I lost?

Several weeks later, I got on a scale at the post office, and the weight measured less than forty-eight kilos—less than one hundred and five pounds.

Who knows how little I weighed that afternoon?

I decided to spend the winter in Rishikesh to regain my strength and rethink my life, as Obi-Wan said that year in a *Star Wars* movie. Taj's abandonment had kicked up a typhoon of emotions. I hadn't heard from him or my family—or any of my old friends, for that matter. Pain, like shards of glass, surfaced and moved up and down my spine.

For the next several weeks, I took long walks and engaged in conversations with Swami-ji, asking him, "I hope to learn yoga and Hindu philosophy. Music, too, if I could. I've heard about the raga system."

I tried not to think about Taj, but I often did—the way he moved through crowds with a leopard-like grace, his deep voice, crescent moon eyebrows, and angular cheekbones. How he attracted others to him like honey to a bee. I missed his eyes the most; liquid-brown pools of flashing fire.

"Yes, yes. Get involved. Study. Learning is best, you know. Maybe Swami Vibhodananda-ji can teach you. He lives at the Sivananda ashram, very close to here. I'll ask if he can come here to teach you in the afternoons. In exchange for his teachings, maybe you make him lunch." His smile stretched from cheek to cheek.

The next day, a small, older man with a bald head and orange robes wrapped tightly around his diminutive frame came through the front entrance. The man clutched a bulky cloth bag to his chest. He called out, "Swami-ji. Swami-ji."

The two men laughed lightly together, like old friends catching up. Swami-ji waved when he saw me standing outside my hut and pointed to the man. "This is Swami Vibhodanada."

I walked toward them and bowed, putting my hands in the traditional prayer position at my chest. "Namaste."

"Namaste, namaste. So, Swami-ji says you want to learn our Hindu mythology and yoga system, no?" His English seemed even better than Swami-ji's.

"Yes. I've decided to spend the winter here in Rishikesh and learn about this remarkable country. Thank you for agreeing to meet with me. My name is Sharon."

"Aaraa?" he replied.

I repeated my name, spelling each syllable out carefully.

He tried again but had difficulty with the *r*. "Maybe, first thing we do is change your name to Shanti, which is a revered name in our language. Directly translated, it means *peace*. It is an honorable name."

"Hmmm. Shanti. Revered, you say?" The name sounded unique, different.

"Yes, yes. Shanti it is, then." Swami-ji seemed pleased with this quick resolution. He handed me three thick books: *The Gospel of Sri Ramakrishna*, *Vedic Universal Prayers*, and *the Upanishads*. "Okay, Shanti, first you read these, and then I will come in two days, and we will talk."

"Uh. Thanks." I doubted whether I could get through one chapter of one book. It did take me quite a few weeks to get through what Swami Vibhodanada thought I should get through in two days.

He chastised me, saying, "Work harder. The spiritual life requires all your heart and all your mind. Go to one of the main ashrams. Meditate. Do yoga. Wake up early."

It sounded noble and good, but I preferred to sleep in late and feel sorry for myself, which justified trips to the chai shop or staying behind for an afternoon in the bazaar. Besides, showers were cold at sunrise.

"What did you think of the Vedic scripture one-twenty-one through one-fifty-two?" Swami Vibhodanada made several attempts to coax higher learning from me.

"Haven't read that yet. Still working on the first two."

Later, Swami-ji disclosed, "Swami Vibhodanada is one of the best scholars in our area. You are lucky he has agreed to meet with you. He gets up at four o'clock every morning, meditates for an hour, then does yoga, studies, and translates scriptures into English, all before breakfast. He only eats two meals a day before noon. He leads an exemplar monk life."

Instead of taking the hint, I continued to lag behind in my studies.

The days matured like the bananas on the nearby trees.

Shouldn't this be fun? Maybe learning music would be better.

One morning, while Swami-ji trimmed his rose bushes, I sat on a nearby rock and asked, "Could I learn a bit about the raga system?"

"Urdu might be able to help you. He studied music when he lived in Madras. He can at least teach you the basics."

Swami-ji invited Urdu for chai, and we talked about music.

"You should get a harmonium," he instructed. "Next, I can teach you the Indian musical system, and maybe you could learn some simple hymns. We call them *bhajans*." Urdu looked pleased and turned his head to face Swami-ji. "She can buy a second-hand one in the bazaar for maybe forty rupees."

Forty rupees, equivalent to one month's rent and food, seemed too much for my limited budget, but I wanted to learn Indian classical music. Images of Taj playing his sitar flashed through my head.

21 India – September 1977

The days matured like the bananas on the nearby trees. Mondays and Wednesdays, I studied Vedanta with Swami Vibhodanada. Thursdays were dedicated to music with Urdu. On my off days, I took long walks in the countryside or shopped in the marketplace.

The internal whirling tornadoes settled down.

The nights cooled. Life became unhurried.

Most evenings, I sipped tea and watched the sun head for the horizon, blue and pink strokes frequently lighting up the sky. Sleep came easily.

The days waltzed toward Christmas.

"You should visit the Sivananda ashram for New Year's Eve," Swami Vibhodanada said. "We meditate from six o'clock at night until six o'clock in the morning and bring in the New Year with Vedic chants. Come, meditate with everyone. It is an auspicious occasion." His teeth showed through his wide smile. "You will understand your studies much better once you begin to meditate more. How is your yoga going?"

"I can touch my toes." I tried to cover up my pathetic attempts at yoga. Swami believed yoga should be practiced six days a week before sunrise. I did maybe one day a week, long after sunrise, and a leisurely breakfast.

"Best if you do yoga on an empty stomach. Now let's read the Upanishads." Swami opened his book and took a sip of his tea.

Swami told Hindu mythological stories: life lessons draped in fairy tales and parables; universal truths wrapped around allegory; peace in prayer. He spoke about the Hindu gods, demigods, and spirits. He elaborated on how Hinduism was more philosophical than doctrine, emphasizing the dichotomy of being in the world and denying it at the same time, a renunciation of sorts.

I attempted to understand this myriad of information, yet I often felt besieged. I nodded at the appropriate moments, hoping I'd remember at least some of what he said.

Whenever I recall my time with Swami Vibhodanada, who died many years ago now, I tip my head back for a moment and close my eyes. I know he can't hear me, but I thank him anyway. He was an honest, kind-hearted man who taught me something about being a decent human being. A few of his books still sit on my bookshelf. Inside one book, an inscription reads, "To Shanti, our warmest blessings for you always, Swami Vibhodanada Puri and Swami-ji."

Although I also listened to Urdu's advice, I never could summon the same respect as I had for Swami Vibhodanada. Urdu talked incessantly about India's musical traditions.

"Yes, yes. Our music can be traced back to the twelfth century, stemming from ancient Persian and Indian folklore. The music is divided into twelve semitones with seven basic notes in ascending order: *Sa Re Ga Ma Pa Dha NiSa.*" His voice carried an enthralling sound, slightly off-key. "Emphasis is on improvisation, monophonic, a single melody. Understand, yes?"

I tried to pay attention. "Yep. Got it."

"Our music has always been passed down from the guru to the student." He paused for a moment. "Some musicians spend their entire lives practicing and practicing to achieve the guru's respect."

A flicker of Taj's blistered fingertips. "That's interesting."

"So, the *tabla* is a type of drum and keeps the rhythm." He tapped his hands on his knees. "A *tanpura* is a tall string instrument made of wood and maintains a steady drone, and you know the sitar is our most famous instrument. But, just as important are the violin, *sarod,* and *sarangi.*"

I nodded. Of course, I knew this already. An image of Taj's splendid sitar raced through my mind.

"The other style of Hindustani music is the repetition of Vedic chants, which you are learning from Swami. But this Bollywood stuff... Phew! Useless!"

I remembered the blaring of popular Bollywood music from countless radios across the Middle East—a mixture of rock, pop, and ancient styles.

"The Indian musical scale is quite similar to the Western scale. You just have to practice," Urdu explained. "You take one verse and repeat it over and over." He placed his fingers on the harmonium and quickly ran through the *raga* scales, his rich tenor voice echoing off the adjacent wall. Next, he lifted the harmonium and placed it in front of me.

I replicated his instructions, trying to recap the day's lesson. The noise coming from my mouth didn't sound like music. "This is hard."

"Yes, of course. It takes a long time to be good at anything." Urdu set down two cups of steaming sweet coffee. "Just don't give up. One day you will understand our music. Look how you dress now, in your saris. Your skin is almost as brown as mine." He held out his arm alongside mine. His skin, ten times darker, glistened in the morning light.

"Okay. If you say so."

I accepted Swami Vibhodanada's invitation to meditate at the Sivananda ashram for New Year's Eve.

Christmas morning was nothing special in Rishikesh, as Hindus do not celebrate this Christian holiday. Yet, I wanted to make merry. I bought butter for *chapattis*, a few sweets, several yards of homespun cotton, and a simple lined notebook.

The soft wind swirled the scent of curry around the market stalls. I let out a deep breath, grateful for my health and a slight sense of well-being, and I waved to the vendors as I passed them.

When I got back to the ashram, Swami-ji said, "This is the Christian Christmas, no?"

"Yes, it is. First warm Christmas I've ever had."

"So, you make special today? I see you have a guest."

I looked in the direction of my hut and saw someone seated cross-legged on the straw mat in front of my door. When I got closer, I noticed he wore the traditional white Hindu dress, and the breeze lifted his long dark hair. The golden globe of the sun peeped out behind him, casting a pastel glow.

My heart seized in my chest.

Taj.

22

Toronto – 1972-1973

What happened? Where was that orphanage?
Why did you leave me? Where did you go?

After a difficult discussion with my college admissions advisor, I realized I needed to find full-time employment if I intended to continue at the university. I quickly found a job waitressing at a diner. It was more than hard to work full-time and simultaneously be a good student. Always worried about money, I often woke in the middle of the night, unable to fall back asleep.

It wasn't long before I found out where my dad lived—in a spacious downtown penthouse apartment. I stood outside the building and checked the address several times before I mustered enough courage to go inside and take the elevator to the top floor. When I knocked on the door, Mary answered.

Not sure what to say, I blubbered out, "Mary. It's me, Sharon. Is my dad here?"

She eyed me suspiciously and closed the door slightly. "Hey, Babe. Your daughter is here."

I heard him say "What?" and then their voices lowered as they chatted.

I chewed my lower lip.

My dad opened the door. "What a surprise... Come in for a moment. We're just on our way out, but let's set up a time to meet. What are you doing in Toronto?"

His fake smile did little to mollify my growing unease.

I sat on their white living room couch. "Uh. I'm trying to go to school, but it's so expensive, and I have to work. I'm not quite sure how to do both." Suddenly hesitant to ask for help, I abruptly changed the subject. "But mostly, I'm here to see you. I haven't seen you for, what, six years? Not since you got married." I looked over at Mary.

Her dyed blonde hair, coiffed into a classic 1960s-style pageboy, fell stiffly to just above her shoulders. The ice from her cocktail clinked against the clear glass. She tapped her foot several times and said, "We should set up a time for dinner. Where are you staying?' Her high heels made little clicking noises. "Babe, we could meet at a nearby restaurant."

My father got up. "Yes. Let's do that. We can talk then."

I noticed his hair had thinned, and he wore glasses with thick black frames.

"Oh. Okay." My ribs seemed to tighten, restricting my breath. "I should have called first."

Mary quickly answered, "Yes. That would be best."

She doesn't like me.

We met a week later at a city center restaurant. The dark interior had private booths, and the dim lights hung over the table. The two of them sat across from me in the booth.

Dad ordered martinis for him and Mary. I ordered a Coke.

"So, what brings you to Toronto?"

"Just trying to figure things out—what college major would be best, where I want to be. I'm not sure of a lot of things right now." I wanted to ask him about my childhood, my mother's confession, and if he could loan me some money.

A waitress in a starched red shirt and carrying a black writing pad came to our table. "What can I get you guys to eat?"

"Steak, baked potatoes, and salad for us all," my father said.

I tried to open my mouth and tell him I'd become a vegetarian, but somehow the words never left my lips.

"Anything wrong with your steak?" My dad eyed the cold meat on my plate.

"No, no. Just not hungry is all." *Just ask him.* "Hey, Dad, um, Mom mentioned before I left things were, ah, difficult for you when I was young and you, uh, sort of left me in some kind of home or foster care. Can you tell me a bit about that?"

He set down his fork and knife, swallowed, and then took a swig of his drink. "Well, it was your mother's fault, really. You are old enough to know that your mother had an affair, and that's why we split up. Yeah, she blames everything on me, but it's her. I was just trying to work and take care of you. And then your brother came along. They were hard years."

> Have to go.

I chewed on my fingernail and wondered how they fought. Did he hit her?

Mary touched his hand. "Let's not talk about this now. It'll ruin our dinner."

I looked at my steak swimming in pink juice, cotton wrapped around my tongue, and nodded.

Outside, the wind had picked up, and I pulled the collar of my coat around my ears. "Well, thanks for dinner. Hope we can get together again soon."

Mary's words seemed to run together. "Yep, some other time then. Hang tight, kid."

My dad leaned back, creating space between us. "Call sometime. We're off to Florida for a couple of weeks but should be home after that."

I watched them get in their shiny new car. The door shut with a resounding slam as if they couldn't wait to escape.

Later, I called him several times to get answers to questions swirling in my head: What happened? Where was that orphanage? Why did you leave me? Where did you go?

His responses were always short, and I never could get a word in before he said, "Have to go."

23

India – December 1977-May 1978

*My stomach felt like a hummingbird
suspended over a nectar-filled flower.*

I tried to harden my heart when I saw him, even summon up some respectable anger. But when he looked into my eyes, my willpower lasted only a few seconds.

"What are you doing here?"

He spoke in English. "Can we walk?" His lush hair, washed and silky, rippled over his shoulders.

I held my packages close to my chest. "Need to put these away, and then we can go to the river, if you want to." I felt my cheeks warm as I opened the door to my hut.

Taj stood and followed me inside. "Leave my bag here? Okay?"

"Yes. It's all right. Everything is safe here."

We walked in single file. On both sides of the alleyway, pink blossoms spilled over. An early rain had fallen, leaving the air fresh and bright.

"I learn English," he beamed. "At the university. With my music. I meet many peoples speaking this English." He turned to face me. The sapphire blue sky sparkled behind him and his eyes, alive with mirth, shone like topaz stones.

I had a thousand questions, but one in particular. "How are Stephan and Roberto?" I purposely looked away as if whatever he said wouldn't bother me. "And Karina?"

Taj hung his head and kicked the ground. "We not together now."

In his newfound way of speaking English, choppy with emphasis on the wrong vowels, and with phrases in Hindi and Spanish, he talked—beginning with what happened when they left Rishikesh.

"Soon we get to Varanasi, Karina no *me gusta* the fact you were with me," he said. She started nagging him, and after two weeks, she left for New Delhi and never came back. He continued, "I no think about her. But I did think you."

I didn't respond. But inside, my heart lifted.

He said Stephan and Roberto gave him hell for how he treated me. "I thought maybe you come back to Varanasi. I studied hard. Played music every day and found two good teachers. I asked for teacher for your English." He grinned. "You didn't come, so I decided to see if you still here."

After every explanation, he'd look in my direction, assessing my reaction. I tried to stay calm. But just being with him again made the little hairs on the back of my neck stand up. I sat on my hands to keep my desire to touch him in check.

We spent hours by the river, letting our feet dangle in the water. I chose my words carefully. "I've been learning the Indian musical system and even bought a harmonium." The smile I tried to hide erupted across my face. "I met a swami who is teaching me Vedanta. I'm going to stay in India for maybe a year. My name is Shanti now."

India felt like home.

I told him about Swami Vibhodanada, Swami-ji, Urdu, learning how to live one day at a time, doing yoga, studying the Vedas. "I'm slowing down and enjoying it here."

He listened, nodded a few times, then picked up my arm and let it drop. "You very thin now." The sunlight seemed to dance, weave, and romp around him.

23 India – December 1977–May 1978

I recapped getting sick and my long recovery. "Wasn't fun."

Taj didn't say anything, just stared at his empty hands.

I forced a laugh. "Hey, no big deal."

I stood up, found a stick, and wrote some Sanskrit words in the sand. "This means peace, and this means compassion. That's what I'm trying to learn about myself, about life." The river water churned over the boulders as a couple of rocks dislodged, followed by a loud splash. I glanced quickly at Taj.

Taj crossed his arms over his chest. "Interesting." He said the word slowly as if he had just learned it. Maybe he had.

We wandered back to the ashram just as the sun dipped toward the horizon. Taj touched my shoulder. "Stephan and Roberto are at inn. They ask see you. Is okay?"

I should've known Taj would not have traveled by himself. Still, I found solace in the fact that he came to find me. "Yes, it'd be nice to see them."

"Shanti, Shanti, Shanti. Good name."

We strolled past the ashram and continued up the pathway to the hotel we first stayed at when we went to Badrinath. Stephan and Roberto sat on a bench in the alleyway. Roberto sported a new beard and wore a bright purple shirt. When they saw us, they jumped up and ran toward us. Stephan twirled me in the air. "You're here!"

"It's good to see you, too." I hugged Stephan and Roberto. The late afternoon sun flickered behind them. Roberto's blue eyes found mine, and a few seconds passed before I could look away.

Taj clapped his hands together and asked, "Chai?"

I smoothed the wrinkle in my sari. "Tea sounds good." I hadn't had a drink of water since morning. "We've been talking all afternoon."

Later, at the teahouse, the three men took turns summarizing their last few months in Varanasi: studying and playing music every day, late night parties, meeting new people. It all sounded quite familiar. Now and then, I caught a whiff of the woodsy smell of Taj's favorite soap. My stomach felt like a hummingbird suspended over a nectar-filled flower.

Stephan turned to me. "What do you think of Taj's decision to return home?"

Taj's head jerked up.

Stephan winced. "Oops..." The tip of his ears turned red.

A few awkward seconds passed before Taj spoke in a mix of English and Hindu.

"Mmmm. Yes. Yes. Home. Study visa finished. Now time to see family. Maybe come back in *Julio* month, maybe longer. Don't know. Lease kaput on place in Varanasi. We pack everything." He struggled for the right words. "Some of our instruments in storage in Delhi. Stephan, Roberto, Domenico and his family, me—we're all flying home in few days." He rubbed his right temple with his finger.

I exhaled, unsure how to respond. Sadness crept in at the thought of him going back to Europe, but I didn't want him to know that. "Well, I'm glad for you."

An uncomfortable hush fell between us like the moments before a sudden spring storm on the plains. The sun had sunk, creating crimson imprints across the sky. "Guess it's getting late. Should be heading back."

Stephan and Roberto got up quickly. They glanced at Taj. "We'll see you later?"

Taj stood and took my hand. "I'll walk you back."

I hugged Stephan, then Roberto. "Glad you came." My words seemed too polite. "Good luck, you two."

"No problem." Stephan held me for a moment longer than was comfortable for both of us.

Long silences tumbled into one another as Taj and I walked to the ashram. I reflected on his departure from India. Would we ever see each other again? My emotions sparred. I felt happy to be next to him and yet, also fearful I'd get hurt again. *Should I just forget about what happened or what might happen?*

When we got to my hut, Taj bent down and kissed me on the lips.

We spent two evenings and a day together, indulging in young love. On the last morning, I held him close but held back what I wanted to say. *I'll miss you. Please, don't go.*

Instead, I managed a weak smile and faked interest in cleaning up. "Guess I'll get to those dishes."

He pushed the hair away from my cheek and brushed his knuckles against my mouth. "Salut," he said and kissed my forehead, the touch so gentle it nearly made me cry.

I watched him walk through the entryway and disappear behind a rose thicket. A blackbird cawed after him, and a few clouds passed over the sun.

I wanted to run after him, hug him one more time, but I didn't.

Instead, I took a deep breath and went back inside my tiny hut.

Many people crowded the main meditation room at the Sivananda ashram for New Year's Eve. A cohort of musicians played and chanted songs and mantras.

Swami Vibhodanada showed me where to sit—with the women. A plump Indian woman smiled and made room next to her. The scratchy mat felt prickly, and I kept changing positions.

The woman frowned a few times, and I got the message: *sit quietly and behave.*

After what seemed like days, but was really only a few hours, the music stopped. Everyone closed their eyes and started meditating.

Having had no formal training in meditation, I shut my eyes and pretended to know what to do. My legs felt anesthetized. My back throbbed. Discomfort took on a new meaning.

Close to midnight, the fleas from the mats started jumping all over the place. The bites stung, and even after wrapping every exposed part of my body with cloth, the nips simply hurt.

I got up, feigning a bathroom break, and left.

The next afternoon Swami-ji asked, "How was your meditation evening?"

"Oh. Fine." I quickly changed the subject. "Need to go to the market to buy milk and tea for chai."

The brilliant sun lit up the market stalls filled with local merchants and native peoples buying staples for their families. A white woman dressed in a cream and bright green sari, carrying a basket on her arm, talked to a shopkeeper next to the booth I was bartering at. Her brown hair was neatly plaited. "Yes. Yes. These bananas are good. I'll take a few guavas and tomatoes, too." She glanced in my direction. "Hello. Are you living in Rishikesh?"

I tried to place her accent. England? Australia? "Yes. I've been here since August. You?"

"I came in December and I am staying at the Yog Niketan ashram. Name's Mudita." Her eyes were a deep chocolate brown. "You're the first white female I've seen in the bazaar."

I nodded. "You, too."

We walked together and exchanged a few more pleasantries as we continued shopping. When we came to the end of the food stands, I pointed. "Want to get some tea and a late lunch at the tea shop over there?"

"Sure." Mudita didn't seem in a hurry to get anywhere.

We talked for more than two hours, the conversation easy and comfortable. I hoped we could meet up again soon. "Want to stop for lunch when you come this way again?" I already felt as if I'd known her all my life. "My ashram is not far from the Ganges. We could go for a walk or just hang out?"

"That would be lovely." Her smile was so wide that it bunched up her cheeks.

23 India – December 1977–May 1978

Mudita studied yoga and meditation with Swami Yogeshwaranand, who she called *Maharaj*, at Yog Niketan, an ashram about two miles from mine. We had a lot in common. We were both alone in India and about the same age, searching for what we wanted in life.

I told her about Taj, and she shared her recent heartache.

From January through April of that year, Mudita and I became the best of friends. I attended lectures, yoga practices, and meditation at her ashram. Sometimes she fixed dinner for us in her tiny room. Often, she came over to my ashram. We'd sit on my bed and talk for hours, swapping stories about Australia and Canada, who we were, what we did, what we hoped for. You know, the obvious things young women of my generation were all hoping for—wealth, fame, love, enlightenment.

We toured the countryside, went for long walks, and even once visited a leper colony.

"Let's see how brave we are?" she said, bouncing from foot to foot.

> I kept hearing the howls and wails of the lepers long after we left.

Men, women, and children with missing limbs and baseball-sized open oozing sores filled the filthy streets. Two children, pockmarked with hundreds of abscesses and wearing threadbare clothing, tugged at our saris.

"Ma'am Sahib, rupees, please..."

Before long, at least twenty lepers trailed behind us, some dragging their half-eaten bodies. A few women wept openly. Sweat slid down my forehead, and panic rose in my chest. We walked fast, keeping our heads down. I was afraid even to breathe.

"That's the last time I'm going to complain about carrying a few extra pounds," Mudita said. "Seeing that...oh, my God, makes me feel ashamed about all the things I worry about. Can you believe what we just saw?"

My eyes shimmered with emotion. I sighed, crossed my arms, and held on to my shoulders, afraid I might catch their disease. "No. I agree. I don't think I could ever go back there." I shivered as a cold sweat formed in the palms of my hands. "What were we thinking?"

Mudita stared at the ground. "I don't know."

We hailed a rickshaw and rode to town, each lost in our thoughts.

I kept hearing the howls and wails of the lepers long after we left. The ghost-like image of a blind young boy, with two large lesions on his forehead, a shrunken nose, and swollen lips, missing his left leg and arm, haunted me for years.

My Vedic studies and yoga practice improved, although pathetically behind more serious yogis. Swami Vibhodanada, Swami-ji, and Urdu continued to offer encouragement. We'd have lengthy conversations about contemplation versus meditation, good versus evil, family life versus a monk's life. Sometimes Mudita would join in on the spirited and animated discussions.

Mudita, fascinated by the harmonium, loved the *bhajans*. "Play some more, play the one with the words *Om Shanti* in it." She clapped her hands. "You're good, you know."

I got to know some of her ashram friends. They became my friends, too. By spring, I had a solid group of people to hang out with. A fresh confidence flourished like the pink and white blossoms all around town. India felt like home.

Toward the end of April, Mudita came to my hut with an armful of spring flowers. "Here. These are for you."

I had a feeling there was more to her gift than just the flowers, by the way she kept nodding her head. "Okay, what is it?"

She blurted, "You've just gotta come to Kashmir!"

"Kashmir? What? Wait. What are you talking about?"

She explained that she and several other ashram colleagues planned to travel to Kashmir to study with *Maharaja* for the summer. "You should come with us. Come and talk to *Maharaj*."

"Okay, question first. What does *Maharaja* mean, or *Maharaj*, as you call him? I don't know why I never asked you that before."

"*Maharaja* is a Sanskrit title meaning *great king*, given to a high-ranking individual to honor his achievements. Swami Yogeshwaranand Saraswati-ji is known as *Maharaja* or shortened to *Maharaj* for all of us who study with him. The title was given to him for his lifelong dedication to the study and practice of yoga. He personally practiced all yoga postures, pranayamas, mudras, *samadhis*, and renunciation—a Brahmachari Yogi of great repute."

"Oh." I understood half of what she said.

To schedule a meeting with *Maharaja* and ask to join the group going to Kashmir seemed more than intimidating. When I visited Yog Niketan, I was introduced to him once but had not spoken with him or even had eye contact.

Mudita talked about his astute sense of insight. "It's as if he can see right through you. His eyes have an intense penetrating quality. You know he's ninety-four and can still do a headstand for fifteen minutes. Everyone admires him greatly. Javier thinks he's God on Earth."

I hesitated, unsure of my spiritual qualifications. "You think he'll let me go with you guys?"

"Yes, yes. I've already talked to Sonya, his main devotee. She said it's okay as long as you are willing to study and do everything the ashram expects."

"And what is that?"

"I think we have to sign an agreement of sorts. I'll get you that. But first, come on, meet with *Maharaj*. Please?"

"Okay, okay."

Maharaja sat perfectly still in half-lotus position on a raised platform. He wore robes made of bright tangerine cloth and sported a hat of the same color. The cushion under him was also orange.

Sonya had long black hair that fell to her waist. Her primrose-yellow sari, stiff from starch and ironing, fell in long pleats. She sat on another podium several inches lower than *Maharaja*'s.

I knelt, sitting on my calves with my feet tucked in my sari, a foot lower than *Maharaja*. I was told we should always be seated below *Maharaja* to show our respect. Sonya, fluent in English, interpreted. Mudita listened from her place in the back of the room.

Maharaja cleared his throat and looked directly at me. His stare reminded me of an encounter I once had with a mountain lion in Banff National Park a few years back. My heart started to beat double speed when *Maharaja*'s tiger eyes looked right into mine.

He spoke, and Sonya interpreted. "Are you ready to study Ashtanga yoga, pranayama, meditation, and be exposed to *samadhi*?"

I nodded. "Yes."

"Are you ready to study Raja yoga, to be concerned with the cultivation of mind using meditation to further your understanding of reality, and to be open to achieve ultimate freedom from the Sutras of the Patanjali?"

"Um. Yes." *What's that?*

"Are you ready to wake in the morning at four o'clock and bathe in cold waters before arriving at the meditation hall at four-thirty sharp for meditation?"

I nodded again, too scared to ask what that meant.

"Are you ready to sit, unmoving, in a cross-legged position on a simple cushion no more than two inches thick and direct your gaze inward for hours at a time?"

I replied weakly. "Yes." *Can I do that?*

"Are you ready to refrain from all tobacco and intoxicant products, abstain from eating meat, garlic, onions? Are you prepared to eat a simple vegetarian diet and maintain celibacy?"

Taj was gone. "Yes, yes, I can do that."

Maharaj said something to Sonya, got up, and left.

The meditation sessions are hard.

Sonya smiled. "*Maharaj* has agreed for you to join us this summer. You can sign your contract when you next visit." She glanced at Mudita. "You will share a tent with Mudita, and you should begin to gather the clothing and other essentials you may need to live in the mountains. We will be a day's bus ride away from Kashmir. Please, plan to arrive by the end of May or the first of June. We will have a Karma yoga week when everyone gets there." She unfolded her legs, bowed in the direction of *Maharaja*'s seat, and seemed to waltz out of the room, her poise as lovely as a swan drifting on a calm lake in the middle of summer.

I turned around and stuck my tongue out at Mudita. "Okay. What in the hell did I just agree to?"

Mudita placed her index finger over her mouth. "*Sh-sh-shh*. Let's go back to my room."

Once there, she explained. "Ashtanga yoga is the physical aspect of the program. It's all the yoga postures. We'll be practicing for at least one hour a day. Pranayamas are the breathing exercises. Here, watch me." She placed her thumb on one side of her nostril and breathed in. Then, she put her ring finger on the other nostril as she exhaled. "There are lots more." She smiled. "The meditation sessions are hard because you'll have to sit still for at least one hour without moving."

I thought about New Year's Eve and trying to maintain composure for ten minutes. "Whew. That'll be tough."

"Yeah. It is. The Sutras are easy enough. We can study with Javier, Zelio, and Alex."

I smiled, thinking about our friends who would meet us there. "Should be a great summer." I counted the days in my head. "Looks as if we have two weeks to get supplies."

We skipped meditation that afternoon, ate sizzling hot *samosas* at the market, and browsed the stalls for blankets, shawls, and material. The day drifted toward a lavender evening.

"Thanks, Mudita, for everything." I held my hand to my heart, excited about traveling again. "I'm really looking forward to this. Kashmir—wow—and *Maharaja*. I wonder what this *samadhi* thing is?"

Mudita's chestnut eyes twinkled. "I don't know, but I have a feeling this will be a summer we will never forget."

24

Canada – Spring 1973

*I held my Grandma Katherine's
delicate frame and felt her heart beating
steady and strong, matching my own.*

Living in poverty and with no financial prospect to afford college tuition, I quit my day job, disenrolled from my university course, and decided to head back out West. Before I left, my dad invited me to dinner.

At a cheap fast-food place near the city center, I asked him, "Where is Grandma Katherine these days?" I crossed my leg and bounced my foot up and down. "You know, I haven't seen her since I was six."

"Oh, she lives with Aunt Toni, Uncle Frank, and your cousin Donna in Oakland, California. Toni took her in. Why do you ask?"

"Well, I've been thinking. I don't have enough money to stay in college, even with a forty-hour workweek." I crumpled my sandwich wrapper into a tight ball. "So...I bought a train ticket for Vancouver with the monies from my last paycheck and thought, well...maybe I'd go visit her...you know, see how she is." I forced myself to relax, suddenly stopping my swinging foot in midair.

"Hmph." He tapped one of his fingers against the booth counter. "You should at least write her first." He tore off a piece of his napkin, wrote down her address, and gave it to me; then he looked at his watch, seemingly disinterested in anything else I might have to say. "Well, got to go. Need to catch an early flight to Cleveland tomorrow." He zipped up his leather jacket and popped a white-and-pink-striped mint into his mouth.

I reached out to give him a hug, but he put his hands in his pockets and winked at the passing waitress. "See ya, kid," was all he said.

I quickly let my arms fall to my side. "Well...okay," not knowing what else to say. "Bye."

He walked to the restaurant's lobby, and before opening the door, he paused and turned, offering a stiff wave.

I didn't know it then, but twelve years would pass before we'd ever see each other again, a brief encounter in an airport, and then one more time before he died—a lonely, embittered man.

However, I did see my Grandma Katherine. She answered my letter with a brief note. "Yes, please come visit. We'd love to see you."

When I got to Vancouver, I stayed at a hostel and counted my meager savings, knowing full well I did not have near enough monies for even a bus ride to California. So, I ended up hitchhiking instead.

Lucky for me, nothing happened. Kind strangers gave me rides and offered overnights in their homes where I joined their families for dinner and breakfast, without any thoughts of the possible dangers.

I like to think it was a different era then, but it certainly seems reckless to me now.

On a sunny May afternoon, Uncle Frank picked me up near Market Street in downtown San Francisco. Tall, robustly built, and sporting a mustache, he hoisted my bag.

"My car is parked just a few blocks from here. It's a short walk." We made small talk. I instantly felt a rapport.

He opened the car door of his shining Mercedes-Benz. "So, how did you get here? I thought maybe I'd be picking you up from the airport." He narrowed his eyes, focusing on my face.

"Uh. I hitchhiked."

His jaw fell. "What?"

"I don't have much money." I quickly added, "And I wanted to see Grandma, you, Toni, Donna. I'm not sure what I'm going to do next. But this seemed important."

His eyebrows raised. "Well, your grandma won't approve."

We rode in silence across the bridge to Oakland, driving through forest-green suburbs until we came to a quiet street. Frank parked in front of a white house with buttery trim. Two pug dogs sat on the manicured lawn. Red rose bushes bordered the sides. A large orange tree flanked the western edge.

When Frank got out of the car, the dogs yelped and jumped on his leg. If the dogs could talk, their high-pitched squeals would be, "Hey, where were you? We missed you."

Aunt Toni opened the screen door. She wore a berry-colored summer dress, her hair falling in one thick wave. Her suede high heels matched her lipstick.

"My, my. The last time I saw you ..." she grabbed my hand, "... you were two. Look how you've grown. Come, come. Your grandma is dying to see you. And you're going to love Donna."

Grandma Katherine's rich black hair tickled my nose as I hugged her. When I pulled back, I noticed a tear in her eye.

A few years younger than me, Donna, with long eyelashes circling her wide, round eyes, seemed uncomplicated. She stood behind her mother. "Hi." She shuffled on her feet back and forth.

> I held hope in my heart like a hundred stars.

For the next several days, Aunt Toni, Uncle Frank, Cousin Donna, and Grandma Katherine proudly showed me around the San Francisco area. Uncle Frank drove us to Lake Tahoe. In

Big Sur, we ate thick hamburgers and homemade French fries outside under a big umbrella, the spring breeze playing with our hair.

Aunt Toni, however, constantly criticized Donna. "Sit up. Fold your legs. Don't look at those guys. Close your mouth when you eat. Why are you wearing that?"

I felt sorry for Donna, and it wasn't long before Toni's icy edge began to irritate me. *Would she just shut up?* She reminded me of my father—cool, aloof, disconnected.

I tried to spend as much time with my grandma as I could, sitting close to her on my aunt's couch, breathing in her rose and lemon scent. Her English had improved, although it was still thickly accented by her native French. She showed me pictures of my ancestors.

"This is my mother, your great-grandmother, and my father. Here is a picture of me when I lived in Nova Scotia. I was thirteen then. You remember your godfather? Uncle Eddie, my brother? Here he is in Saudi Arabia."

"Where is he now?" I asked.

Grandma sighed. "He died last year." The fold in the middle of her forehead tightened. Then she gathered up all the photographs. "Want to help me hang the laundry?"

As the sun peeked through the trees, I passed the wooden clothespins to Grandma while she skillfully clipped the clothes to the line. In the quiet, I reflected on Uncle Eddie's visit when I was ten, saddened that I'd never see him again.

"I know we have a dryer, but fresh linen warmed by the sun is the best." She gathered a towel in her hands and buried her nose in it.

I kind of wanted to stay with my grandma. Cuddled under the sheets that smelled of the outdoors, I had secret daydreams of living with her and going to school there. But I had already worn out my welcome.

Toni made a comment at breakfast. "When are you leaving again?"

Later, Frank took me aside. "Listen, we bought you a plane ticket for Vancouver. It's a gift. We want you to be safe."

The day I left, Grandma Katherine bought me a blouse I had yearned for at a store; creamy soft cotton, the edges embroidered with daisies and violets. "Oh, wow. I love it! I'm wearing it on the plane."

Grandma laughed. "Come here, you silly girl." She took me in her arms and said, "No more hitchhiking."

When I held my Grandma Katherine's delicate frame and felt her heart beating steady and strong, matching my own, I held hope in my heart like a hundred stars.

I never saw Grandma Katherine, Aunt Toni, Uncle Frank, or Cousin Donna again.

Before passing away in the late 1980s, Aunt Toni grew increasingly hostile, primarily because of Donna's affiliation with a notorious motorcycle gang and a heroin addiction. Both Donna and Frank died a few years later.

Grandma Katherine moved back to Canada and lived out her final years in a small industrial northern town.

25

Kashmir – June–August 1978

*Those moments with Sonya are still fresh,
vivid, and pregnant in my memory.*

"I wish the damn train would get here on time for once." Mudita let out a slow sigh. "You'd think I'd be used to nothing being on time in India, especially the train, but I get my hopes up every time. I think maybe I'll only have to wait an hour or two. Eight hours. This is ridiculous." She wiped her flushed face and smoothed her sari, wrinkled from sitting on top of our luggage. Her long hair had wispy curls on the ends.

I noticed a tea *walla* coming onto the platform. "I'll go find chai. Want anything else?"

"No. What time do you think we'll get into Jammu?"

"Don't know. Maybe tomorrow?"

I brought back two clay cups of steaming tea with fried potato *samosas* wrapped in paper; then, I heard a distinct screech and shrill echo off the concrete platform.

"Hey, is that a whistle?"

Mudita perked up and peered down the length of the railway tracks. "Yes, yes! Finally." She stood. "I've been looking forward to this moment all day, heading north to Kashmir and studying with *Maharaj* for the whole summer. I'm so excited!" She clapped her hands and danced a little jig.

An hour later, we boarded the packed train, found our assigned seats, and stuffed our bags around us. We each had two soft canvas traveling bags with leather handles holding clothes, blankets, cooking supplies, a few books, and miscellaneous items. For the last few weeks, we'd spent hours in the market, haggling over things we needed.

The train car filled with Indian families; their belongings crammed into a tied cotton sheet instead of suitcases. Babies cried, and their mothers quickly nestled them close to their breast while the rest unpacked stacks of *chapattis* and chopped fruit. The train chugged and clanged for a bit before picking up speed and propelling us into the late spring air, the white sun blazing the path ahead.

I pulled out *Maharaja*'s book, *First Steps to Higher Yoga*, and read the first chapter.

"This *ahimsa* thing, not to kill or hurt any being or wound its feelings, does that mean mosquitoes, too? How about a spider or if an ant gets in our tent? I mean, really, isn't that taking it too far? How will I know if I hurt someone's feelings or not anyhow? Jeez."

> He'll forgive us when we can't live up to these standards.

I gazed over the top of my book at Mudita. "What do you think?"

"Just reading about that now. Okay, listen to this. *Maharaj* says that it is a sin to kill any living being, from the smallest insect to the biggest elephant. The soul is the same in all living beings." She put the book in her lap. "Guess that answers that."

"What happens if I do kill a mosquito or use someone else's soap they left in the shower stall? Does *Maharaja* know all that stuff? I mean, can he read minds or something? And can I call him *Maharaj* now, too?"

Mudita giggled. "I don't know. Maybe. Suspect we just do our best, and he'll forgive us when we can't live up to these standards. You can call him *Maharaj* if you want to."

25 Kashmir – June–August 1978

"Great. Just try my best. Okay."

I looked out the window at the passing scenery: earthy brown villages dotting the leafy green hills; water buffalo swishing their tails; fields of wheat and barley.

I closed my eyes and daydreamed of sitting in perfect lotus, unmoving, *Maharaj* admiring the dedication, my ashram peers in awe and exclaiming their surprise, "Wow, you are something. Never seen anyone do that before. Your handstand is perfect."

Pathetic.

In traditional Hindu philosophy, Raja yoga, derived from the Sutras of Patanjali, involved cultivating the mind using *dhyana,* or meditation, to further one's understanding of reality and achieve ultimate freedom or liberation.

Ashtanga yoga, founded by Krishnamacharya of Mysore and promoted as classical Indian yoga, was popularized by K. Pattabhi Jois in the 1900s. *Maharaja* had studied with Krishnamacharya when he was young.

Ashtanga, a Sanskrit term meaning "eight-limbed," encompassed moral codes; the study of physical postures or *asanas*; breath control; sense withdrawal; concentration; deep meditation; and *Samadhi*, a state of consciousness where the mind is entirely still, fixed, or one-pointed. The physical part of the yoga incorporated diaphragmatic breathing and muscle contraction to create internal heat, which increased circulation, necessary for extended practice.

In Jammu, we stepped off the train and quickly found a rickshaw driver. The air, moist from a recent rain, felt damp and cool. A friend of Mudita's suggested we stay at a hotel not far from the bus station. From there, we could easily find our way to Srinagar.

I pointed to a covered quadrangle surrounded by mowed grass and small shrubs. "Look, we can even cook our food under that common area over there." Two rustic picnic tables sat empty underneath.

That evening, we fixed a rice dish and talked with two male westerners coming back from Kashmir.

The thin man, with slightly crooked teeth, spoke about what to do in Srinagar.

"You got two days there, you say? Well, you should really take a *shikara* ride on Lake Dal and visit the infamous houseboat community. Huge lily pads border the islands, and thousands of birds feed there as well. It's something to see. I'd check out the main marketplace, too, and buy what you need there. Pahalgam won't have much. And you are going to be at the ashram for, what, four months? Might want to stock up on medicine. I got a bad bout of dysentery hiking up there. But so beautiful. You two are fortunate for the opportunity."

I nodded in agreement. "Hey, thanks for the info."

Back in our room, Mudita and I decided to try the *shikara* ride after we found our hotel in Srinagar.

The Srinagar bus station resembled every depot in India: covered in soot, crowded, and loud. A layer of dust clung to our clothes, hair, and face. Mudita flagged down a rickshaw driver, and thirty minutes later, we stood outside our hotel.

Bunches of flowers sat in earthenware pots of varying colors: apricot orange, china blue, rose red, juniper green. The sun slipped behind a cloud for a moment before lighting up the midnight-blue sky.

I took a deep breath. "It's so nice here. I love the air. Srinagar doesn't seem near as humid or busy."

Indeed, Srinagar appeared to be a picturesque mountain town with old-world temples, charming shops, and attractive people. Our small, no-frills hotel had six rooms, with ours on the second floor overlooking the street. The smell of cooking oil made my mouth water.

"Let's find something to eat and check things out."

25 Kashmir – June–August 1978

Kashmir, in the northwestern region of India, was a large valley lying between the Himalayas and the Pir Panjal mountain range with a rich historical past: Sultan and Muslim rulers, Hindu and Buddhist gurus, the British regime.

Boundary disputes between Pakistan, India, and China had been ongoing for years, all fighting for control over the entire country, resulting in each governing a different part. Pakistan controlled the northwestern portion, India the south, and China the northeast. During the nineteenth century, Kashmir became a popular tourist destination for Europeans and Indian residents because of its favorable climate.

The Jhelum River meandered through the ancient city, creating canals, lakes, and the famous *Hokersar* wetland area, home to thousands of migratory birds. Dal Lake, with its famous houseboats, skirted the city. Dozens of *shikaras*—wooden boats bowed in the center and covered with a tarpaulin to protect passengers or cargo from the summer sun, similar to a Venetian gondola—sat idle in the morning light. Dal Lake's shoreline seemed to go on forever; the Himalayan foothills flickered in the background.

"Let's hire one of those boats to take us around the lake and see the houseboat community," I told Mudita. "I'd love to get a glimpse of all those lilies, too. What do you think?"

"Yes, yes. I can't think of a better way to spend our day tomorrow than out there." She opened her arms and danced around, making footprints on the green grass beneath her.

A cloudless Mediterranean blue sky greeted us the next morning. We chose a *shikara* driver who had a young son helping him put up the canvas cover. A family man seemed a better choice for two young women. We got in the boat, perched like two birds on a fence, and clapped our hands. The sailcloth provided just enough shade for the Ma'am Sahibs.

Our boatman spoke a little English and showed us things along the way he thought might pique our interest. Attractive birds flew overhead. Other *shikaras* sailed past. We toured the houseboat community, homes on the water dotting the inlet shores. A few were beautifully maintained with fresh paint and pots of flowers outside. Some appeared to be only summer cabins, while others looked rundown and needed repair. A few looked outright abandoned. Our driver spotted a sizeable lily pad area. I mimed that we wanted to see it.

> I inhaled the cardamom scent from the tea.

The soft pink and creamy white lilies opened to the sun, their flawless petals like a thousand hands in prayer. I touched one and rubbed the velvety smooth blossom between my fingers. "I understand why they use this flower as a symbol for perfection. Look how big these are." I turned to face Mudita. "Have you ever seen anything so beautiful?"

"No." She took off her sunglasses and let her hand dangle in the water. "Pretty impressive."

Midway through our journey, our companions made chai on a small gas stove. The son, barefoot and smiling, carried two tall glasses of sweet tea. "Namaste," he said.

"Thank you. Thank you. Namaste." I sipped the hot liquid and closed my eyes. When I opened them, a single, gauzy cloud drifted above. Dainty yellow wildflowers on a nearby island reflected seamlessly on the lake. I inhaled the cardamom scent from the tea.

I looked at my friend. "You know, Mudita, I think I'll remember this day all of my life." The hours passed in the space of a heartbeat, but that moment has not faded from my memory.

A few days and shopping trips later, we boarded a congested bus for Pahalgam, placing our luggage and purchases on the torn vinyl seat.

I laughed. "This is going to be uncomfortable."

25 Kashmir – June–August 1978

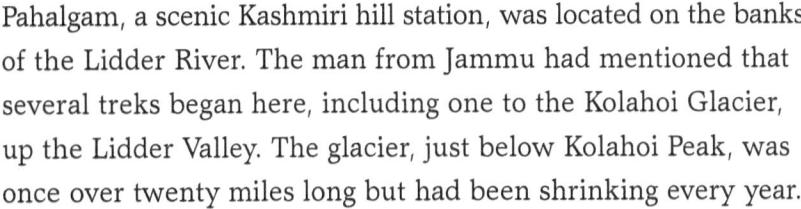

Pahalgam, a scenic Kashmiri hill station, was located on the banks of the Lidder River. The man from Jammu had mentioned that several treks began here, including one to the Kolahoi Glacier, up the Lidder Valley. The glacier, just below Kolahoi Peak, was once over twenty miles long but had been shrinking every year.

The valley, surrounded by lush green meadows, snow-capped mountains, and conifer forests, contained a hint of winter, the air fresh and cool. Muslim families, sheepherders, farmers, and local merchants moved around us, ambivalent to our white skin.

I filled my lungs with the clean mountain air. The ashram, a mile or more walk from the bus depot, sat at the end of a small dirt road northwest from the town center. Because of the high altitude, we often stopped to sit on our luggage and catch our breath.

"Maybe we should've hired someone to carry our bags. Would've just cost a few rupees." Mudita stretched her back by hanging over her two bags and touching the road with her fingers.

"Not much further, I hope." I looked ahead and noticed a new two-story building. "Is that it?"

Mudita sat up and squinted. "I think so."

Fresh white paint on the trim of the recently sided building made it appear contemporary amongst the long-standing farmsteads. Mudita opened the black iron gate. One set of stairs went up into the ashram and the other down to a patio.

We took the latter and set our bags down on the smooth stones. A worn footpath meandered through a mowed meadow. A dozen canvas tents scattered the field like army barracks.

"Wonder if that's home?"

We climbed up to the ashram and found a caretaker.

He smiled broadly. "Oh. Ma'am Sahibs. You early. *Maharaja* no here yet. Few days come. But...okay, pick tent. Best you get bedroll ready. Sun soon go. *Brrrrr*." He rubbed his arms to show us it would get cold.

Mudita picked our new home for the summer, the furthest tent from the ashram, with western exposure. The undulating Pahalgam valley and a snow-covered peak to the north came into view from behind a cloud.

We tied back the tent flaps, found a broom, bucket, and water, and scrubbed the rough wooden platform floor before setting down our straw mats. A slight breeze came over the meadow and combed the grass below us.

Mudita and I spent the last week of May and the first part of June setting up our living space. We bought extra blankets for warmth and white tennis shoes to wear if we needed to get up in the middle of the night. Flimsy and poorly manufactured, the shoes were still better than flip-flops. I wished for my old hiking boots.

We spent Karma yoga week in the front garden pulling weeds, cleaning the smooth river stones, and planting flowers. Ashram life was to begin the next day. I shuddered at the thought of the four a.m. wake-up bell.

"I'm not bathing in this," Mudita laughed in the communal shower stall next to me. The water was ice-cold. *No way.* I folded into my comfy shawl and walked up to the meditation hall. *Who's going to know?*

> A sonata of chimes traveled through the room.

We entered the ashram through a set of heavy wooden doors with cut glass in the center. Protocol required footwear be left on a shoe rack outside in the hallway. To my left, I spotted a small library with two big soft chairs. I contemplated curling into one and skipping the morning sitting.

Maharaja sat cross-legged on a raised platform, not a crinkle in his tangerine robes. Behind *Maharaja*'s podium, the western wall had high windows with no coverings, keeping the room bright and cheery, even when it rained. However, at four in the morning, I could not see the verdant valley and the snowcapped mountains.

The bottom windows opened to let in the churning noises of the fast moving Lidder River below. A large overhead fan in the middle of the elevated ceiling circulated the air. The north wall displayed pictures of *Maharaja*—photos from around the world, some with important diplomats. To the left of *Maharaja* stood a fat vase with fresh-cut flowers: daisies, marigolds, roses, violets, and baby's breath combined with splashes of mountain greenery.

Dressed in her yellow wrap, Sonya sat straight and majestic on her own pedestal just below *Maharaja*. Sonya was a poised beauty, emanating light and kindness. At times she appeared ageless, but I guessed her to be about thirty. Twirled in a tight bun at her neck, her ebony hair gleamed against her skin and her golden-brown eyes. I hoped for a fraction of her loveliness.

I chose a maroon cushion, the farthest seat from *Maharaj*. Within minutes, yogis filled the hall, and *Maharaj* tapped a bronze bowl with a thick, short stick. A sonata of chimes traveled through the room, the echo lasting for many seconds. Everyone closed their eyes and placed their hands neatly in front of them, one on top of the other to form an empty cup.

I took my time getting settled, making sure my shawl was draped and tucked just right. One last look around and, then I, too, shut my eyes.

One-hour meditation time, four-thirty to five-thirty a.m., followed by chanting and yoga. *I can do that*, I thought. However, within fifteen minutes, my right knee and hip started to ache. I opened my eyes. Everyone sat motionlessly. Any sound seemed magnified in the tranquility.

What if I had to sneeze or cough?

I painstakingly tried to lift my leg from its torturous position without making any noise, but the rustle of my skirt gave me away. I tried again. Another ten minutes and my left leg started to throb—and then, my back. I must have moved two dozen times during that first sitting. When *Maharaj* tapped the bowl and the symphony of vibration rang out, I almost applauded.

Maharaja's melodious voice filled the hall. Each syllable of his Sanskrit chant was distinctly pronounced. Then, silence. *Maharaj* unfolded his legs and nodded to one of his senior devotees in the front. We remained seated until *Maharaj* exited, leaving us to practice a ninety-minute Ashtanga yoga class.

The senior student *Maharaj* motioned to was our instructor. He spoke English and guided us through a rigorous series of physical postures, some seemingly impossible.

I limped back to our shelter for breakfast. Mudita formed small balls of dough to make *chapattis* sprinkled with a little sugar and cinnamon. I chopped up bananas and papaya, placing them in a small bowl with toasted almonds. We ate in silence. A silver mist cloaked the peaks and valleys.

By the end of June, I could meditate steadily for thirty minutes, do a few yoga postures, and learned one chant.

"We should celebrate," I said to Mudita. "Let's spend our day off this week shopping in town. I want a pair of those dangly earrings the local women wear and I wouldn't mind eating something fried in oil or drinking several cups of chai. Just do nothing."

> The ashram, often quiet and calm, felt a little bit like how I imagined heaven.

"*Maharaj* is going to extend the meditation time to one hour and fifteen minutes. He expects us to remain motionless for two hours by September." Mudita gathered her clothes into a neat pile next to her bedroll.

My delight quickly evaporated. "Oh."

Our ashram friends, about twenty western yogis, were fast becoming family, each of us taking turns to host dinner and afterward, leisurely sipping cups of tea before the evening sit.

The ashram, often quiet and calm, felt a little bit like how I imagined heaven. Pink and white flowers speckled the paths. Faint, sweet smells of their blossoms filled the air. Vivid blues, soft greens were everywhere.

Zelio and Sasha, a married couple from Switzerland, had studied with *Maharaj* for years. Both were proficient in more advanced yoga postures, such as full bending or balancing on one hand. Sasha's beautiful face lit up whenever she smiled.

Alex and Caroline, single when they arrived, flirted constantly. "Oh, Alex, you don't have to do that for me..." Alex was from Germany and spoke English with a thick German accent, while Caroline called Ireland home.

I liked Jerry from America, a big burly man with a sense of humor who often lightened my mood. His quick wit helped when I fell out of a posture or when I forgot to bow when *Maharaj* entered a room. He'd wink or crack a joke: "Hey, did you see Jovin pick his nose? Glad *Maharaj* wasn't looking."

There was nothing romantic between us, which suited me just fine. I enjoyed the platonic relationship we shared.

In July, the weather warmed, and some yogis left while new ones arrived, all from Europe. *Maharaj* gave talks, interpreted by Sonya, and conducted evening meditation outside in the courtyard. We brought our cushions and placed them on the flat stones. I continued to position myself at the very back, trying to be inconspicuous.

I enjoyed these sessions even if I couldn't maintain stillness for the entire time. When everyone had their eyes shut, I'd watch the sky light up with beautiful brushstrokes of scarlet, sunflower, and amber, wings of birds fluttering in the dusk. If the training was more prolonged than usual, stars came out, flecks of bone scintillating in the bruised sky. The schedule became easier to follow, and I didn't mind getting up that early anymore but continued to skip the four a.m. bath. Instead, I placed a large bucket of water in the sun after breakfast. By late afternoon, the water sometimes became even hot, and I'd wash in warm luxury.

Sundays—our one day off—was devoted to laundry and cleaning the tent, walks to town for supplies, and lunch with friends at a favorite spot.

In the final days of July, something extraordinary happened. *Maharaj* informed us that Sonya would be going into Samadhi for three days. I did not know what that meant, nor did I ask. For the next several days, a palpable excitement filled the air.

Several older Indian people, some in distinguished clothing and fancy cars, came to the ashram. A large dome tent was erected in the terraced area with a small stage covered with bright cloth and blankets.

Maharaj encouraged more profound dedication to our meditation and yoga. His steely expression matched his voice.

> **A soft, lustrous blue light surrounded her.**

"Meditate longer. Sit completely still. Stay in your postures for all five breaths. Study. Don't eat too much." The ashram's atmosphere took on a zealous quality. People walked fast. They looked at the ground, quiet and serious.

I tried to stay out of the way.

The sun rose, spreading a golden light across the horizon the day Sonya situated herself on the stage. The entire ashram community gathered below her, motionless figurines on a sea of grape-colored cushions. *Maharaj* stood off to the side and ordered two attendants to wrap her gently in cloth, including her head but not her face.

Maharaj chanted for a long time. Then, silence. It seemed no one but me moved for the hour and fifteen minutes. When the ring of the bell pealed through the tent, *Maharaj* said to us in Hindi, "Time for you to leave. Continue to practice meditation in your tents." As stately as the Himalayan mountains behind him, *Maharaj* stayed and meditated with Sonya.

Group meditations occurred throughout the next day and into the late evening. Sonya did not move. At all. An eerie silence fell over the ashram. Two guards protected the area, pacing the perimeter.

The second night, my curiosity piqued.

She can't actually sit for three whole days without moving, can she?

After Mudita fell asleep, I crept up to the pergola and peered inside. Sonya, regal as a high empress, sat utterly still, and the air around me seemed to be infused with a hushed peacefulness.

I tiptoed closer and kneeled a few feet in front of her, blinking a few times to clear away any illusions of what I may be witnessing. A soft, lustrous blue light surrounded her. The hovering luminosity appeared to be about four inches thick. I wanted to touch it but thought, *"No, I shouldn't even be here."*

And then, my heart seemed to swell with a sensation of warmth coursing through my veins. My vision blurred, tears pooling in the corners of my eyes, and I stayed there—for how long, I don't know. It could have been seconds or even minutes. All I remember was a feeling of a hundred hearts pulsing in the light and a voice inside my head, more like a whisper: *be still.*

Was it my voice or Sonya's?

I heard the guards as they made their rounds back toward the patio and abruptly backed out into the cool evening. The moonlight grazed the tips of the trees, and a bat or an owl flew overhead, the hush of its wings in the dark. I lay awake until the early morning hours, struggling to make sense of those moments with Sonya, unexpectedly changed, but having no words to explain it.

Sonya emerged from her three-day Samadhi in the middle of the afternoon, sunlight bathing her in liquid gold. The guards and attendants dismantled the gazebo. *Maharaj* and two other higher-ranking students helped her stretch and lay down on the cotton blankets that had supported her for three days. She exhaled noisily and muttered the sound *ahm*.

Maharaj cried. Students in attendance cried. Mudita cried.

I took a deep breath and looked at the sky, the summer brightness warming my face, the air stagnant and quiet. The senior devotees massaged Sonya's legs, arms, face, and she slowly started to move, eventually leaving about an hour later, gently escorted by two helpers.

I watched her until she entered the main ashram. No one spoke, and serenity enveloped us like a warm fog, creeping stealthily into everything.

After *Maharaja* departed, Mudita and I cleaned the courtyard and picked wildflowers for the meditation hall, each deep in our own thoughts.

I turned to Mudita. "What happened to Sonya? Did she have some out-of-body experience or something? It feels pretty weird around here." I debated whether or not to tell her about sneaking up to Sonya's tent.

Mudita placed several delicate flowers in a small vase. "I overheard *Maharaj* talking to some of the visiting elders. He said that Sonya was in some kind of super-consciousness thing. When one of the elders asked what that was, he told them there were no words to explain it, but he went on to say that Sonya's mind and body had entered a state of bliss and peace where all mental functions stop—all thinking ceases. I don't know what really happened, but we witnessed something so extraordinary I doubt we'll ever be able to describe these last three days to anyone." Her eyes watered and seemed to glitter in the light.

I cleared my throat. "Well, I'm going to ask when I see her."

I got my wish the next day. When I left the communal shower area, I saw Sonya stretched on a bench looking at some violets, their plum petals swaying in the light breeze.

I waved. "Hey there."

She lifted her head and motioned with her hand. "Come, come. Sit with me for a moment."

I walked over and flopped down on the uneven earth. Sonya's eyes shone like two suns, their lustrous brightness blinding my eyes as if someone had shone a flashlight right in them. She beamed. "Aren't these flowers beautiful?"

I looked at the blossoms. "Well, yeah. I guess they are really nice." I felt shaky, suddenly uncertain, and unsure how to form my words. "Um. Sonya, can you tell me what happened to you? I don't understand."

Sonya tilted her head to one side and touched my hand with the greatest of care, the contact feeling as gentle as spring rain. "I saw everything." That was all she said. She patted my hand again, got up, and walked away, her lithe movements reminiscent of a ballerina on pointe.

I sat there and watched the sun dance on the green leaves. A single leaf, translucent as a baby's skin, trembled in the breeze. When I looked up, Sonya was almost at the top of the stairs. The space between us shimmered—or maybe it was a trick of the light, I don't know.

Sometimes I forget the name of someone I met just yesterday, but those moments with Sonya are still fresh, vivid, and pregnant in my memory.

August, a month of renewed commitment to ashram standards, was filled with longer meditation sessions, sustained yoga practice, long walks in the surrounding hills, and a deepening of my friendship with Mudita. She listened to my problems, never judged or disapproved, and encouraged more than dissuaded. One time, she bought henna in the marketplace and dyed my hair an exquisite auburn color.

Toward the close of that month, we trekked to Amarnath Cave.

The natural Amarnath Cave, high in the Himalaya mountains and surrounded by snow for most of the year, attracted hundreds of native pilgrims in the summer. Most hiked from Pahalgam to see the ice stalagmite inside the cave, formed from freezing water drops that fell from the cave's roof onto the floor, growing vertically to form the stalagmite, or in the Hindu tradition, a Shiva *linga* dedicated to their mythological god Shiva.

The roundtrip hike to this well-known Hindu shrine took around five days. For the first ten miles or so, we walked over fairly flat terrain in our cheap tennis shoes. After that, the topography became steep as we climbed about seven miles to a deep mountain lake the color of sapphires. Snow covered the nearby peaks, and a waterfall fell over black rocks on the distant shore.

We stopped to rest above the half-mile-long lake and watched sheep grazing on the tundra grass and several Nomadic tribes shepherding goats. Wind gusts dragged the clouds over the sun, and the tinkle of livestock bells could be heard in the distance.

Mudita rested against a rock. "I've decided to return to Australia after our time with *Maharaj*. I'm out of money. I've been thinking about it a lot, actually. Seems anything after this would be a letdown."

My heart contracted slightly. "Oh."

"I had thought of studying with another teacher this fall. His name is Goenka, a Vipassana teacher from Burma. He'll be teaching in Rajasthan soon. Vipassana is similar to what we are learning here, although no one can hold a candle to *Maharaj*. His energy is so formidable. Anyhow, I think you should go—study with Goenka, I mean."

I let this piece of information settle a bit before answering, listening to the hum of a bee buzzing around a meadow daisy, the cry of a hawk overhead. "I guess I just assumed we'd both spend the winter in India. Tell me more about this Vipassana thing."

We picked up our light shoulder bags, slung them across our chest, and began to walk toward Mahagunastop, the high mountain pass, approximately eight miles away.

Mudita talked. "Goenka is a leading teacher of Buddhist Vipassana meditation and a student of U Ba Khin. He was originally from Burma but now lives in India and conducts silent Dharma retreats where he offers instruction and gives inspirational lectures called Dharma talks. Vipassana means insight or mindfulness in English, and the meditation style is to observe the constantly changing nature of the mind and body. Not much different from what *Maharaj* teaches."

"What does Dharma mean?"

"Dharma means truth. To see things as they are, not as we may wish them to be, but just how they are." She spread her arms wide to convey the present moment, everything we were experiencing.

> We continued to walk until purple shadows danced across the sky.

I listened to the sigh of the wind in the grasses and remembered the Buddhist monk in Marpha. "Sounds interesting. What do I need to do to sign up for that?"

"I'll put you in touch with a contact person in New Delhi. You'll have to take a train to Rajasthan from there. The retreat starts toward the end of September." She counted on her fingers. "That's not too far away. And now that I'm returning home, we should really go to Srinagar and make plans."

I didn't say much because I felt a mixture of emotions; happy to stay in India and experience new things and yet sad because Mudita would be traveling back to Australia.

We continued to walk until purple shadows danced across the sky and spent the night in a primitive Hindu pilgrim camp—

which was nothing more than a rustic wall tent, the flaps fluttering in the late-day wind.

―⁓―

Many people stood in line to enter the cave and pay their respects: nomadic tribes in tattered clothes, wealthy Brahmins in pristine whites, barefoot *sadhus* wearing just a loincloth and covered in white ash. We approached the linga, rang the bell, bowed, and kneeled in front of the ice stalagmite. When the customary moment of silence passed, enough to show reverence, we left.

After all the work of getting to this legendary cave, I was disappointed. "Well, I don't know what the big deal is. Just some ice formation in a cave that people have decided is holy. An ancient fairy tale if you ask me." I looked around at the hundreds of people in prayer.

Mudita put a finger over her lips. "*Shh.* Someone might hear you." She let out a nervous laugh.

"Mudita, you are such a rule follower."

> I froze like a creature seeking camouflage.

We hiked back as quickly as possible. Cold and rain welcomed us at the mountain passes and low clouds hung in the valleys obscuring any views.

Maharaj greeted us when we returned two days later. He fixed his gaze on me first, his X-ray eyes staring into mine, the look so intent, I feared he could see all my secrets. He moved his head back and forth. "No. No."

He did the same thing to Mudita. "No, no, no," and he continued to shake his head as he mounted the steps back into the ashram.

I turned and smiled. "We didn't measure up, did we?"

She slowly shook her head. "I wonder what he was looking for. He probably won't tell us, either."

"Nope. I doubt it."

25 Kashmir – June–August 1978

The evenings began to cool, and the neighboring hills seemed to turn the color of wheat overnight. I could sit for an hour without moving but continued to enjoy opening my eyes to admire the view or glance around at everyone.

I often stared at *Maharaja*. It was hard to believe he was born in 1884. His light cinnamon skin was smooth, not wrinkled, and he sat straight, not hunched over, carrying his five-feet-ten muscular frame with effortless grace. He had a booming laugh; I sometimes heard him from our tent. His bright and clear eyes never seemed to look at people as much as *into* them.

One time, *Maharaj* opened his eyes at the exact moment I opened mine, and he looked directly at me. His broad smile made his eyes crinkle. I froze like a creature seeking camouflage. He held my gaze and chuckled. I quickly shut my eyes and remained motionless for the rest of the hour.

After the sitting, he said something to Sonya.

Sonya glanced at me and said, "*Maharaj* wants to know what you look at when you open your eyes every time you meditate?"

Busted. "Nothing." I dropped my head. A flush worked its way up my face. I tried to ignore the muffled titters of the other meditators.

Maharaja turned to Sonya, who translated my response. "She says nothing, but I think she looks at everything." He laughed quietly.

I fixed my gaze on a spot roughly two feet in front of me and did not hear the rest of what he said. Several uncomfortable moments went by.

Sonya addressed the group. "*Maharaj* says you should dedicate yourself as much as possible these last days before you leave. One never knows when or how things will change. This is an auspicious time; use it well."

I stayed in the mediation hall after everyone left, too embarrassed to face my friends, feeling a pressure building in my chest.

Mudita came to find me.

"Let it go. *Maharaj* has given each of us a lesson when he felt it was appropriate. You just had yours." She rubbed my shoulders. Light streamed down onto the wooden floor.

I moaned. "I'm such an idiot."

"No more than the rest of us. Come on, let's make breakfast."

Winds swirled around the tent. A few scattered drops of freezing rain fell. I shivered. "Wow, it's gotten cold fast. Do you have an extra blanket by chance?"

"No." Mudita poked her head out from under her wool shawl. "I was thinking. Maybe we should just go now. Let's stop in Srinagar so I can confirm my flight. We could make train arrangements there, too. Do you want to spend time in New Delhi at all?"

I wasn't quite ready to leave Kashmir. "Do you want to see Ladakh before we leave? We're so close. I don't know if I'll ever get back here, and it'd be nice to spend just a few more days here."

"Hmm." She fell silent for a few moments and then nodded. "Let's do it." She clapped her hands. "Our last adventure together before I leave."

I grinned. When we made our way up to the ashram to tell the lead attendant our plans, I noticed red petals spattered against the grass.

Our time here, delicate as a suspended breath, was ending.

26

Canada – May 1973-September 1976

*Sometimes I could barely sit still,
my insides vibrating with excitement.*

Sherbet swirls of pink and orange lit up the sky when I met Rick in downtown Vancouver, British Columbia. He was sitting on the other side of the small park, leaning on his backpack. His long hair, shaggy beard, and tall frame made him appear a bit on the wild side, kind of like a modern-day Rasputin. He waved. I put down my journal and waved back.

He sauntered over and introduced himself. "Hey. Name's Rick. What are you doing up so early?" We were the only people in the square.

"Truth?" I gazed into his blue eyes. "I didn't sleep."

"Really?"

"Yep. Just flew in from Oakland and couldn't afford a hotel, so I just walked around until it got light."

He nodded slowly. "Well, I've been known to stay up all night, too." He stroked his beard. "C'mon. I'll treat you to breakfast."

We ate at a natural foods restaurant on Fourth Street and talked over whole wheat pancakes with real maple syrup. He paid the bill. Later, we crossed the road and browsed in a new age bookstore. Rick bought me a small book on Taoism. "A gift," he said.

"Uh. Thanks." I didn't know who the heck this Chinese philosopher was—or Rick, for that matter—but I was flat broke and not about to refuse the thoughtfulness.

We spent the day together. I found out Rick worked on a trail crew for the national parks, specifically Banff and Jasper, and was on his way back to Lake Louise. He offered, "Why don't you come with me? I'm sure I could talk to Joe and get you on the campground crew. He's looking for a few seasonal workers. Pay's good and includes room and board."

And, so I did. Without any other immediate alternative, I decided why not and hopped into Rick's pickup truck. Within a week, I had a job and a place to live.

In those days, the national park housed its employees in small cabins and fed them in a communal cafeteria. The cook packed brown paper bag lunches with sandwiches, chips, brownies or cookies, fruit, and juice.

I shared a cabin with two young college women from Calgary: one studying to be a naturalist and the other a botanist. I couldn't believe my good luck.

I fell in love with the Rockies and became infatuated with Rick, fifteen years my senior. He'd wait for me after work, and we'd walk back to the cabins. He was an avid hiker and mountain climber and asked me one day, "Do you want to go hiking this weekend?"

Almost every weekend after that, Rick and I hiked a new trail: up and down ridges and passes; fording streams; fielding encounters with bears, mountain goats, and sheep; negotiating questionable rock faces. By September, my stamina and hiking ability improved significantly, and I accepted his invitation to travel that winter to the American Southwest. Two of his friends joined us, and we explored Zion National Park, Bryce Canyon, and the Canyon Lands.

> **I refused to pay attention to some obvious red flags in our relationship.**

26 Canada – May 1973–September 1976

We traveled to the Pacific coast, visiting Point Reyes National Seashore and a dozen other parks in the California area. I spent all the money I had earned and was back at work the following spring, the snow still on the ground.

Rick and I dated for a few years. There were things, however, that bothered me about him. He'd say: *I don't want you hanging out with those people. It's just going to be you and me this weekend. Don't wear those shorts. Don't eat that. Don't listen to that music.*

I refused to pay attention to some obvious red flags in our relationship, and instead of going on my merry way, I joined him on a second and third tour of the Southwest after our summer work season. Unfortunately, we argued and bickered—a lot.

Long silences fell between us.

When we got back to Lake Louise, I could barely stand to be in the same room with him and declined his invites to climb on the weekends. Instead, I went into Banff and hung out with members of the mountain rescue crew or friends from my work team. Sometimes, I even went to the pub and drank beer.

Rick loathed the bar scene, and he became jealous and mean. "Only floozy women go to saloons. I saw the way you looked at Steve. People are talking."

One time, he hit me. My stepfather's face smoldered in my mind. Without thinking, I said, "Buddy, it's over. We're done. I don't want to see you again." After that, I refused to talk to him.

Rick's resentment grew. One time after work, he followed me and yelled, "I got you this job. You owe me."

I turned around and shouted, "Stay away from me!"

He tried to catch up with me. "You're nothing without me, bitch!"

I ran as fast as I could back to my cabin and locked the door, but I worried about being alone at night.

One night, Justin, a member of Rick's crew, said, "Why don't you travel? Get out of here and let Rick cool off. He's still in love with you, but we all see you don't feel the same." He added, "You got your whole life in front of you."

He was right. I saved every penny and chose to go to Europe. There, I could decide where and what I wanted to do. I applied for a passport, got vaccinations, bought some touring equipment.

> Remember, you can do anything you want.

Justin helped. He had toured Europe and offered valuable advice. He loaned me books about the Himalayas. I bought maps and made plans. Sometimes I could barely sit still, my insides vibrating with excitement.

The whispers stopped when I walked into the communal kitchen. I looked around. "What?"

Justin spoke up. "Rick went ballistic when he heard you were leaving. He stormed into the office and quit."

"Oh." I felt bad, but not too much. My resolve to travel and see the world grew stronger with each passing day.

I watched everyone leave at the end of the season. Justin went back to school at the University of Calgary. The day he left, I walked up to his van and gave him a small gift, a book of poems. "Thank you for everything."

"Good luck. Drop me a postcard occasionally." He tucked a note with his address and phone number into my hand. "This is your chance for a new start. Be happy. Enjoy yourself. Remember, you can do anything you want."

I bought a one-way ticket to London, England.

27

Ladakh – September 1978

*Then the space around me seemed to thicken
as if I was in the water, and the room
began to spin, around and around.*

We placed our bags on the patio and walked up the stairs to the main meditation hall to say goodbye to *Maharaja*. When I opened the door, dust danced in the thin light.

Mudita approached first. Tears streamed down her face, and her words cracked with emotion. I barely heard her whisper.

Maharaja cupped her face tenderly between his large hands, his grandfather eyes soft and radiant. He spoke, and Sonya translated. "*Maharaja* wants you to continue with your studies and not to forget everything you learned. Meditate every day. Do your yoga in the early morning. Remember to love all things, Mudita. May you be free, happy, and have a life of peace."

Mudita bent over and touched her head to the ground, her sobs audible now. She repeated, "Thank you" at least a dozen times. Lifting her head, she retreated to the back corner of the room, plucking some tissues from her pocket to blow her nose.

My chest contracted slightly, and I quickly contemplated my spiritual progress. I could sit motionless for an hour, had diligently worked on my yoga practice, weeded the upper garden until only flowers shone through, did extra chores around the main ashram, and had a newfound respect for these wonderful teachers. But I believed *Maharaja* did not care about me in the same way he cared for Mudita.

In those final moments with *Maharaja* and Sonya, my heart felt heavy and an ache pulsed at the back of my throat.

I lowered my head respectfully and sat cross-legged in front of him, my eyes glued to the floor. With my hands in a prayer position, I said, "Thank you for this amazing opportunity. I have learned so much from you and will continue to work on all the things you have taught me."

Sonya said softly, "Lift up your face and look at *Maharaja*. Don't be afraid."

> **This place, this feeling of peace, like being suspended in time.**

Maharaja's eyes, like two magnetic stars, seemed to pierce right through me. He said some things—things I can't remember now—the words hollow compared to the light encircling him. His face split into a huge smile.

A sensation of warmth filled my heart and spread to my fingertips, suddenly feeling good and strong for a few moments. I clutched my hands as he continued to talk, not knowing how to respond but nodding accordingly. Afterward, I tried to recall his words and evoke the feeling I felt in his presence, but nothing came—and self-doubt silently trickled in.

Mudita picked up her luggage. "That was beautiful. I'll never forget *Maharaj* or this summer. I think I've said it a thousand times, but I'll never be able to describe this to anyone." She looked up at the morning sunlight. "This place, this feeling of peace, like being suspended in time."

I didn't reply. Instead, self-loathing brewed inside me.

Mudita's lovely face glowed, and her eyes sparkled. She chatted all the way to town. I drifted behind like a flower petal being carried away by the breeze. She continued to talk on the bus, making small talk with the locals and a few visiting tourists.

I feigned happiness but the tips of my nerves burned beneath my skin. The green-eyed monster jumped on my shoulder and spoke in my ear, "She's so much better than you. You are such a loser. Selfish. You'll never make it." A hot mixture of rancid feelings and vinegary thoughts was running through my body and mind unchecked.

It took years for me to understand this negative internal dialogue was fueled by things my mother often said to me.

It also took years for me to realize *Maharaja* taught Mudita and me different lessons, each important, each equally as loving.

I sometimes think I had some of my peak life experiences that summer with Mudita and Maharaja, many of which have taken most of my adult life to comprehend, digest, and integrate.

At the time, I had thought I would see *Maharaja* and the ashram again, perhaps for a more extended period of study—but I didn't. *Maharaja* died in 1984, and I lost contact with everyone I met that summer.

Some days my memories seemed like prayer flags flapping in the wind.

Clouds drifted in the cool pewter sky as we sat on our gear, waiting for the bus. The only way to get to Leh in those days was via the Srinagar-Leh Road, a difficult journey climbing up and over Zoji La Pass in the great Himalayan wall, which included an overnight stop in Kargil.

I turned to look at Mudita, the dark veil of uncertainty lightening slightly. "I'm going to do that retreat with Goenka in Rajasthan. I get it that you are ready to go home and that you've learned enough for now, but me—I'm just beginning."

"That's great," she said. "You've been so quiet, withdrawn these last two days. Everything okay?"

I wasn't brave enough to discuss my problems. "Yeah. Everything's cool. Just thinking is all."

"When we get back to Srinagar, we'll write to the retreat manager. I'll give you directions and contacts." She pointed. "There's our ride."

The wobbly old bus creaked and groaned its way up into Ladakh, bouncing into and over potholes the size of small cars, through overflowing creeks, and around herds of sheep or goats. I gripped the seat in front of me to prevent falling into my neighbor's lap.

Although the ride was uncomfortable and at times nauseating, the landscape proved to be all we had hoped for—burnt orange, mustard yellow, persimmon-red gorges, and chasms like the great canyons of the American Southwest, set against towering snow-capped mountain ranges. Sunshine glowed along the sapphire horizon, shifting into a striking marigold color when the light pierced the clouds.

We stopped in ravines, havens of lush green trees thick with oranges, dates, and walnuts. Rustic shops served sweet milk tea flavored with cardamom and cinnamon. We lounged under the trees in heavy bloom, the sugary scent filling our nostrils, as we munched fresh fruit and sipped rich tea.

"Wow, this is something. I didn't know it was going to be this spectacular." I watched the light clouds skid past.

The province of Ladakh, sandwiched between the Kunlun mountain range in the north and the Himalayas to the south, supported a primarily Tibetan population. Chinese guerilla uniformed officers with semiautomatic rifles examined our passports at various checkpoints along the way. They stood rigid in their stark plywood barracks while thousands of prayer flags next to handmade *stupas* blew in the ever-persistent wind.

At our last checkpoint, I pointed to the army garrisons and then the *stupas*. "Well, if that isn't an oxymoron..."

27 Ladakh – September 1978

Mudita laughed. "You're not kidding. I heard they've been doing that since 1949, when China closed its doors and blocked the old trade routes. Seems strange, though, this political strife in a land full of peace and harmony."

By midafternoon, we reached Leh, the largest town in Ladakh. The wind whisked across the earth, the air cool and dry. Leh was once an important link on an ancient commerce road between Tibet and Kashmir for items such as cashmere wool, silk, salt, and grains.

My skirt beat against my legs. "It's a lot colder up here. What's the name of that hotel again?"

> The air was like a thief, stealing any moisture from my body.

Mudita looked at the piece of paper and read the directions. "It should be just around that corner over there." Up ahead, a row of two-story houses rested next to a mound of large stones.

I surveyed the miles of gray-brown landscape and white-capped mountains against the cobalt sky—a spectacular trifecta only Mother Nature could produce. The constant hiss of the wind flapped the tattered sun-bleached prayer flags strung from the roofs. Little dirt funnels swirled in front of us like dancing Sufi dervishes.

I tightened my cotton scarf around my head and shoulders. A Tibetan woman in a navy-blue wool skirt and a matching long-sleeved top bowed from her post as we passed. Two small children played in the sand near her feet.

Far behind the industrialized West, Leh felt as if I had stepped into a different world, a land of simple needs and wants. The nine-story Leh Palace, built in the sixteenth century and abandoned in the nineteenth century during a Kashmiri invasion, dominated the northern horizon. It used to house Ladakhi royals and was similar in style to Tibet's Potala Palace in Lhasa. Shops and terraced homes lay nuzzled beneath. It was a remote and beautiful place.

I swallowed; my throat already parched with thirst. The air was like a thief, stealing any moisture from my body.

We arrived at our hotel—cottage might be a better description—as the sun crept toward the horizon. The host family lived on the first floor and rented out the top two rooms to foreign visitors. They served us a dinner of salty barley gruel and sour tea.

I stirred the tasteless mush around and around with my spoon. "Let's check out the bazaar tomorrow and see if we can get any fresh fruit and vegetables. Maybe walnuts and dates? I don't think I can live on this for the next few days. You?"

Mudita laughed quietly. "Not much flavor. Let's check out the market in the morning and tour the Palace in the afternoon."

We visited Leh Palace, bought food, and watched the amazing Tibetan culture float around us for most of the next day. Charmingly behind the times, Leh had an ageless way of life at every corner and in 1978 was just beginning to experience tourism. In the evening, we bought tickets for a trip to the La Myna monastery, located about sixty miles away.

Early the next morning, we clambered aboard a local run-down-beat-up-no-shocks bus, the windows and seat springs long gone. The constant motion and screeching of the brakes and gears made conversation impossible. I clung to the rail of the next seat to keep from spilling into the aisle. The natives seemed unfazed.

After an hour or more, I saw what resembled a medieval castle perched precariously on a high, hilly outcrop overlooking the valley and a small village. The fortress, made from stones of slate gray and rich sienna brown, blended seamlessly with the landscape below the steely blue sky.

27 Ladakh – September 1978

We zoomed past the citadel and began a switchback ascent on the other side. Everyone clung to anything bolted down as the bus squealed past the turns. After that, the vehicle stopped abruptly in a dusty parking lot. The driver shouted something in Tibetan and then in English, "Now, here. Time, go!"

Mudita and I brushed the soot off our saris and marched in single file off the bus. We followed a small path that rose sharply toward the monastery. A Tibetan couple in front of us began to slow down. I almost bumped into the man.

I let out a sigh, looked around, and noticed a less-prominent trail to my left. I whispered to Mudita, "Hey, let's take that."

We didn't encounter anyone as we hiked up to a massive door the color of chestnuts. I ran my hand over the elaborate carvings. Tibetan gods were depicted as Buddhas with six arms, deities carrying skulls, dancing warriors.

I turned to Mudita. "Wow, this is something. Should we go in?"

> **I had trouble believing what I was seeing.**

Mudita shrugged. "Sure, I guess."

I undid the latch and pushed the heavy door. The creak echoed in the large, vaulted room. It took several seconds for my eyes to adjust to the small dimly-lit entryway that led into a chamber. It was so quiet. I could hear the sound of my breathing.

Mudita whispered, "Oh, my God..."

The room was filled with enormous gold Buddha statues, gigantic Tibetan paintings hanging from the tall ceiling, piles of carved chalices, elaborate statues illustrating Tibetan folklore, books covered in cloth, stacks of engraved woodcuts, mounds of prayer flags, etched stonework, ornate clothing, and beadwork. I had trouble believing what I was seeing.

Then the space around me seemed to thicken as if I was in the water, and the room began to spin, around and around. I blinked a few times, feeling dizzy and confused.

The earth did not feel solid, and for a moment, time felt angular and spherical instead of linear. That's the only way I can describe it.

I looked over at Mudita. Her eyes were round and full; her mouth open in a perfect little circle. A resounding, wordless echo vibrated and filled the hall. I tried to speak, but no words came. Instead, I let out a deep breath, one I hadn't realized I was holding. Then, I heard the sound of feet scurrying over hard stones.

A short elderly monk, less than five feet tall, darted around the corner. "Oh, oh, oh. You no allowed here. Leave, leave, leave. Oh, oh, oh."

We quickly retreated into the daylight. Without a word, we found the main trail and passed a notice. *No one is allowed past this sign. Strictly forbidden.* Underneath, the same message was written in the Tibetan and Hindu language.

We located the core group and explored the permitted area of the monastery, but we didn't take in much, lost in our own thoughts.

On the ride back, I asked Mudita, "Did you experience something in that room?"

She nodded and looked out the window. "I can't talk about it right now. I'm still blown away."

"Me too." Sometimes words are inadequate.

We never talked about it again, but now and then, when I see a Buddhist artifact or hear Tibetan monks chanting, I think about those few moments in a secret chamber of that ancient monastery...and wonder.

On the return ride to Srinagar, two Tibetan monks sat behind us. One of the monks tugged on my long braid. Whenever I turned around, he'd burst out laughing. I smiled and tried to be polite by not showing he was bothering me.

He pulled at my braids again. *That's it,* I thought.

I rotated and glared at him. He erupted into great big chuckles before he once again pulled at my hair. I whispered to Mudita, "This is getting old."

The two monks got off a few hours—and many braid yanks later—and walked into a barren countryside, no buildings or people in sight. The monk waved to me and then burst out laughing.

I never figured out what was so funny, but I have often thought about how joyful they seemed.

Early one morning, a few days afterward, the sun rose, scattering a golden light across the horizon.

Mudita boarded the train for New Delhi. She shouted, "I'll see you in New Delhi. Remember, the Thai Buddhist Guest House. Let's see the Red Fort together." She waved both arms overhead. "I'll miss you."

The outside light stretched and quilted as the train pulled away.

I picked up my bag and walked farther down the concrete platform to wait for the train to Rishikesh. I wanted to take that train to New Delhi, too, but I needed to collect the rest of my belongings and say goodbye to the swamis. The time passed slowly without my friend.

The drumbeat of the train on the tracks matched the rhythm of my own heartbeat as I watched the lush green landscape roll by. The day drifted toward evening, and I fell asleep dreaming about the summer.

When I arrived in Rishikesh, Swami-ji said, "There's been a flood."

On September 4, 1978, the worst ever recorded flood struck northern India because the monsoons had continued past their usual time. Many rivers, including the Yamuna, had risen six feet above the safe level, sweeping away buildings and roads, telephone and electricity lines, disrupting train travel and leaving millions homeless.

Swami-ji continued, "The ashram was under water, and all of your things were destroyed. I had to throw out your clothes because they were covered in mildew. All your books are gone except for this one." He handed over a slightly warped version of one of my books.

I couldn't quite grasp the reality of losing most of my things again. A year ago, someone stole my sleeping bag, western clothing, and backpacking equipment. Now, the flood ruined Vedic books and the clothing I bought or made this past year. The pungent smell of mold filled the air.

I tried to open the book, but too many pages were stuck together. I left it out in the sun and half-listened to Swami-ji talk about his flood experience. A heaviness filled my stomach.

"... We stood on our roofs. An American woman, visiting the ashram while you were gone, missed her flight because no trains were running. The railway tracks were destroyed south of here."

"What?" I asked.

"Yes, yes. No one can travel to New Delhi for at least one week. Terrible."

"Oh, no."

"What?"

"I was supposed to meet Mudita in New Delhi. I'm not going to catch her before she flies out in a few days. Oh, man, not good." The heaviness in my stomach spread to my limbs.

Telephone lines were down. The post office, exasperatingly slow even in the best of times, was not delivering mail. I didn't know how to let her know about the floods.

27 Ladakh – September 1978

I hoped we would see each other again, but I wasn't optimistic. I imagined worst-case scenarios: the water would never go down; I'd be stuck in Rishikesh forever; and decay and rot would permeate everything I owned.

After six days, the flood receded enough for the trains to begin their regular operating times, and I bought a one-way ticket to New Delhi. I decided to leave that day, but not before I said goodbye to Swami-ji.

When I got back from town, he was pulling weeds in his front garden. I sat down beside him. "Hey there."

Swami-ji lifted his face. "Did you get a ticket to New Delhi?"

"Yep." I ran my fingers through my hair. "Thank you, Swami-ji." I'd never been very good at goodbyes. "I don't know when I'll be back to Rishikesh." I didn't want to tell him maybe never. "But I'll send a postcard from Rajasthan." I didn't tell him that after the retreat, I wanted to go to Bombay and Goa, maybe Kerala. "I'll be in New Delhi for a few days to renew my passport and I will stay at the Thai Buddhist Guest House." I wrote down the address and handed it to Swami-ji.

"You must come back someday and see us. You are always welcome here." Swami-ji rose from his seated position and folded his arms across his chest. "Oh, I hear a rickshaw. Must be your ride, yes?"

All my belongings fit into one small canvas bag. The trip back to Rishikesh had been pointless, as almost everything I had left there was gone. The rickshaw driver lifted my bag and set it on the seat next to me. "Train station, Ma'am Sahib?"

"Yes, yes. Thank you."

I waved to Swami-ji. "Be well."

Swami-ji adjusted his straw hat and knelt down next to his rose bushes. The rich, loamy smells of the earth filled my nostrils, and I turned my face to the light of the new sun.

28

England – October-December 1976

My eyes sparkled like diamonds
all the way back to the hostel...

With no plan, I arrived at the Heathrow Airport in the early morning on a clear, sunny day. The clipped, quick pronunciation of England's English sounded foreign, and I had to ask the airline attendant to repeat himself several times.

"Your luggage is not here. Seems as if it was left in Montreal."

I opened my hands. "So, what do I do?"

"Where are you staying?" He peered over his glasses.

"At the Hyde Park Youth Hostel in downtown London."

"An airport worker will bring you your luggage, hmm—backpack, rather—to the hostel within twenty-four hours." He gave me a lost baggage claim ticket.

"Okay. Now, how do I get to downtown London exactly?"

"The tube."

"The tube?" I visualized a long capsule, like something out of a science fiction novel.

"Yes, the subway is over there." He pointed to a long hallway.

I zipped up my sweatshirt and tucked my passport securely inside my security pouch.

A portrait of Queen Elizabeth hung high on the wall above the lobby, a replica of the one in my K-8 grade school. Many childhood daydreams were spent gazing up at her striking profile, and I took a moment to remember that child, fantasizing about getting away.

Here I am.

The lengthy corridor was nearly empty of travelers, and I found my way to London's fast and efficient transportation system quite easily. Within minutes we were off, and before long, the shriek of brakes announced our arrival. I followed a man and woman holding hands to the front door of the centrally located youth hostel, minutes from Hyde Park and Piccadilly Circus, SoHo, and Buckingham Palace. I hadn't researched much about England; I just thought I'd learn as I went along.

The hostel attendant gave me a quick tour of the dormitory, the shower area, and the lockers. "We'll let you know when your pack arrives. The hostel is closed for the rest of the day. Do enjoy the city, and check in with us later this evening."

I bought fish and chips from a street vendor in Piccadilly Circus, a public road junction of signs, people, and shops—the equivalent to New York City's Times Square. Thick slices of deep-fried potatoes with milk-battered haddock sprinkled with salt and vinegar. *Delicious.*

Is this a special street or something?

I walked and walked and walked all day, visiting London's Big Ben and the Tower Bridge with the River Thames flowing underneath. All sorts of boats and ships dotted the brown waters, a reflection of England's extraordinary past.

When I retraced my steps back into the city, I noticed a beautifully maintained street: ceramic flowerpots filled with blooming flowers, washed brick buildings, forest green vines clinging to the fronts and sides, no litter. I strolled through the luxurious neighborhood of a seemingly long-standing quarter of central London and envisioned about who lived there—kings and princesses, dukes, and knights.

28 England – October–December 1976

On the other side of the street were parked four flawlessly polished Rolls-Royce automobiles, one behind the other; two a deep azure blue, one black, and the other a rich wine color. I noticed a man in a black suit buffing the wine Rolls-Royce with a soft cloth. I saw my reflection in the car's luster.

"Wow, that's some car," I said to the man.

He tipped his black cap in my direction and continued to rub the side of the car.

I sat down on the curb and watched. "Is this a special street or something?" I opened my arms to indicate the whole area.

"Hmm," he mumbled.

Not to be deterred, I carried on, "This is my first day in England, and I've been walking all day. Hope you don't mind if I rest a bit. I've never seen cars this beautiful before. Is this one yours?"

He stopped and straightened his back. "If you wait a moment, Prince Philip will be coming out that door." He gestured to a dark-colored entryway. "You just might have a chance to meet him." His words were short and snappy.

"Really?"

The man once again tilted his cap in my direction.

I looked up and saw a number ten above the elegant door. A few minutes later, the door opened, and two men walked out.

I stood and wondered what to do... Bow? Curtsy?

Smiling at the older man, who I recognized from newspaper and magazine photos, I made a slight genuflection as if entering a church pew, the closest I could think of as a form of obeisance.

His arctic blue eyes seemed to twinkle around the edges. "Hello," he said.

I blurted, "Hello. I am so honored to meet you."

"Where are you from?" he asked, his British English sounding so much better than my words.

"Canada. I want to spend some time in Britain, travel around, see the sights." I felt shy and unsure of what to say next.

"England is a wonderful country. I hope you see many of our famous spots. I must say it is a beautiful day for walking. Goodbye then and best of luck." He turned and walked to the polished Rolls-Royce.

The man behind him opened the door of the Rolls-Royce, and Prince Philip climbed into the car, the darkened windows obscuring any view of the inside.

The man in the black suit folded the cloth, winked, and then climbed into the car's driver seat. The four Rolls-Royces' engines started up and left at the same time.

I stood on the silent street for a moment and thought, *my first day in England and I meet Prince Philip. Wow.* In today's age, I could've asked for a selfie, but at the time, I didn't even own a camera or have anyone to share the moment with.

Still, my eyes sparkled like diamonds all the way back to the hostel.

The hostel was filled with travelers from all over the world. Some were returning from Greece, others were on their way to Africa, and a few talked about the "overland trip." Their exotic tales compelled me to ask questions: *What is the overland trip? How do you get visas? Where do you stay? Could I do that?*

Sammy, a tall blonde woman from South Africa, had toured most of the Middle East and Asia. She now planned a journey to America and enthusiastically answered all of my questions.

"The overland trip is the trek from Europe to India via the Middle East corridor, through Turkey, Iran, or Syria, Afghanistan, Pakistan, using the local transportation. You have to find your own way, and get visas as you hop from one country to

28 England – October–December 1976

another. The further east you go, the cheaper the travel. Your money can go a long way."

I listened attentively. "Is Europe as expensive as people say it is?"

She nodded. "Absolutely. If you want to see the east, skip Europe. Have you ever heard of the Magic Bus?"

"You mean, from The Who song?"

"I guess. I don't know. But it's the cheapest way to get from London to Greece. In Greece, I camped out on the island beaches before jumping over to Turkey."

I wondered what "jumping over to Turkey" meant, but didn't say anything.

That night I planned: I'd visit the English countryside, Scotland, Wales, take the Magic Bus to Greece, and then make my way to India.

An *Alice in Wonderland* adventure, falling down the rabbit hole.

29

Rajasthan – September 1978

My thoughts were not rushed.
They did not tumble into one another.
It was the closest thing to peace
I had ever felt.

"Yes, your friend gone now. She left this."

A petite Indian man, dressed in impeccable white clothing, handed me a folded piece of paper. I guessed him to be about forty years old, and I could tell he took his job as the caretaker of the Buddhist Guest House seriously—flowers in clean, clear glass vases, the floor tiles buffed to a glossy shine. The lush green inner garden was enveloped in silence behind a heavy metal door.

I nodded, clutching the paper. "Thank you."

"Your room this way." He pointed down an open hallway and gave me a key. I found number twelve at the far end. The space had been freshly washed, and a sheet and blanket lay folded on a bed frame. The metal-grated window allowed some afternoon sunshine into the room, the rays dancing on the pallid walls. Next to the bed sat a small stand, with a jar of violet flowers placed on the bare surface. I dropped my bag and sat cross-legged on the woven mat, eager to open my note.

> *Shanti,*
>
> *I waited for you and hoped you'd be able to get out, but I guess the manager was right about the trains from Rishikesh not running because of the flood. Hey, sorry we missed each other. I went ahead and toured the Red Fort; you should too. It's so old, very historical. Can't believe I'm headed back to Australia today.*
>
> *Best wishes for a wonderful retreat in Rajasthan. Write often about your adventures and I'll daydream I'm traveling with you. I think I'm going to head down to the orchards to pick grapes near Adelaide; hope I make some good money so I can return to India and see you next summer. Tell me all about the retreat and any good-looking guys you might meet there. Just kidding. I know you are not going there for that. But it might help you get over Taj. Okay, must go. Hugs. I miss you already,*   *—Mudita*

I laughed quietly and spoke to the small lizard scurrying across the ceiling.

"I'm going to have a good time here. See the Red Fort. Shop. I have to be here until my passport is renewed anyway. It'll be fun. Positive thinking, right?"

The wait to apply for a new passport at the Canadian embassy tried my patience. One day I had to sit for several hours before even seeing an agent. Another day I again sat for several hours before the same agent agreed that all my papers were in order. And finally, another day sitting for several hours before that same agent said, "Okay, Ma'am Sahib. You come back in two weeks and your passport will be ready."

"I'm going to Rajasthan in a few days. Can I pick it up on my way back through New Delhi in three weeks?"

He bobbled his head back and forth. "Oh, yes. It will be here."

I wondered how long I would have to wait the next time. "Okay, thanks very much. Namaste."

Annoyed and frustrated, I decided to visit the music industry area, a street full of sitars, harmoniums, tanpuras, and other Indian instruments. I hailed the nearest rickshaw.

The harmonium shop was located on the second floor of an old building. At the top of steep and narrow stairs, a fan circulated the stale air. On soft cotton blankets, rows and rows of harmoniums lay next to each other as if they were related somehow.

An older man approached me. "Ma'am Sahib looking for something special?"

"No. I don't have a lot of money. Do you have anything for fifty or sixty rupees?"

He let out a heavy sigh. Clearly, he had hoped I would be spending much more than that. "We have a few back there for that price." He indicated a spot at the back of the shop.

On an orange and purple cloth, two beautiful harmoniums were positioned facing one another. I hated to break them up. I could see my reflection in the wood. "Beautiful. How much?"

"Oh, that one. A hundred rupees."

> The flapping sound of my flip-flops on the creaky wood-paneled steps echoed down the narrow staircase.

I flexed my fingers and realized I would have to bargain. "Hmmm. That's a lot. I'll think about it."

"Oh. Okay. Ninety rupees."

I was going to spend sixty rupees on a new harmonium, and that was that. "Hmm. Think I'll go for chai and come back a little later."

"Okay. Okay. Eighty rupees." Red pan juice glistened between his yellowed teeth. He faked a defeated smile.

"I don't have eighty rupees to spend."

Two more rounds of bargaining, and I bought the harmonium for sixty rupees. He wrapped it in a marigold-colored chamois cloth and tied it up with thick red string. At the ends, he made a woven handle for easy transport.

I smiled. "Thank you."

He jiggled his head back and forth. "Ma'am Sahib. You good bargainer. You live here long?"

"Yes, I've been in India for eighteen months now."

"You think my India a good place, then?"

"Yes, very much. Feels like home."

"You be one of us." He pointed to my sari and the bindi on my forehead. "Come again and tell your friends where they can buy best harmoniums, yes?"

"Of course. Thanks again. Namaste, and I hope you get a lot of customers today." I peered around at the empty shop.

The flapping sound of my flip-flops on the creaky wood-paneled steps echoed down the narrow staircase. Light from the street shone into the dark entryway. I could hear the call of rickshaw drivers and the shouts of the chai *wallas*. It was indeed time for tea.

A lean man with thick, long dark hair passed in front of the shop entrance. He laughed, a great big burst of life, so infectious I wanted to catch it. It reminded me of the violet and tangerine butterfly I had seen in the Himalayas.

Could it be?

I ran out into the street and yelled, "TAJ!"

The man stopped and turned. "Shanti?"

I was stunned. How many millions of people were in New Delhi? What were the chances of running into somebody I knew outside a reclusive music shop—in a foreign country? Not only

29 Rajasthan – September 1978

that, but someone I cared deeply about. The odds seemed incredulous.

Bewildered, we said nothing for several moments.

Then Taj ran toward me and cried out, "Can't believe it! What are you doing here?" When we hugged, I felt his heart beating fast, as if he'd just finished a run.

I pointed to myself and then at him. "What am I doing here? What are you doing here?"

Taj shook his head. "It's unbelievable." He turned to face a good-looking man standing to his right. "This is Shanti. Shanti, this is Ricardo."

I shook Ricardo's hand. "Nice to meet you." *Another one of Taj's groupies, no doubt.*

A woman peeked from behind Ricardo. She was about my height, carried an extra twenty pounds, and had a lovely smile. Large gold hoop earrings fell gracefully from her ears, matching the highlights in her tawny hair. She exuded self-confidence.

She spoke in heavy, accented English. "Who this?"

"Krista, this is Shanti." Taj pulled her to his side. "Krista's my new violin player." He looked at her the way he gazed at Ricardo...friendly, brotherly.

My insides relaxed. *Okay, not a girlfriend. Good.*

He let out a breath, and his eyes brightened. "We're going for lunch. Join? Too noisy to talk here." He shuffled back and forth, rocking on his heels, and breaking into a boyish grin as he peeked at me through a strand of his ebony hair.

"Yes, love to. Oh, see what I bought. A new harmonium."

Ricardo offered to carry my purchase through the crowded street until we found a little outdoor restaurant a few blocks away.

Taj ordered food for everyone. Some things hadn't changed. "Shanti, where are you headed?"

I told him about Rajasthan, meeting Mudita, my time in Kashmir. Taj listened to every word. He nodded respectfully and appeared genuinely attentive. Ever so slightly, with a glint of admiration in his eyes, he'd look at Krista and Ricardo. They'd nod, glance at Taj, and then at me.

"So, enough about me. What about you, Taj?"

"I'm headed back to Varanasi for nine months of study. Ricardo and Krista are with me this time. I want to go...hmm, how do you say in your English—deep, yes?—into the Indian raga system and possibly invent some new sounds." His English had improved.

"What about home? What have you been doing these many months? How are Stephan and Roberto?"

"Stephan went to university and Roberto working with family in Madrid. I helped my family, too. Personal stuff." He didn't offer anything more.

Taj had always been secretive and elusive when he talked about his family. I knew not to press. Stephan had mentioned once that Taj did not want his family to suspect his feelings for me.

After another round of chai, stories continued about Ricardo and Krista. Ricardo, a talented drummer, hoped to study the Indian tablas. His girlfriend, Fatima, lived in Spain's countryside. He got misty-eyed talking about her.

Single Krista called Florence, Italy, her home and was noticeably devoted to her music as well. Her eyes lit up every time she talked about her violin, which she named *the madonna*.

I yawned. "Well, time for me to head back." I wanted to stay but wasn't sure where our relationship stood at that moment.

Taj jumped to his feet. "I'll walk you back." He pulled me up and brushed my hair off my face.

"It's too far to walk from here. Will need a rickshaw, but hey, thanks." I took a quick look at the congested street.

"Oh, I'll get a rickshaw. Ricardo, Krista, I'll see you back at the hotel." Taj offered to carry the harmonium, and we talked until the rickshaw driver announced my stop. "You had most amazing time this summer, it seems."

29 Rajasthan – September 1978

Maharaja and images of Kashmir rested in my mind like the notes of a cello. "Yes, it really was a great summer." I turned to face him, trying to ignore the way my stomach fluttered. "It's great to see you, Taj."

He slipped a piece of paper into the palm of my hand. "This is our hotel. Please, come tomorrow. We'll spend the day together before you leave."

Taj's touch lingered on my skin like a shimmer of heat on the road, my insides going soft as melted chocolate. I moved my head up and down. "Sure."

He broke out into a childish grin, helped me out of the rickshaw, and placed the harmonium on the ground. "Tomorrow," he said.

I watched the back of the rickshaw slip into the sea of New Delhi traffic. The late day sun flickered against the tall gate.

I closed the heavy door and listened to the sound of my heart, like glass smashing into glass.

The "we" was Taj, Ricardo, Krista, and two other musicians traveling with Taj—not the "we" of just the two of us I had hoped for.

We spent the day touring the Red Fort, a seventeenth-century octagonal complex built by the Rajput king in the walled city of Old Delhi. The fort, bordered by moats and walls, lay along the Yamuna River. The red sandstone walls gave the complex its name and covered an area of about two hundred and sixty acres. The height of the walls varied from sixty feet on the river side to over a hundred on the city side and the walls were topped with turrets and citadels. The artwork within the fort was a fusion of Persian, European, and Indian art—rich, expressive colors, marble with floral designs, domes, gold columns, canopied alcoves, spacious courtyards, and arches.

> **But we maintained our engineered indifference, the hesitancy thick as oil.**

Taj grabbed my arm. "Did you see this?" An emerald pool of water reflected the mosaic colors of an Indian sculpture displaying a goddess and her consort.

I focused on his warm hand on my skin for several moments before responding, "Wow. Gorgeous."

Later, we ate at shops for lunch and then dinner. Taj paid for everything. Soon after, he escorted me back to the guest house. I would be leaving in the morning.

"You must come to Varanasi after your travels." There was no doubt in the tone of his voice as he touched a strand of my hair. "Beautiful."

"Hmm. I'll think about it."

We were like fire and ice together. I wanted to touch him. I think he wanted to touch me. But we maintained our engineered indifference, the hesitancy thick as oil. Or was it my hesitancy?

"Okay, but please do come to Varanasi." A bright moon shone over his head, and a slight breeze brushed across his face.

I studied his eyes for a moment, and a dull pain spread through my chest as I watched him flag down a rickshaw as if he were hailing a taxi in New York City. We were both so good at wordlessness, waiting for the other to offer the first sound.

Polite? Afraid of getting hurt? Fearful of appearing the fool?

"Salut, Shanti. See you soon. Yes?" His question was more an affirmation. And then he was gone, lost in the pandemonium of the New Delhi night.

I stood outside the guest house gate and watched the moon rise higher and higher in the sky.

A well-used bus with glassless windows rattled and squeaked its way along a narrow dirt road, leaving plumes of dust that settled like sugar crystals on my new tie-dyed sari. There were three other white foreigners on the bus. The rest were east Indians, all riding together toward Goenka's ten-day retreat in the Thar Desert.

29 Rajasthan – September 1978

The Rajasthan state, located in northwest India, was comprised mainly of the inhospitable Thar Desert, the climate protecting the archaeological ruins of the Indus Valley civilization. A primarily Hindu population lived in Rajasthan, an ancient land full of classical music, traditional dance, colorful art, block prints, and the vibrant multi-colored Rajasthani clothing: bold blues, bright yellows, deep oranges, reds, and purples.

The day before, I had visited Jodhpur's museums and famous landmarks. There might have been a few other tourists, but I didn't see anyone as I toured rooms filled with ancient artifacts.

Jodhpur, the second-largest city in Rajasthan, was about two hundred miles west of Jaipur and had numerous forts, palaces, and temples to explore. The desert, a land of uneven sand dunes, extended west from the Sutlej River and was surrounded by the Aravalli Range to the east and a salt marsh in the south.

We arrived in the late afternoon. Several large cream-colored canvas tents stood straight and tall against an open blue sky. A few workers went from tent to tent carrying blankets, cots, and buckets. I caught a whiff of garam masala.

"Registration is at the first tent." A slim Hindu man in sparkling white directed the way.

> **I watched the trail of dirt flow out of the stall.**

The bus crowd walked in a single file to the welcome table.

"Ma'am Sahib, you are in tent five in the female section. The wash area is close by." The attendant lifted his arm and waved his hand to a sizable canvas wall. "Best find your cot and proceed to the main dining area." The clang of pots echoed in the desert silence.

At the end of a long row of green cots, I placed my two bags on top of a bed, the farthest away from the main door and facing a cloth partition. On the upper right-hand corner of the cot, a folded blanket lay underneath a pillow. The rough plank floor reminded me of my summer home in Kashmir, and I wished for

Mudita. I leisurely made the bed and took out a few toiletries, hoping for a shower before dinner.

The provisional bathhouse was divided into separate stalls. Water in a large urn warmed in the sun. Smaller metal buckets sat next to the pot, and light towels lay on a rustic table. I watched the trail of dirt flow out of the stall as I poured a third bucket of almost-hot water over my head.

I strolled quietly to the dining tent, thinking about the upcoming retreat.

The words of our welcoming host played through my head. "Enjoy your evening meal. Tonight, you will take the five precepts, which will include the vow of silence for the next ten days." My stomach rumbled, whether from hunger or anticipation, I wasn't sure, but the smell of curry made my mouth water.

Looking around for a place to sit among long picnic tables took me back to high school. I saw a vacant spot next to a lovely Indian woman. She wore an exquisite ruby sari, her hair in a fashionable updo.

I asked. "Is this spot taken?"

"No, no. Please, sit down." Her well-spoken English matched her flawless skin.

"Is this your first Goenka retreat?" I carefully put down my food tray, trying not to spill the steaming tea.

"No. I do a retreat every year for my sanity." She grinned and scooped up a mouthful of rice and lentils. "You?"

"Yes. Any words of advice?"

"You'll do fine. It's a wonderful experience. Truly." She smiled.

Her name was Kati, and she was also assigned to tent five. She lived in Jaipur and worked as a lawyer in a high-ranking position for the government. A modern Indian career woman living in her own home, she was truly ahead of her time.

We talked until the sound of a bell, a deep resonating gong, indicated that it was time for the opening discourse.

29 Rajasthan – September 1978

Blankets covered the inside floor of the huge meditation tent. I glanced around at the gathering and set my shawl down next to two American men. I had seen them on the bus and had listened in on their conversation but didn't say much except for a brief hello. I guessed our retreat group numbered around a hundred.

Everyone sat cross-legged on the floor facing a raised podium wrapped in white fabric. A large cushion, about twelve inches high, was placed in the center behind a microphone stand. Only a few whispers could be heard in the near quietude.

I closed my eyes and waited.

Maharaja had taught me well.

After about a half-hour, Goenka came in and took his position on that silky-smooth pillow. His silver hair shone in the evening light, and he wore a long-sleeved Nehru-style shirt and vest. His full face looked healthy and strong.

Goenka talked about the Dharma—the "truth," he called it— and mentioned the word *mindfulness* several times before telling a story about the Buddha. I thought about the Tibetan monk from Marpha. Then, he asked us to take the five precepts, or vows for the retreat: not to harm any living thing; not to steal or take anything that was not ours; not to use any intoxicants such as tobacco, drugs, or alcohol; to maintain celibacy, and to be honest in thought and action.

Like the rules in Kashmir, I thought.

He invited us to take the vow of silence, no talking to deepen the meditation practice, and to cultivate a sense of aloneness by suspending preconceptions about ourselves, relationships, and other people. He spoke about not looking into other people's eyes while on retreat and encouraged us to experience ourselves in a genuine way.

"There is no hurry, no place to go, nothing else to do but be here. In all your activities, be mindful. Your meditation practice will deepen through the continuity of being aware." He looked around the room, smiled, got up, and left.

Before I had a chance to process his words, a man seemingly sprinted to the microphone and talked about the logistics of the retreat—the schedule, mealtimes, washing areas, medical concerns. "Oh, and this is the Thar Desert. Scorpions, snakes, and spiders are plentiful. We will have patrols at night monitoring the area. Don't be alarmed if you are awakened by flashlights. You will notice our retreat is surrounded by red rope. Please, do not leave the secured zone. There are other dangers in the desert as well. Thank you. Have a wonderful retreat. Good night." His words seemed rushed and frantic after listening to Goenka's soothing voice.

I found the retreat schedule and the vow to maintain silence unproblematic. In fact, I relished being with more than one hundred people and not having to talk to anyone. All I had to do was meditate.

We got up early, but not nearly as early as in Kashmir. Effortless. We only meditated for an hour or less each time—painless compared to the summer. In between sitting meditations, we had walking meditations. Nice.

We had long lunch breaks. In the evenings, dharma talks or sermons on Buddhist teachings were inspirational: be kind; more alert; awake to the moment; we are all in this together; no one will be left behind; we are all connected.

I slept well in the desert peace.

One day after lunch, I decided to take a walk past the red roped area. I checked to make sure no one was watching before I ducked under the line heading west toward some low-lying trees. The boiling ball in the sky was blistering hot, and I covered my head with the end of my sari. I loved the feel of the sand beneath my feet, cushy like luxurious carpet.

The desert had a primal beauty, not a breath of wind, quiet colors everywhere. After maybe a half-mile, I came to a stream. Exotic trees stood on each side with tufts of golden grass

29 Rajasthan – September 1978

underneath. I decided to meditate in the still surroundings. Before long, I heard a loud rustle.

When I opened my eyes, a camel, less than five feet from where I sat, lowered her head and began to drink from the clear water. I remained motionless and admired her soft velvet coat and bottomless brown eyes. Then a huge frog, the biggest one I had ever seen, leaped out of the water, forming a giant arc of water droplets, creating a hundred mini-rainbows.

> **I am not in any hurry to get to Bombay.**

That moment encapsulated the retreat for me.

Another evening, I woke in the middle of the night to the sound of several guards talking outside our tent, just inches from my head. I only caught the word "scorpion."

The next morning several workers cleaned our tent area. One woman whispered, "Many scorpions tried to crawl into our tent last night. The deadly ones." She lifted her eyebrows. We all checked our sleeping area carefully before dusk.

Ten days slipped by quickly. On the last morning, after early meditation and breakfast, our logistical assistant told us we could talk. I found Kati and immediately fell into a relaxed conversation about the retreat, things we appreciated, things we didn't care for. She invited me to stay at her house.

"Do come. I have an extra bedroom, and I want to show you some beautiful places around Jaipur." She grabbed my hand and squeezed it.

"Okay. I am not in any hurry to get to Bombay (note: in 1978, Mumbai was still called Bombay)." How could I refuse her kind offer?

"Yes, and I'll have my maid do your laundry so you can be ready for your travels. Oh, how exciting! I want to introduce you to a few people." She looked so happy.

We landed in Jaipur that evening. Kati hailed a taxi, and before long, we were at her home on the outskirts of Jaipur, a two-story cement home with a sizeable courtyard. A large iron gate with hefty sharp spikes on top kept Kati safe within her private residence.

An older woman met us. She talked in rapid Hindustani. Kati's serene face began to tighten.

"I have to make some phone calls." She introduced me to her housekeeper, Amma. "Please, make yourself at home. Amma has prepared food for us, and tonight is Bollywood night." Her face softened a bit. "I just have to make one phone call and will join you soon."

Her one phone call turned into three, and I ate in silence, similar to the proceeding days in the Thar Desert. Amma placed a steaming cup of chai down next to me when Kati hurried in.

"Oh, sorry. Work stuff already." The place between her eyebrows was taut and wrinkled. "The kids will be here soon."

"Kids? I didn't know you had kids." I blew soft breaths on top of the hot liquid.

"They're not mine. Just the neighborhood kids. I'm the only one with a color television in my area, and I offer to host Bollywood night here. It's fun. Amma makes them treats." She shoveled in mouthfuls of food; the hurry already evident in her movements.

Twenty to twenty-five children arrived soon after and gathered on the floor of the courtyard. Amma set up the television and brought out little cookies in a bright yellow bowl.

As soon as the television came on, a hush fell over the kids, and not another sound was heard until the movie finished. I had tried to follow along but got lost early, most of the Hindu dialogue too difficult to follow, but I picked up something about enduring love and past lives.

When the film ended, the children cheered. They thanked Kati repeatedly and left respectfully. I admired them.

Amma showed me the guest room, a nice, quiet space at the back of the second floor. She said something in Hindustani, but I couldn't understand her, except for "Namaste."

I closed the door and fell asleep quickly.

In the middle of the night, I heard the phone ring. Kati answered and began to have a fiery conversation with the person on the other end. Later, the phone rang again. Kati's voice rose and fell, sharp notes echoing in the muted night.

Dark half-moon circles were under her eyes at breakfast. Her fingers tapped the table in rapid succession. I missed her beautiful smile.

"Listen, Shanti. I will not be able to tour with you today, but please stay and enjoy the city. Amma can help with anything you need. Get your clothes washed. Make yourself at home." She folded her arms tightly.

"Uh. Okay. Are you sure? Should I leave now? It's all right if I need to."

She shook her head. "No, no. You'll need to get your train ticket anyway." She repeated, "Stay. Enjoy Jaipur."

Jaipur, the capital and also the largest city of Rajasthan, had several historical forts, monuments, and temples to visit: Jantar Mantar—an astronomical observation site built in the eighteenth century; Jal Mahal—a palace in the middle of the Man Sagar Lake; and Albert Hall Museum—a government-run museum with a complete collection of paintings, ivory, stone, metal sculptures, crystals, carved objects, and pottery. The City Palace, in the heart of the city, featured a vast array of courtyards, gardens, and buildings, to name a few.

The afterglow of ten days in silence, having the opportunity to look within in such a quiet and secluded environment, evaporated quickly for Kati but not for me.

A warm feeling spread through my chest as I spent the day sightseeing Jaipur. I felt connected to the world around me. My thoughts were not rushed. They did not tumble into one another. It was the closest thing to peace I had ever felt.

I cherished the continuity of awareness, the value of slowing down. Colors appeared more vibrant, smells rich and full. Sounds seemed to pulsate in ways I had not noticed before. In the market, I bought a bright cotton shawl and laughed with the vendor. I naïvely thought the feeling would last forever.

After lunch, I purchased a train ticket for Bombay via New Delhi to pick up my passport.

I returned to Kati's home just before the sun sunk low, stretching my shadow in front of me. When I rang the gate, Kati was on the phone and she did not come to dinner. Things felt tense and I was glad to be leaving in the morning.

When I went to say goodnight and thank her for her kindness, she was sitting at the kitchen table, papers spread everywhere, her face stretched with concern.

I tried to cheer her up. "Thank you for your kindness, Kati. I think Jaipur is a wonderful city." I wasn't sure if I was helping. "I hope you'll get to go back to the desert again soon."

"We'll see. I have a great deal of work ahead. Sometimes I wonder if it is worth it. Being gone for ten days seems such a bad idea right now. Sorry I could not spend time with you today. Best of luck." She smiled quickly and gazed back down to the pile in front of her. An awkward silence followed.

I never want to be like that, I thought.

Once again, the train was late by several hours.

I sat on top of my luggage and pulled out a book. Next to me, two elementary-school-aged children with their parents and an elderly gray-haired woman sat huddled around a pile

29 Rajasthan – September 1978

of belongings. The older woman lay on the concrete platform in a fetal position, her grandson waving a flat woven fan to keep her cool. Her eyes were closed, and she seemed to be muttering something.

> Whenever I imagine things are difficult, I remember her.

The sounds of an approaching chai *walla* filled the air. My stomach rumbled, and I waved the man over. "How much?"

I paid his price, not bothering to haggle. The tea tasted extra sweet, and the samosas were so greasy, the oil dribbled down my chin. The two kids watched me eat every bite. I felt a little self-conscious under their scrutiny, so I ate fast.

The frail, tiny grandmother began to whimper and pulled her legs up to her chest. She looked incredibly thin and frail. I watched for a moment. She stretched out, and her dirty white sari opened to reveal a gaping hole, the size of a large softball, in the middle of where her stomach should be, revealing her insides.

I swallowed the acid taste of my stomach contents that crept back up my throat and looked away, forgetting everything for a moment.

Over the course of my lifetime, I've often thought about that woman on the bare concrete floor writhing in pain—and whenever I imagine things are difficult, I remember her.

Europe 1976 -1977

30

Greece – January 1977

Goats and sheep munched on the wild grasses, and a three-hundred-and-sixty-degree view of the magnificent Mediterranean Sea stretched out in front of us, our home for a few days.

"WAIT!" I yelled, running as fast as I could down the street toward a timeworn-looking tour bus. I was thankful it was a Sunday morning and not Monday rush hour in downtown London.

"Hurry, hurry, hurry. Run! We are just about to leave. We've been waiting for over an hour for you!" the bus driver shouted.

I was too out of breath to answer and simply gave the driver my ticket. Thirsty and hungry, I got on the full bus. Hippies, gypsies, drifters, wanderers, an old woman, and a middle-aged couple glared at me. I humbly apologized, found the one remaining seat, and closed my eyes.

I couldn't believe I had made it.

Earlier that morning, I had walked down to the train platform from Allison's apartment.

Allison, a friend I made on my two-month tour of the British Isles, lived in the north London suburbs, a sixty-minute train ride from downtown London. I had looked at the train schedule posted on the fridge in her apartment. The first train left at six in the morning. Plenty of time to get downtown, find some food, and catch the eight-o'clock infamous Magic Bus.

I failed to notice the asterisk and the tiny print at the bottom of the schedule indicating that the first train on Sundays left at seven-thirty, not six.

When I got off the later train, I sprinted to the bus stop. Minutes seemed like hours. Sweat dripped down my armpits as I raced to catch my ride that was supposed to leave at eight.

My heart still slammed against my chest when I opened my eyes to peek at my surroundings. The Magic Bus seats were torn and stained, and the springs were shot. Some of the windows were cracked and several side panels hung by flimsy bolts. It was a no-frills, cheap way to get through Europe all right—a hippie version of casual.

> You definitely win the prize for tardiness.

A guy in a leather-fringed vest rolled tobacco in thin paper, pinching the ends like a joint. An older man with hair to his waist sat cross-legged with his eyes closed. A couple kissed. A woman in a beaded skirt munched on cut-up melon.

We passed the White Cliffs of Dover and sped through the underground tunnel. The driver was trying to make up lost time. I struck up a conversation with the man sitting next to me.

"Sorry about holding up the bus. It's a long story, but I'm glad the bus driver decided to wait."

The long-limbed man with light brown hair said, "Ah. No problem. There were a few other late ones, too. But you definitely win the prize for tardiness." He unfolded his legs.

I guessed him to be in his late twenties. His white T-shirt showed beneath a plaid, long-sleeved button-down shirt, worn loose over flared denim jeans. His English had a hint of an accent. "Where are you from?" I asked.

"Holland. You?"

"Canada."

He nodded. "Nice to meet you. Haven't met many Canadians before. Name's Johan, by the way."

Before we could finish our conversation, the bus driver alerted us to the approaching Belgium customs. "Passports out. We'll quickly go through and stop for lunch. I know a great place."

The bus paused at a quaint village for an hour or more, enough time to buy food and stretch our legs. I purchased fresh bread and cheese. Johan took out a bag of dried fruit and sunflower seeds.

We talked after we got our food. Johan was traveling to Greece on an art scholarship. He planned on living there for three months, painting several watercolor portraits.

"Hey, mind if I join you two?" asked a fellow bus rider who was wearing a tie over his multi-colored T-shirt.

"Sure." I cleared a space for him to sit at our small table.

He extended his arm and offered a handshake. "I'm Mike from California."

That afternoon it rained, and we did not see much of the passing countryside, but Mike, Johan, and I formed an alliance of sorts and conversed well past dinner. I learned Mike had lived in Greece for the past few years teaching English, recently returning from a two-week vacation in Scotland. He laughed easily, and his azure blue eyes sparkled when he talked. He appeared to enjoy watching the other travelers.

"You see those two over there?" He pointed to a man and a woman who wore matching coats that fell to their ankles. The man looked as if he had not had a shower in a while, and he wore sunglasses, even though it was dark now. "They're junkies."

I pretended to understand and nodded.

At our first stopover, we stayed at a small bed and breakfast place in south Germany. I shared a room with two other women, one being the "junkie." The next morning, she was first to use the shower and all the hot water.

After a hearty breakfast of muesli and yoghurt, we headed south through the Alps. The sun grew increasingly bright, highlighting the spectacular views. I watched and daydreamed.

Yugoslavia rolled by the bus windows, a lush green landscape. The sun streamed through the windows. Dust mites boogied in the air. After three days, we passed the border into Greece.

One of the two drivers started to sing. A few passengers joined in while a man jumped out of his seat and began to dance. He passed around a bottle of ouzo, a Greek liquor made from grapes and herbs such as aniseed, licorice, and mint.

Mike and Johan took big gulps. I took a sip. It tasted bitter and burned the inside of my mouth and throat. When the bottle came around again, I declined.

Mike quickly glanced my way and then focused his attention on the roof of the bus. "Where are you staying in Athens?"

"Don't know yet. Do you have any suggestions?"

"Matter of fact, I do. There are a few hostels, but by far the nicest is in the historical part of Athens. I can take you there." He made soft drumming noises with his fingers.

I assumed his offer was for both Johan and me and turned to face Johan. "What do you think? Sound good?"

Johan nodded. "Yah," he said with a slight Scandinavian inflection. "Thank you."

True to his word, Mike navigated the streets of Athens with complete ease and found the hostel, even with no sign out front. We would've never have found it on our own. He spoke to the attendant and even escorted us to our assigned dorms, segregated by gender.

"I'm headed home for a shower and will swing by here in about two hours. There's this local place I go for dinner. Great authentic Greek food and cheap as hell."

I marveled at his goodwill. "Gee, thanks, Mike. That's nice of you. See you soon."

The restaurant was in the basement of an old building. Large barrels of wine stood like soldiers against the bare whitewashed walls. Eight round tables covered with red-checkered tablecloths were sporadically placed around the barrels.

When we walked in, Mike waved to a gray-haired man talking to a lively bunch of guests. He spoke to Mike in Greek and sat us at one of the tables.

"They are serving only one dish, so I went ahead and ordered. Wine, yes?"

We nodded. The man brought three full glasses of red wine and placed them on the table without spilling a drop, along with steaming fresh bread and olive oil.

Our meal took a long time to arrive. So began my introduction to the art of eating in the Mediterranean, and later, the Middle East and Asia—the unhurried luxury of savoring every bite. I had never tasted tomatoes so fresh, oranges so sweet, or puff pastry full of such rich, tangy flavor.

"I think I'll gain weight here." I glanced quickly in Mike's direction. "This is delicious. Thanks for taking us here."

Mike smiled. "Hey, no problem. Look, I have a few days before I head back to work and wouldn't mind spending the time showing you some of Athens' finest."

Johan and I responded together, "Yes, yes," and then laughed. "That'd be great."

We toured the city with Mike as our teacher and guide: the Parthenon on the Acropolis; the National Museum of Athens, which houses the world's greatest collection of Greek art; the Byzantine Museum with its assembly of metamodern figures dating back some three thousand years; Roman monuments; sampled street vendor food; and browsed bazaars and flea markets.

I bought a stainless-steel bowl and a purple silk scarf in a quaint shop near the sea. "This should help keep my hair out of my face. And this bowl should come in handy on the islands."

We stopped at a small park and ate our lunch. "I plan on visiting those two islands you suggested, Mike—Paros and Rhodos. You sure I can camp for free?"

> The rest of me wanted to be all by myself.

Mike grinned. "You bet. I've done it, as well as many others. I'll write down directions and don't forget to buy food in the local market. You can live like a king for just a few dollars a day."

Johan sat in the shade of a nearby tree, sketching in his journal. "Mind if I join you? I'm thinking of traveling the islands, too, and we can keep each other company. Don't know if it's such a good idea for you to camp alone."

"Okay. But only if you want to. Really, I'll be okay." A tiny part of me wanted Johan to come. A larger fraction wanted Mike to come. And the rest of me wanted to be all by myself.

On our final day, the three of us walked to the harbor. Mike showed us where to buy tickets for the Paros ferry.

"It's been great hanging out with you guys. If you decide to stay in Greece, do look me up. Here's my address." He placed a small piece of yellow paper, folded in half, in the palm of my hand. He reminded me of Justin.

"Thanks again, Mike, for everything." I meant it. "I wish you were going with us." I meant that, too.

"Yep. It'd be nice. But I gotta teach tomorrow. Have to pay the bills, you know." He pushed back his long hair over his ears. "Take care." He opened his arms and gripped our shoulders. "It's been fun."

We watched him climb the stairs. At the top, he waved.

Johan tucked his satchel underneath his arm. "Nice guy."

I sighed. "Yeah."

30 Greece – January 1977

Expensive yachts lined the wharf of Paros, a ten-mile-long, pear-shaped island with a single mountain in the center. Following Mike's directions, we hiked through a quaint village, bought fresh food, admired the views, and climbed a goat trail to the top of Mount Marpissa.

When we reached the crest, the path leveled, and we walked toward a flat meadow with a few interspersed trees. Goats and sheep munched on the wild grasses, and a three-hundred-and-sixty-degree view of the magnificent Mediterranean Sea stretched out in front of us, our home for a few days.

For shelter, we used my blue plastic tarp and a thin piece of climbing rope to make a lean-to. Lucky for us, it did not rain.

Numerous beaches surrounded the lovely island. Traditional Cycladic-style houses with flat roofs, whitewashed walls, blue windows and doors were enveloped by orange and pomegranate orchards. The first night, Johan and I watched the light drain from the sky, eating juicy oranges and fresh bread, mesmerized by the aquamarine blue of the sea.

For the next two days, Johan stayed at camp and sketched while I walked down the mountain to tour the town, bringing back food and stories. "I saw the most amazing boat. I'm sure they were movie stars. They drank champagne out of tall skinny glasses on the deck. At one shop, I saw a beautiful green dress."

Johan chuckled. He cut up bread and made a Greek salad, pouring fresh olive oil over everything.

I continued, "I got the ferry schedule. The ferry for Rhodos leaves tomorrow."

Johan finished what was in his mouth and nodded. "Mike suggested we camp on the beach south of the main town."

I fell in love with Rhodos, a quaint island with rural towns and beautiful cream-colored beaches, the tranquil waves softly bumping into each other. Johan and I camped outside the port city on a southern beach and bought fresh food each day in the market.

I talked about Turkey. "I heard that for a price, you can hitch a ride to the tip of Turkey on one of the sailboats that come to town."

Johan set down his flute. "Yes, I heard that, too. What? You're thinking of doing that?"

"Well, actually, I thought about traveling along the southern Turkish coast and into Syria. Seems as if it might be an awful lot of extra travel to go back to Athens, take a bus up north to Istanbul, and then start the journey through Turkey."

Johan set down his bowl and shook his head. "I've been thinking."

"What?"

"My art scholarship is about painting landscapes. I can do that here on these exquisite islands, or I can travel anywhere I please, really. Why not India?"

I paused a moment to let the news sink in. I liked Johan as a brother and didn't want him to get too attached, but camaraderie through the Middle East might be a good idea. "It'd be great if you wanted to come with me, but where will you go when you get there? I'm planning on heading straight to Nepal for the trekking season." I wanted it clear that I had no intention of Johan joining me in Nepal.

Johan picked up his flute and played until the first stars came out; the sound soft and tender.

The white sails caught the wind, and we skipped over the turquoise blue waves of the sea. I tied my scarf tightly around my head and looked up at the steroid-big sky. A few white puffy clouds skimmed overhead.

A Greek couple, and Johan and I were the only passengers the captain and deckhand had that day. The sailboat's polished wood interior glistened in the afternoon light. I smiled brightly at our good fortune at securing a ride to Turkey on such a fine-looking vessel. The day was picture-perfect—one of my memories which has stayed fresh and vivid, unwilling to fade.

We landed at the Marmaris marina as the sun turned burnt orange, perched on the horizon and ready to fall into the indigo sea. The port of entry was nothing more than a small shed. A gruff-looking man stamped our passports. The Greek couple left quickly, leaving Johan and me alone on the wharf.

I looked around and noticed no other women.

With each step on Turkish soil, with each question—"Where should we stay? Where do we get food?"—I began to realize I had crossed a threshold.

This was Muslim country.

31

Goa – October 1978

In all my years since that day,
whenever I've had to visualize a "safe place"
or even recall the most beautiful place I've
ever been, I always envision that beach.

The cities, roads, people, and muted hues of the countryside blurred together in a peaceful collage. Lulled by the drumbeat of the train on the metal tracks, I found myself daydreaming about Taj, wondering if he'd rent the same place or if he was with anyone. Our last moment together in New Delhi played like a broken record, boring a vinyl groove in my mind.

On the way, I stopped for an overnight at the Gandhi Ashram in Ahmedabad on the banks of the River Sabarmati and toured the museum before leaving on the next southbound train to Bombay.

Inspired by Mahatma Gandhi's dedication to simplicity, spinning cotton for his clothes and fasting one day a week to never forget the hunger of his countrymen, I bought two things: his autobiography and a blanket made of organic cotton.

I still have that dusty rose coverlet in the trunk of my car, now tattered and stained, but I can't seem to throw it away. I fold it carefully each summer. And, when I first returned from

India, I tried fasting one day a week, but that faded, too, just like my once-bright plum scarf left to dry too many times in the hot sun.

The hot, sticky air and the human density of Bombay made it hard for me even to breathe. Moisture puddles formed in the creases of my arms, legs, and back. I had never seen so many people in one place, moving in a mass as if individuality did not exist.

Crammed into a commuter railway car with people on top, on the sides, in the aisles, with children on parents' shoulders and heads, a slow tingle of panic worked its way up my spine, and I closed my eyes, willing myself to stay calm. Images of rolling sand dunes, miles of open space, a thousand twinkling stars, and Goenka's melodic voice played in my head.

Nestled next to the Arabian Sea on the central western coast of India, Bombay (renamed Mumbai in 1996) was one of the most populous cities in the world—the commercial and entertainment center of India (Bollywood). Migrants from all over India hoping for a better life flocked to Bombay, which created a diverse culture. Many of them formed makeshift communities—or slums—in and around the city.

The train stopped in downtown Bombay, and I got off and walked to the YWCA, a place for young women to find moderately priced safe lodging. I booked a room for three nights, giving me a little time to tour Bombay and learn how to get to Goa.

The dormitory room proved to be nice: clean, whitewashed walls; four beds, each with crisp sheets on top; a large ceiling fan circulating the stale air. A modern Indian woman sat at a tiny desk, brushing her thick short hair into a flip. She then applied a heavy layer of ruby lipstick.

"Hello. Welcome." She motioned to the two least attractive bed spaces, one by the door and the other shoved against a wall. "You can take either of those two beds." Her bed sat under a big window.

"My name is Maela, and the other roommate is Janet from America." Janet's bed faced the southern wall with a large pile of books stacked on the floor next to it. "She's studying yoga near Poona." She smiled. Two dimples appeared.

"Thanks. Whew, I'm beat. Long trip from Rajasthan." I placed my bags on the bed against the wall. "I plan on touring Bombay for a bit before heading to Goa."

Maela replied, "Nice." She set her lipstick down. "Dinner will be served shortly. Just the typical Indian fare—rice, dhal, *chapattis* —but it's included with the room." She turned. "Well, nice meeting you." Her sari swished as she walked out the door.

At dinner, I sat with Maela and listened to her chat. I guessed her to be about mid-twenties. She was studying at the university. I never did meet Janet.

The next day, I took a ferry over to Elephanta Island to see the historic Hindu and Buddhist rock sculptures. The vessel, crowded with tourists, had little sitting space. What was available went to the elderly or mothers with young children. I stood and looked out at the harbor. A gust of wind whipped around my ears.

Seven islands constituted Bombay, or as it is now known, Mumbai. The islands were once fishing communities but have been since transformed into a major seaport and a giant economic-financial hub. Some of the islands are home to ancient Buddhist and Hindu artifacts, such as the Kanheri and Elephanta Caves.

The Elephanta Caves are made up of two groups of caverns with sixteen-foot-high engravings on the walls of the larger caves. In the 1970s, Elephanta Island had just begun a restoration project for the extensive artwork there; mythological sculptures, statues, bas-reliefs on the walls, and figurines. The seven caves and adjoining areas are now protected and designated as a UNESCO World Heritage Site. Touring these magnificent caves often gave me goose bumps.

After a few hours, I sat on a grassy ledge and ate a sandwich I had packed from the YWCA cafeteria, the wide-open sky such a contrast to the heavily populated panorama. I lifted my face to the warm sun, feeling sleepy, and closed my eyes for a short siesta before exploring a smaller group of Buddhist caverns. On the return late afternoon ferry, several children cried in unison, their tired shrieks annoying. Even worse were the mothers trying to shush them.

> I felt claustrophobic and longed for clean, open spaces.

The next morning, I woke covered in a rash, my face swollen with hives. I felt and looked terrible. I fretted, wondering if I'd touched something nasty in the caves or if I had somehow come in contact with a poisonous plant on the island.

One of the women running the YWCA wrote down the address of a nearby health clinic. She looked at me, her hands moving up and down. "You should go now before that gets serious."

"Can I walk there? Do I need a rickshaw?"

"Yes, yes. Easy walk from here."

Haggler calls echoed in the crowded streets, and the stench of congestion stuck to the insides of my nose. I felt claustrophobic and longed for clean, open spaces.

Suddenly, three days in Bombay felt too long.

At the clinic, a young Indian doctor said, "You've had a severe allergic reaction. I am giving you a shot." He rolled up my sleeve, injected something, and left. The visit took all of five minutes.

I didn't even ask what he had given me, but the hives and swelling reduced quickly. Feeling much better, I took a leisurely stroll back to the Y.

The smoky light spilled into the streets as I took in the pandemonium. Women carried baskets of raw dung. Music blared from some open-fronted stall. Hundreds of people walked or stood in groups. Side-by-side shops filled the streets. Language, music, and smiles changed with every step.

31 Goa – October 1978

The boiling air affixed to my skin. Men with wagons and handcarts wiggled their way through the heavy traffic like ants rushing to their colonies. Garbage was heaped in piles on the roadways. Diseased beggars pleaded for something—anything, probably.

The retreat calm suddenly evaporated, and I longed for two things: a quiet beach and Taj.

Goa resided three hundred and sixty miles south of Bombay on the western coast. A Portuguese territory for four hundred and fifty years, until India took back possession in 1961, Goa was India's smallest state. The Portuguese influence abounded, everywhere from architecture and Christian churches to women in western clothing.

Several foreign tourists got off the bus in the historical town of Vasco de Gama, looking for a piece of paradise on the world-renowned beaches of Goa. Several local children circled us like Australian sheepdogs rounding up the cattle.

"Ma'am Sahib, come. We have best place." A small boy showed off his white teeth. He wore frayed denim shorts and a dirty T-shirt.

I laughed. "I'm looking for a quiet home away from these tourists." My hands formed a wide circle to indicate all the people on the bus.

Another youngster barged in front of the small boy. "Oh, Ma'am Sahib. We have best place for you. Far away from town. Very quiet. Very special." He bowed.

I laughed at his attempt to win me over. "All right. How do I get there?"

"Oh, oh. I take you with this rickshaw driver. You pay?" He tilted his head to the side, and the sun lit up his dark brown hair.

"Yes, I'll pay. Is it far away?"

He grinned. "Not far."

The rickshaw drive took a long time. At some point, I began to question where we were headed and if I had been shanghaied.

The boy's smile broadened after each question, "Where are you from? What are you doing here? How long are you here for?"

The rickshaw veered off on several smaller roads until we came to a dirt path with barely enough room for the cycle. I squirmed in my seat. "How much further? How much will this cost, again?"

The boy looked up. "Oh, oh. Not much. Only fifteen rupees. Maybe twenty. My name is Prabu."

Twenty rupees! "Prabu, that's a lot of money."

"You must leave tip, Ma'am Sahib. Such good driver for such long way." He gave me a toothy grin to show his sincerity.

I sighed. "All right. Now, tell me once more who I will be staying with?"

Prabu inflated his chest. "My auntie. She lives in such nice house with two daughters, Maria and Karla."

Interesting... Christian names. "Well, thank you for all your help, Prabu."

He bobbed his head from side to side. "Welcome. Ma'am Sahib." He shouted something to the rickshaw driver, who speedily swerved off onto a narrow passageway, the wheels brushing up against thick foliage.

We jostled along for several hundred feet until a corridor of foliage opened onto a brick patio with cashew and banana trees lined like soldiers alongside the courtyard. Behind the terrace, a small two-story home with a screened-in porch stood quiet and humble.

To the left of the house, a cute thatched roofed cottage looked more than inviting. A middle-aged woman, in a dress falling just below her knees, rose from a wicker chair. The screen door slammed, and two girls followed her down the stairs. One of the

31 Goa – October 1978

girls I guessed to be a young teenager, the other maybe eight or nine. The woman hugged Prabu and looked up at me.

"Welcome, Ma'am Sahib. My name Basanti." She couldn't have been taller than five feet, had rich dark skin, a little belly, and gray-streaked hair tied in a tight bun near the base of her skull. She grabbed my hand. "Where from?"

"Canada originally, but I've been living in North India for a year and a half."

"Oh, so you know about our India now, yes?" Basanti nodded from side to side in the typical Indian way. She might be of Portuguese decent, but she was Indian in every other way.

The rickshaw driver unloaded my bags, and I paid him well. I gave a few rupees to Prabu, who never stopped smiling. Prabu had to return to town with the rickshaw driver, no doubt ready to wrangle in the next tourist. I waved to them as they left. The bicycle whistle tinkled as they turned the corner into the profuse underbrush.

"This be where you stay." Basanti pointed to the cottage, then took my arm. "Come."

> I took in the views of the most beautiful beach I had ever seen.

As her full lips curled into a soft smile, I let my shoulders drop as if relaxing into a bubble bath. The place was absolutely what I had been seeking.

She spoke to her elder daughter. "Maria, take her bag."

Maria's cinnamon eyes held mine for a moment.

I woke the next morning to a gentle knock on my door. "Ma'am Sahib, breakfast?"

"Yes, yes, please come in," I answered.

Maria opened the door slowly and poked her head in. "Morning. My mother has made chai and *chapattis* with fruit. Please join us. I'll show you where the bathhouse is, our well for your water and, of course, the latrine." She giggled.

The bathhouse was situated at the back of the house. The well resembled old-fashioned American farm wells with a crank to lower the bucket down several feet to a cold spring. Down a short path toward the beach, the latrine was positioned among several tall trees, an outhouse with a cracked toilet seat over an open cement area. A water spigot and bucket were placed out front. I happily noted the cleanliness of the cement—no feces, urine, or odor.

Back at the house, I ate a leisurely breakfast and talked with the family. Maria offered to show me the path to the beach after I settled my account with Basanti. I did not quibble over her price. It seemed fair, and I felt thankful for the luck of running into Prabu.

Maria walked ahead on her bare feet. "My dad died in a fishing boat accident several years ago. He left us this house and farm. We're lucky, but we need to board tourists to survive. My mom also sews dresses and scarves that she sells in town." Her English held only a slight Indian accent. She looked back, and her kind eyes held mine once again.

A breeze lifted the hair off my back, and I tasted salt in the air. The trail led to a small open space surrounded by a thick hedge. Once through the gap, I took in the views of the most beautiful beach I had ever seen. Cream-colored sand oozed over my flip-flops. The ocean tide softly caressed the shoreline. A bird hovered over the blue-green water.

I felt a warmth radiate across my chest. "Oh, my gosh, Maria. This is incredible. Holy cow."

"Yes, it is special, isn't it?" Maria put her hand over her eyes to shield the intense sun.

I looked up and down the beach and saw only a few people walking along the seashore. "Maria, this truly is spectacular. Can we sit for a while?"

"I have to get back. But you enjoy." Her long hair fell over one eye. "When you are done, just walk back the same way."

I watched Maria disappear through the hidden thicket before I sat on the hot sand and watched the water's edge: wide-open sky; slight breeze; warm sand on my back; the gentle waters licking the shore; the coo of a pigeon; sunlight dancing on my face; the sweet scent of roses; and everything feeling as natural as it should be.

> Taj crept into my thoughts like a burglar, invading my peace.

Lulled by the ocean waves, I closed my eyes and dozed off...dreaming of Taj.

In all my years since that day, whenever I've had to visualize a "safe place" or even recall the most beautiful place I've ever been, I always envision that beach.

Basanti cooked using many things from her little farm and a nearby market: fresh fish, coconut, mango, cashews, rice, flour, raisins, eggplant. I ate two magnificent meals each day.

A routine developed: early morning meditation, chai, and breakfast, a walk to the beach, hours spent writing, reading, yoga, siesta, dinner, and visits with the family, playing bhajans on the harmonium, meditation, sleep.

The days flowed into one another, one quiet heartbeat at a time. Three weeks went by.

You'd think it'd be bliss, but it wasn't. Taj crept into my thoughts like a burglar, invading my peace. My meditations turned into fantasy: Taj and me together on the beach, Taj and me together in Bombay, Taj and me together, forever.

I tried to expunge these thoughts like erasing words on a chalkboard, but the censoring only seemed to foster my longing. Desire grew feral and rampant.

That, and the latrine, nullified any attempt at spiritual illumination.

The second time I went to use the latrine, a large hog trotted behind me. I placed my hands on my hips and mustered a stern voice. "Shoo. Shoo. Get out of here."

The hog stopped and grunted a few times, clearly not impressed with my effort to deter him. Next, I waved my arms over my head and kicked the earth. The hog grumbled a few sounds and stood his ground. I decided to return to the cottage, wait a few minutes, and try again.

No hog followed me. *Good work*, I thought.

I sat down on the toilet seat and began my business. No sooner had I finished when the hog came running up the cement trough, squealing at the top of his lungs. *What?* Yep, he ate everything I had dropped and licked the cement clean. Horrified, I gagged. *How gross!*

When I got back to the house, I asked about this practice.

"Oh, yes. The pigs eat all our refuse. Keeps everything clean," Basanti replied.

I never got used to it and no matter how hard I tried to break from any schedule, the hog outsmarted me every time. Once, I even tiptoed out there and took great effort to not make a sound. Sure enough, that hog came wailing up the trench as if to say, "Found you, hurry up, I'm hungry."

I choked back the need to vomit every time. It still makes me shudder a little now.

It was no use.

In the fourth week, I decided to travel back to Varanasi and see Taj.

"I'll be leaving in about five days," I told Maria. "I'll need to go into town and buy a bus pass back to the city and then a train ticket for Varanasi. Do you think your mom would let you come with me; into town, I mean? We could shop and have lunch?"

I wanted to thank her for all the special things she did for me each day. Once she found a black scorpion in my room and quickly crushed it with a stone. From that time on, she took extra care cleaning and bringing me chai in the mornings.

"Oh ... yes, yes. I'll ask." She reminded me of my sister.

On the day I left, Maria gave me a picture card of the Virgin Mary with an inscription on the back: *In loving memory of Raffaele* (her father).

Her eyes were moist with emotion. "Please, I want you to have this. Remember me. I hope I can travel someday, too."

I looked at the ground. A daisy swayed gently in the morning breeze. "Maria, I can't take this. It's too much, really."

"I want you to have it. Please." She closed her hand around mine.

I still have that card, nestled in the pages of a book somewhere, frayed around the edges, creased with a tear on the right corner.

The Middle East and Asia 1977

32

Turkey – January 1977

*My heart raced like a hundred wild horses
across the American western plains.
Where am I?*

An ant scurried across the hot pavement. I looked up. Not a cloud in the sky.

I moistened my parched lips and looked around for shade. Nothing. Only lines of men waiting for the bus. Sweat slid down my forehead and caught on my eyelashes. Moisture pooled in the middle of my back and underarms.

I let out a long sigh. "Not easy to find water around here, is it?"

Johan glanced up from reading the bus passes. "Sure is a different world. Seems the bus will leave in about an hour. I'll see if anyone speaks Dutch or French." He went in search of cold water and food for the journey from Marmaris to Antalya. There, we would ask for visas to enter Syria.

I put a scarf around my head and shoulders in a feeble attempt to fit in and reduce the stares of the men, but my jeans and checkered shirt did little to help. My knowledge of the Islamic faith, culture, and tradition was extremely limited. I did not know women were discouraged or even forbidden from being in public places without proper attire and company. I should have sought shelter indoors.

Later, I would learn women who openly shared the public domain were considered freely available—in other words, prostitutes.

"Here, found these." Johan held two cold bottles of soda. "They cost a dollar each. We'll have to find good drinking water soon."

On the bus, I sat next to the window and watched the scenery float by. The southern coastline of Turkey was often called the Turkish Riviera due to its favorable climate, warm sea, and hundreds of miles of exquisite shoreline.

On that day, the intense heat made me feel a bit as if I was inside the sun. The bottle of soda did little to quench my thirst, and within an hour into our journey, my head began to throb. We arrived in Antalya just after sunset, and the pounding in my head felt like a jackhammer.

"Johan, I can't seem to lift my head."

Johan looked at me. "What's wrong?"

"I don't know, but I think I need to throw up. Is there a bathroom anywhere?"

Johan asked for help, but no one seemed to speak English. Unable to stand, I sat on the road curb and waited for the nausea to pass. I put my head between my knees and tried to breathe, in and out, in and out.

A young man about our age tapped Johan on the shoulder. "Is she okay?"

Johan talked fast, "Oh, good, good. You speak English. Listen, my friend here has a terrible headache. She's also dehydrated. Could you help us find a hotel for the night?"

"Sure, sure. I am from Ankara, studying at the university. I'd be glad to help. My name is Davud." Davud took care to pronounce each word slowly and carefully, his heavy accent thick as molasses.

Johan shook Davud's hand. "Nice to meet you. Thanks for your help. Man, I wouldn't know what to do next."

Davud and Johan helped me to my feet, and I leaned on them as we made our way to a small hotel Davud had suggested. The men on the street observed us with watchful eyes. Some laughed, others scoffed. Both felt malicious.

I asked Davud, "Why are they doing that?"

Davud shook his head. "Never mind. Let's get you indoors."

I have little memory of how we got to the hotel that night or how Johan arranged for a room. The next morning, I could not open my eyes. Davud and Johan were both concerned. They left me at the hotel, and when they returned, hours later, I had not moved.

> I just wanted the agonizing throbbing and painful pulsations in my head to stop.

Johan shook my shoulder and explained that Davud found the visa offices but that the nearest Syrian border was closed. He suggested traveling to Ankara and going through Iran instead. "Davud has opened up his home for us to stay until you get well. I think we should go. Generous, huh?"

My "Okay," came out more a whimper than a consent. I just wanted the agonizing throbbing and painful pulsations in my head to stop.

The bus to Ankara went through Konya, and the only recollection I have of that trip was Davud waking me up. "Look, look. There, over there." He pointed to large cone-shaped peaks clustered snugly together like squished marshmallows. "Those are sacred Sufi caves. Have you heard of the whirling dervishes?"

I squinted, with my hand over my eyes, the light bright and sharp. "Hmmm. Very nice." I tried to find something more intelligent to say, but the pain in my neck crushed any attempt to speak. The mountain funnels were indeed spectacular, and I stayed awake long enough to view a few caves when we got closer.

Once in Ankara, Davud took over. We took a taxi to his home and waited outside while he informed his parents of their new, maybe not-so-welcome guests. I briefly wondered if we should find a hotel, but my vision blurred, and I fainted.

Of the next few days, this is what I have not forgotten: a small room at the back of the house; an overhead fan that purred and buzzed; and cold, wet towels left on my head, neck, and arms. Mostly, I slept, and when I woke in the middle of the night, I was confused. My heart raced like a hundred wild horses across the American western plains.

Where am I?

Finally, one morning, I stole a glimpse out of my bedroom door and feeling brave, ventured farther. The house had stone floors with intricately embroidered carpets. Big comfy couches, ready to be pounced on, were in the main living area. A coffee table featuring a mosque in the center dominated the center space, and a large picture of the Turkish countryside hung on the opposite wall.

I heard the clang of a pot coming from what I assumed to be the kitchen.

A small woman, her hair tied in a tight bun at the nape of her neck, filled a kettle with water from the kitchen faucet.

"Good morning," I tried to sound cheerful.

The woman jumped and said something in a language I did not understand. She reached for her scarf and put it around her head. I instantly felt sorry I had startled her.

> **I had a hard time believing I'd slept for three days.**

She patted a kitchen chair and motioned for me to sit. She left for a moment and came back with two towels and a bar of white soap. She talked and moved her hands in circular motions. As I tried to figure out what she might be trying to tell me, Davud came in.

32 Turkey – January 1977

"Ah, you're up. Nice. Feeling better?"

I nodded. "Yes, thank you very much, Davud, for all your help and the gracious bigheartedness of your family. How long has it been?"

Davud gave his mom a hug. "You've been sleeping for almost three days. I've shown Johan a bit of Ankara. He'll be glad you're up."

"Your mom was telling me something, and she gave me these." I showed him the towels and soap. "I probably need a good washing-up."

Davud bit the bottom of his lip and indicated where the bathroom was. After a long hot shower, I changed and went back to the kitchen. Davud and Johan sipped hot tea.

"Ah, you look much better, no?" Johan lifted his eyebrows and blew on the surface of his tea.

"Yup. Worlds better. Do you know what I had?" I had a hard time believing I'd slept for three days.

"Davud's sister came over and said maybe heatstroke, migraine, or dehydration. Maybe all of it. Don't know. Just glad you're okay."

"Me too."

Davud's mom placed a plate of warm bread with butter and honey, boiled eggs, and sliced tomatoes on the table. She spoke to Davud. He stared at the ground.

I looked at his mom and then at Davud. I sensed she might be tired of having these unasked-for guests. "Davud, can we catch a bus out of here and make it to the Iranian border in a day or two?" I swallowed back my desire to stay a little longer.

Davud got up to refill his tea. I noticed he was not that tall and carried a little extra weight around his middle. Funny, I hadn't noticed that before.

"Oh, you don't have to leave just yet." He sat back down and made small puffing noises on top of his tea, creating tiny ripples. "But you're right. You'll have to travel through Iran, not Syria."

"I think it would be best if we left as soon as we can. Your parents have been very gracious. Thank you, really." I gazed over at his mother. She began to scrub the counters.

Davud dropped his chin to his chest. "Yes." He shrugged. "My parents are not used to your foreign customs."

"What do you mean?'

Davud squirmed in his seat. "The way you dress and talk. The fact that you and Johan are traveling together. Women here do not go out alone and especially do not take a trip with single men."

I let this piece of information sink in. "Okay." I glanced at Johan. "Guess we'll see about getting bus tickets to Erzurum." I didn't want to impose any more than I had already.

Johan examined the tablecloth. "Davud, do you mind writing down directions to the bus terminal again?"

We set our backpacks down in the main living area and thanked Davud and his family for their generosity. I gave his mother a box of baklava Johan and I had bought in the marketplace. "Thank you very, very much. You have been more than generous."

I didn't know if I should have hugged them or shook their hands or bowed, so I did nothing, careful not to offend.

Johan sent them cards from the countries that lay ahead.

But I did not. I don't know why. I should have sent them something for their goodwill. I have no excuse.

33

Varanasi – November 1978

*Varanasi greeted me with an explosion
of such energy and liveliness I wanted to
hold my arms out and hug the city.*

The familiar train's drumbeat mollified my growing anxiety about returning to Varanasi. Bands of violet, gold, and rose filled the sky. I wrapped my supple cotton blanket around my shoulders and closed my eyes.

The train roof, baked hot from the autumn sun, provided hardy souls, willing to risk the dangers, a free ride. I wondered how they survived up there. Underneath, in third class, the compartment held too many of us, but we endured it well, finding relief in chai stops and country stations. The air smelled of rotten garbage as the passengers left their rubbish and chewed *betel* on the floor.

As soon as our train slowed for whatever reason—sometimes I never really knew why we suddenly stopped—children of all ages ran up to the windows, shouting *"CHAI! SAMOSAS! CHAPPATIS!"* at the top of their lungs. Many, including me, climbed down the rickety ladder for hot cups of tea in clay cups or food wrapped in newspaper.

After hurried drinks, we smashed the cups against the railway tracks. Evidence of this practice could be seen for miles; pieces of broken terracotta all over the place. When the whistle blew, we'd scramble back on board, sometimes giggling at the thought of missing our ride.

I read Gandhi's autobiography and marked certain inspirational passages: the value of truth, nonviolence, silence, humility. Gandhi's words confirmed what I had learned with *Maharaja*: be kind, disciplined, honest.

When I wasn't reading, I mused on how to find Taj.

Where would he be living now? Near the *ghats* or close to the university? How many friends and band members had congregated in Varanasi? Would he be happy with my choice to come back? Would he be more attracted to me now that I had lived in India for all these many months and had studied and learned about this ancient land?

> **I settled into my smugness like a thief**

The dream of exploring South India, Sri Lanka, and perhaps further east, such as Thailand and Indonesia, quickly vanished once the daydreams of seeing Taj waltzed into my thoughts.

My waist-length hair, in a traditional Indian braid, swished against my back when I stood to smooth out the wrinkles of my light pink sari, my arms the color of a copper penny. I held my head and shoulders straight and high—proud of the things I had learned in Rishikesh, with the swamis, with *Maharaja*, with Goenka, with the places and people I'd encountered.

I meditated for real now, even mastering a few Ashtanga yoga postures. Spoke Hindi in the marketplace. Practiced patience when the train was twelve hours late. I couldn't wait to show off my progress to Taj. I relaxed into my self-assuredness, the conceit luscious and seductive, like a movie star thinking she'd outsmarted the paparazzi.

Crossing my legs and clasping my hands in my lap, I waited to get off the overcrowded train until some of the families had a chance to gather their things.

33 Varanasi – November 1978

The rickshaw driver scrambled through the street traffic: hundreds of bicycle rickshaws, camels, cows, groups carrying heavy bundles on their heads. Children played. Beggars requested baksheesh. Vendors cooked fried chili peppers over an open fire. Bike bells chimed continuously. Car horns blared. People yelled.

The streets narrowed in chaotic intersections. Women in bright saris clutched the hands of young children. Swarms of men carried wads of cloth and bags of grain. Varanasi greeted me with an explosion of such energy and liveliness I wanted to hold my arms out and hug the city.

I told the driver, "Drop me off at the Travel Lodge near the last *ghat*."

He peddled with renewed vigor, sure that I would tip him well. The muscles on his calves bulged, his body taut and fit from years of riding. I did indeed reward him nicely and strolled into the main reception area with renewed confidence. "Yes, I'd prefer a room with a view."

The next morning, I rose at sunrise and made my way to the Ganges River with hundreds of pilgrims. I washed my face, chanted, sat on a concrete step, watched the sunrise, and prayed. "May I find Taj today." Not a very spiritual request, I know, but at least it was honest.

The murky waters of the Ganges River flowed swiftly past the hundreds of people washing their bodies while dead ones burned above on the *ghats*.

After what I assumed to be enough time to appear devout, I walked to a familiar chai house and passed several snake charmers. The memory of me, Taj, and Roberto sipping tea, the sweat pooling under our light cotton clothing, the smell of cardamom, floated through my head. A tender sensation trickled into my heart and spread into my fingers and toes. I knew I had made the right choice to come here.

"Chai, Ma'am Sahib?" the tea maker asked.

The shop, mostly empty except for a few older men who convened in the corner, wearing billowy cotton harem pants, reminded me of an American bar in the middle of the afternoon.

"Yes, yes. Little sugar, please." I handed him a few coins, found a table, and watched the morning street bustle begin, the hubbub matching my thoughts. Minutes, then an hour passed, lost in my daydreams. I had forgotten Taj stayed up late and would probably not be in the market until later.

Back at the lodge, I busied with laundry and writing. I checked the time often: ten, noon, one, two. Would three be too early? I waited until five o'clock.

The teahouse had little space left. A group of Hindu men, two with big bellies, discussed the day's events around a work surface. A university crowd huddled around two tables debated about something. Three young foreigners, dressed in an array of Hindu and Western clothing, sat at another table.

One woman resembled Krista, Taj's violin player.

I waved. "Krista?"

> The thousand butterflies in my stomach started to go nuts when Krista opened the front door.

She turned, and her eyebrows lifted. "Shanti, Shanti. You came!"

I let out a huge breath and walked over to Krista's table. "Yep. I'm here." I tried to appear nonchalant and yawned. "Is... um...Taj around?"

She nodded. "He play tonight with new players from Italia." She pronounced the country's name with flawless enunciation. "You should come."

I pulled up a chair, and Krista introduced her friends. They spoke rapidly in their language. I couldn't understand what they were talking about, but I smiled politely and pretended to care while concentrating on the taste of my tea, blowing little rivers around the rim. I waited just the right amount of time before I asked, "So, where are you living?"

Krista turned away from her comrades. "We live near Carlos and Sophia's place. You remember them, no?"

I twisted my mouth to the side and tried to recall if I had met them or not. "I don't think so."

"Well, Carlos has shop in Paris, buys clothes here, ships them to France. Make huge profit. His house beautiful." She rolled her eyes. "Much money. He thinks he better than most of us."

I laughed. "I'm sure Taj and he get along just fine."

"Well, Taj rent one of his houses. A few streets from here." She pointed her finger to a gap between a rice stall and a small office building.

The thousand butterflies in my stomach started to go nuts when Krista opened the front door. A stream of music, the familiar sitar, floated down the stairs. I let Krista and her friends go in first.

I stood against the back wall and took in the scene. Taj and his band dazzled in their Indian dress. The instruments glowed in the soft light. The packed room didn't seem big enough to hold everyone. I slid down the wall and waited.

Krista slinked through the audience, gave someone a hug, took a puff of a cigarette from another, laughed, and picked up her violin. Taj tapped his foot, and the chatter ceased. They played a beautiful rendition of a popular Indian raga, improvising at the end: first sitar and tabla, then tabla and violin, then tabla and guitar, and so on until each had played with one other and had also soloed. They ended after more than two hours of playing.

Taj jumped up. "Chai?" Then he spoke a few more words in his native tongue. He gave each of his band members a hug. Krista whispered in his ear. He looked up and gazed over the small sea of people.

I tried to think of something clever to do or say but settled on just letting his eyes find mine. When they did, a cascade of emotion fought to come out.

Taj took a while to get to me. Everyone wanted a piece of him, and he loved the attention, the adulation. Watching him, I began to have doubts.

Would music always be his first love?

So many women wanted to touch him. I wondered if Taj could ever be capable of the monogamy I craved with such constant flirtation. Did I make the right decision? Maybe not.

However, as soon as he stood in front of me, his dark eyes holding mine, those thoughts vanished like water droplets touching the hot earth. I sat motionless, feeling time warp and bend as if a thousand lifetimes passed through me. I lost my intelligence.

"Shanti. Where you staying?"

He grinned.

I tried to clear my head. "Taj. Quite a gathering. You never cease to amaze me."

He reached out his hand and I grabbed it, letting him pull me up. We stood for a moment, not speaking. The sounds of the frenzied crowd hushed and subdued.

Krista captured me around the waist. "Good you come. Chai, yes?"

I held up my hands, feeling bankrupted out of the moment, the spell broken. "Of course. Happy to see all of you." It was the right thing to say.

I let out a long sigh. I must have drunk ten cups of chai already.

The packed café felt like something out of a Disney cartoon: the small tables, the unstable chairs, the tea owner beaming, happy for the business. Taj conversed with him in fluent Hindi, and I got drunk watching his magnetism.

I missed this. I missed *him*.

Krista nudged my side and spoke softly in my ear. "Taj looks at you differently. It's in his eyes. When he saw you in New Delhi, he couldn't stop talking about you. It drove us a little nuts. I've never seen him get so riled up about a girl before." She looked at me long and hard.

"Oh." I didn't know what to say. But I was glad, thinking I might have meant as much to him as he did to me.

After an hour or more, Taj leaned his head toward mine. "You never tell me where you stay?"

I turned. "Travel Lodge, near the last *ghat*."

"Okay. I find rickshaw for you."

He called to one of the many drivers waiting to earn extra income, spoke to him in Hindi, and waved at me. I got up, lifting my sari so it wouldn't graze the dirt.

"Thanks, Taj. Good night. Nice to see you." Should I hug him? Unsure, I crossed my arms.

"Yes, yes." He touched my shoulder. "Good night."

I watched him return to his friends and replayed the evening over and over as the rickshaw driver carried me into the late evening mass of Varanasi's humanity, feeling a little like a moth near a Venus flytrap.

34

Iran – February 1977

*I was swept into a human river bursting
with a mania I couldn't comprehend.*

"The roads close at sunset. Iran has strict laws about this and just about everything, it seems," Johan groaned. "There are no places to hang out either at this hole."

I looked at the hard, ugly benches and the gray cement walls of the compound building. "Can we wait here until morning?" We only had thirty minutes until the border between Turkey and Iran locked up for the day.

Naïvely, we thought a bus service would just magically be there. Not only did such a thing not exist, but Iran had travel bans from sunset to dawn.

"I asked the guard that. He rolled his eyes. I assume that meant no."

"Well, what are we supposed to do?" The dark night had settled like a fog from the sea, cool and all-encompassing. "Do they send us back into Turkey or what?"

Johan shrugged. "I dunno." He sat next to me and put his long legs up on his rucksack. I felt comforted by at least knowing one person in this uninviting environment.

We both spotted him at the same time. His brown hair fell almost to his elbows, and he carried a small canvas bag slung across his shoulder. He smiled when he saw us and ambled our way, indifferent to the hostile sentry.

"Comrades, looks as if we're all in the same boat here." He spoke with a honeyed American accent, smooth and soft.

Johan got up to shake his hand. "Yep. Name's Johan from Holland, and this is Sharon from Canada."

"Hi." I gave a beauty queen wave; my arm bent at the elbow.

We sat on the inflexible pew and chatted about what to do.

His name was Larry. He pronounced his name in long, drawn-out syllables, Texas-style: *Laaarrrrreeee*. "You know. Someone told me you can hitch a ride into Tehran with truck drivers from Eastern Europe. They're less strict about company rules and apparently appreciate the camaraderie, especially with a beautiful woman. Wanna try?" He leaned in somewhat.

> Surely Iran would be better than northeastern Turkey.

I blushed and wondered how he got such flawless teeth. "I guess. We don't have a lot of options." I turned to face Johan. "What do you think?"

"Worth a shot. Stay here with our backpacks, and we'll ask around." He looked out the window. "There seems to be a lot of big trucks out there, and they can't drive until morning."

I watched Larry and Johan disappear into the ebony shadows and waited, attentive to the guards' stares. One watchman came over, scoffed, and pointed to the large black-and-white clock on the wall.

I held back the sarcasm and nodded. Yes, I knew the border would close soon. I closed my eyes and let out a long sigh.

The two-day bus ride from Ankara to this boundary had been unpleasant at best: the foul odor of rotten garlic on a packed bus, the overnight at a horrid motel, and the nasty outhouses at pit stops made me gag. Surely Iran would be better than northeastern Turkey.

Larry rapped on my shoulder. "We found two truck drivers from Bulgaria who are willing to take us to Tehran. They don't speak much English—just a few words. It takes about two days." His chest puffed up as if he wore a light down vest. "Come on. Let's get out of here. We can sleep in the front of their cabs."

The two Bulgarian truck drivers shook our hands. The shorter man had a beard and showed us a picture of his family. The thicker man's belly protruded over his belt. Flecks of gray around his temples showed he must've been in his forties. The bearded man's name was Sergey, and the older man was Micha.

The three of us unrolled our sleeping bags and had a restless sleep, bumping into each other throughout the night. I woke early, eager to get going. Sergey and Micha were already up and motioned for us to be ready to leave in five minutes. We quickly used the latrine and left.

Johan and Larry rode with Micha, and I traveled with Sergey. I didn't think to ask why they separated us. We halted for a rest midmorning, and the drivers shared food from their home: chunks of hearty whole wheat bread, cheese, juice, and fruit. In the late afternoon, we took another break at a small settlement and ate at a quiet outdoor eatery—rice pilaf, flatbread, and warm water from a spigot.

At sundown, the two trucks pulled off onto an extended off-ramp and parked at the back of a row of trucks, tucked within inches of each other. They looked like toy matchbox cars.

Within minutes, several semis parked behind us, and we were frozen in place until morning. Darkness descended quickly. Stars appeared, and a cool evening replaced the hot, dry day. Miles of barren hills and parched earth surrounded our little camp. I had spent the day looking at this waterless land, with only a few poor villages here and there to break the monotony.

Get off me!

In the middle of the night, I awoke to Sergey unzipping my sleeping bag. He rolled on top of me and began to fondle my breasts.

"No!" I yelled. "Get off me!"

Sergey laughed and said a few unfamiliar words. He started to unbutton my blouse and held my arms down.

I screamed and tried to wrestle his every move. I pointed to his family picture.

He laughed. I think he thought this was part of sexual play.

We fought for what seemed like a long time, but probably was only about ten minutes. Then, he just froze, apologized, crawled back into his compartment, and fell asleep.

The loud snores kept me awake, but mostly I feared he'd try to assault me again. I thought about what Davud had said about women in this part of the world.

"Unmarried women live virtuously at home until their fathers have arranged for their marriages. Women do not go out alone and do not take a trip with single men."

Maybe Sergey thought I was a prostitute, and that's why he gave us a ride.

The next day we woke at sunrise and departed hastily. I focused my attention on the desolate landscape and avoided any eye contact with Sergey.

At our final rest break before Tehran, Johan stared at me. "What's up? You seem sad."

Sergey and Micha sat near us and laughed.

Johan and Larry thanked the Bulgarian men for their kindness. I sat on my pack and watched. I couldn't bring myself to thank them, even though they did us a huge favor. Sergey glanced my way and waved. I didn't wave back.

The bus, headed to Tehran's city center, squealed around corners, sending the passengers lurching side to side. I hung on to the overhead rail with both hands to steady myself from falling into an Iranian man. The full bus contained men primarily, with one woman in a full-length plain *burqa* in the front.

34 Iran – February 1977

We tried several hotels and inns. At each place, the door slammed in our faces. The keepers shook their heads. I heard one man say in broken English, "Oh, no, no. No foreigners allowed."

We took it personally, not understanding that the launch of an Islamic revolution was underfoot.

Finally, we saw two tourists in the street. Larry yelled, "Hey! Can you help us?"

"Only one place in Tehran you can stay as a foreigner right now," one of the men told us. "Some uprising is going on about America, and they think all of us are from the United States, even if we are from Germany."

The taller of the two travelers tapped his foot. "I detest it here and plan on leaving as soon as my visa comes through. You better go to the embassy tomorrow. I heard it takes at least a week, and there's not much you can do because of the riots at night."

I perked up. *Riots? Uprising? Sounds exciting.* I whispered to Johan. "Let's go out tonight and see what's happening?"

Johan lifted his eyebrows. "First, let's find lodging and food."

Figures. Johan is thinking about his stomach, I thought.

The only place for outsiders to stay in Tehran was a four-story dilapidated dwelling with one shower house for the men and another for women, a cafeteria and office on the first floor, and several rooms on the second and third floor. The crowded, filthy dormitory on the fourth floor reeked of backed-up toilets.

But there was nothing we could do.

We settled into the dormitory until a room opened on the second floor. We ate in the cafeteria that first night and slept fitfully on sagging cots.

Larry pegged it perfectly. "This place is a rip-off."

> **I found the insurgency electrifying.**

The next day we took a bus into modern Tehran and stood in line for hours to apply for Afghani visas. When my turn came, the male clerk barked, "Passport.

Open it up and leave it right here." He tapped his index finger on the work surface. "Do not touch me."

I thought, *who does he think he is? Geez, okay already.*

I did as he asked and offered a smile, trying to appear friendly.

He did not smile back. After several silent minutes, he slid my passport across the countertop, careful not to make any contact with my skin, and said, "You come back in five days for visa." His gaze felt cold and foreboding, like the chills I got once walking down a deserted alley in Vancouver.

On the third night, I convinced Johan to go out into the city. I had heard loud noises and pops of what I suspected to be rifles.

Earlier in the day, I had watched a procession of tanks rumble down our street. Men sat on top and wore white turbans. They shouted things from a loudspeaker. I didn't understand a word. Johan seemed troubled, but I found the insurgency electrifying.

Iranian men—and women in full *burqas*—filled the streets yelling and holding up signs. I couldn't read the symbols. Several had a picture of an older man with a long white beard.

Johan held onto my sweatshirt. "This is not good."

> **Tiny, panicky bubbles began to bounce in my veins.**

Suddenly, a group of men rushed past, carrying torches above their heads. They looked like athletes running in the Olympics. A few screamed something, and then others joined in.

The frenzied crowd's momentum picked up speed, and the urgency tasted acidic and hot. Beads of sweat formed on my forehead, and the air felt saturated and seared like a steak on a boiling grill. Tiny, panicky bubbles began to bounce in my veins.

A loud bang erupted to my left, but I couldn't see because the crowd had strengthened in numbers, and I was swept into a human river bursting with a mania I couldn't comprehend.

Someone grabbed my arm. I turned to face a woman in a light blue *burqa,* who pulled me away from the thunder and onto a street curb. She lifted her veil, and I saw she had the same skin color as me.

She spoke English. "What are you doing here?" Her voice was high-pitched and vehement. "This is dangerous. Get out. *Now!*" She pushed me into a nearby shrub.

I heard Johan holler my name, and I yelled back, "Over here!"

He clutched my hand and pulled me up. "Wow. Let's go." A loud explosion echoed off the walls of a concrete building.

We ran down a side street and made our way back to the hotel.

The Iranian peoples' passion moved and terrified me at the same time. The turmoil lasted into the early morning hours. No one told me revolt could be so thrilling.

In the cafeteria, everyone talked about the upheaval, the opinions as diverse as we were: "Yeah, I heard a few people got killed." "I'm getting out of here as quick as I can." "Oh, this will pass." "They need the Shah." "Better to go into modern Tehran right now." "I'm scared." "No big deal, just chill." "Let's get stoned."

I didn't go out at night again, and we waited impatiently for our visas. Johan and I got ours first.

Larry would have to remain in Iran. "It's because I'm American, I think. You guys go on ahead. I'll meet you in Herat. There's a really nice place there." He jotted down the name of the inn. "It'll be heaven after this."

The uprising of Iran's needs—both oppressive and worrisome—had strengthened during the week. I looked at the filmy disk of the sun and nodded. "I'm looking forward to leaving, too. We'll wait for you."

I began to understand a little of the world around me—a culture built on modesty, with strict adherence to the Quran. A woman should shield her face and body from public view. Many Muslims shunned anything western; handshakes, laughter, movies, books, dancing, alcohol.

We hugged, and Larry gave us a bag of dried fruit and freshly roasted pistachios for the lengthy bus ride across the extensive Iranian desert into Afghanistan, another Islamic country.

35

Varanasi – November-December 1978

The buzzing energy fired up my imagination and aroused something in me I had not felt before — community, a sense of belonging, promise.

The soft knock surprised me. I looked at the little clock on the desk. Eleven in the morning. Did I forget something?

"Yes. Just a moment, please." I untangled my legs from sitting cross-legged in morning meditation and got up to answer the door.

A young boy, missing an arm, turned the corners of his mouth up and revealed a straight row of front teeth. "Ma'am Sahib. Someone here for you. Downstairs. Lobby." He grinned broadly again, clearly pleased with his ability to relay the message.

"Thank you. I'll be right down." *It must be Krista.*

In the reception area, Taj and four of his band members sat in comfortable lounge chairs, chatting in Hindi with the manager.

I waited a moment and took in the view of Taj: his tall thin frame, long fingers, hair a shade darker than night, white clothing against his olive skin, legs crossed with his foot swinging back and forth, and his big expressive eyes. Taj had the ability to blend seamlessly wherever he was, to be at ease in crowds and for crowds to be at ease with him. His allure was like watching rolling tidal waves against the seashore: *whoosh, whoosh.*

"Taj."

He turned and broke out into a huge smile. "Shanti, Shanti. Lunch?"

I laughed. "That'd be great, Taj. Anywhere in particular?"

His boyish grin warmed my heart all over again. I followed his entourage out the door into the thronging streets of midday Varanasi.

> **You could stay with us.**

Taj led the way to a local outdoor eatery—a few tables, authentic fare, owners who did not speak English or cater to western money. Taj had a great infectious laugh, igniting all to join him, like a lit match on dry kindling. Everyone wanting to be around his warmth, and when you weren't, everything seemed less somehow.

It wasn't long before Taj voiced his opinion of my hotel choice. His head slowly moved from side to side. "Shanti, this place you stay." He was becoming so Indian.

I knew what he was going to say, but I played along. "Hmm. Yes, Taj. What about it?"

He sucked in a bit of air and curled his lip. "Too American. Too showy. Much better places."

I smiled. "Yah? And where would that be, Taj?"

He chuckled. "You could stay with us."

I didn't leave the hotel right away.

It wasn't Taj's invitation to stay at his nice home with his band members, but my dwindling budget that convinced me to accept his offer. I had been away from Canada for over two years, and the thick wallet of traveler checks had thinned significantly. I knew Taj would not expect any monies, although I had every intention of paying for my fair share of the housing.

Taj's two-story concrete home had an iron gate out front and a similar one on the second floor. An enclosed staircase separated the levels. A kitchen and courtyard were on the bottom floor.

35 Varanasi – November-December 1978

A large, gnarled banyan tree with twisted branches provided shade for the main living area upstairs, a sizeable area for hosting dozens of practicing musicians. There were four bedrooms upstairs and two downstairs.

Ricardo had become Taj's loyal tabla player, and I could tell the men had grown close. Ricardo adored Taj and looked to him for just about everything. He had the room next to mine. While apparently just friends—or so they said—Krista and Andre shared a room. Maybe Taj told them to room together so I could have one of the bedrooms.

The other spaces were occupied by Alba, the Spanish guitar player; Leo, who played violin; and Mani, the flute player. Sometimes Augusto, who everyone called Gus, came and stayed over. He played harmonium and percussion.

We did not become intimate right away. Cautious at first, I held the silence between us like a fragile flower. However, the attraction proved too strong. Like a magnet next to metal, I got sucked into Taj's mesmeric whirlpool.

One night Ricardo pulled me aside. "Careful, Shanti. I think you scare Taj a little. He's afraid to feel, how do you say in English —*mucho*—too much."

I dropped my head. "What do you mean by *careful*?" My heart picked up speed. I wanted Taj to have eyes only for me.

He hugged me from the side, a tight protective embrace. "Taj has a lot of plans for the future. Maybe a record soon. He's talking of a concert when we get home. He doesn't want to be tied down to anything." He laughed nervously. "No worries, though. Everything okay, yes?"

"Hmm. I guess." I wondered if Ricardo was looking out for me or for Taj. I folded my arms and let it go, glad to not think too much about what he had just said.

The house walls echoed music for most of the days and nights. Sunset signified the time for everybody to come together and play for hours and hours and hours. If you didn't love music and didn't play music, you didn't belong.

And so began my short career in music.

All the musicians studied at the university. Most were incredibly dedicated, and many had natural talent, but I felt out of place, a hippo in a herd of gazelles. Taj acted delighted when I brought up the subject of studying music with them. He talked it over with the others, and they decided I should learn the tanpura. "Easy, and we could use someone to keep time," Taj told me.

> I always felt a bit like a fraud sitting on their temporary stage.

The tanpura, a tall instrument with a four-stringed vertical neck and a bowled bottom, produced a deep, resonant sound. The four strings were simply played, one at a time, in a fluid flow to keep a steady and continuous rhythm for the real instruments.

Truth was, I always felt a bit like a fraud sitting on their temporary stage. I wondered if the cliché *fake it until you make it* would work for me.

Shortly after that, Taj introduced me to a highly respected Muslim elder, who was also a notable musician. "He once trained Ravi Shankar, you know."

"Wow. You're kidding, right? Ravi Shankar? And you want to ask him to teach me? Really?" I couldn't understand why a man of such ranking would want to take on a newbie as myself. Didn't he know I was not a musician?

We traveled to an unfamiliar part of Varanasi and passed a marketplace. Clouds of incense wafted around like thick wisps of smog. The rickshaw meandered through a network of complicated streets and alleyways lined with ramshackle huts, and roadside food stands until we came to a modest home with a black iron gate. The heavy metal bell sounded particularly loud as it ricocheted off the adjacent brick.

With his hands in prayer position under his chin, the elder spoke to Taj. They conversed comfortably, waggling their heads at certain points, laughing at other times. The elder had thick white hair and wore a woven vest over his cream *kirtan* shirt. He rolled a cigarette, and they smoked.

"Shanti, this Baba-ji is great musician. He plays best *Durga* style." Taj looked at Baba-ji affectionately. "Come sit here. He is going to play for us." Taj moved slightly to make room.

I sat next to Taj and waited while Baba-ji tuned his harmonium and voice. His young wife brought tea, and his two little children giggled in the background. I had been told he was close to eighty, and his wife seemed younger than me.

I made a mental note to ask Taj why he married again so late in life.

A soulful note and then another, Baba-ji began to sing an Indian ballad that felt odd and strangely familiar at the same time, as if memory were a butterfly fluttering out of reach.

Sadness tugged at my heart, and countless mental pictures jumped around in my head: waves of people moving toward a sea, a tall, turbaned man riding a camel, women in sheer saris, turrets, citadels, a peacock spreading his wings, a painted elephant, beggars sleeping on train tracks, hands intricately painted with henna, marigold flowers falling from the sky.

Twenty minutes later, my eyes held a pool of tears. When I blinked, the wetness rolled down my cheeks and slid into my mouth, warm and salty.

I looked at Taj. I couldn't be sure, but it looked as if his eyes had misted over, too.

He held my gaze. "He'll come to the house tomorrow around lunchtime."

Taj bowed, spoke a few soft words, and placed several rupee notes in Baba-ji's wrinkled hand. Baba-ji bobbed his head and then watched his petite wife escort us to the door. I hadn't spoken a word.

On the ride back, the dense maze of humanity and noise of Varanasi left little opportunity to discuss what happened, but I tried. "Taj, that was amazing. His voice—so pure. And that style. I've never heard anything, so..." I searched for the right word. "Primordial."

Taj squinted. "Not sure what you mean, but yes, Baba-ji is a master. You must do everything he says." He clasped my hand, threading his fingers through mine.

"Everything?" I wondered what that might mean.

"Yes, if you want to learn. The right way. The only way."

The next day, Baba-ji arrived promptly at noon. Taj's cook served him a large plate of rice, lentils, and vegetables, followed by a cup of tea. He ate in silence, and I waited nervously, unsure what to expect.

How would he teach me if he could not speak English?

He sat down next to the harmonium in a cross-legged position and began to speak. I didn't understand a word. He touched his mouth and sang a note. Next, he pointed to me. Mimic him? I let out a squeak. He laughed.

> My knees ached for release from their prison.

For the next two hours, we practiced the Indian musical scale, similar to a western musical scale but with distinctly different sounds. When he got up to leave, I almost kissed his feet from relief. I could hardly talk, and my knees ached for release from their prison. I wobbled back to my room and slept until evening.

Taj asked. "Good first practice, yes?"

I didn't want to disappoint him, so I lied. "Sure."

Ricardo nudged my side. "Difficult work, no?"

I looked at the calluses on their fingers. "Yes."

Baba-ji came six days a week to teach the basics of classical Indian music: the scales; the ragas; the delicate, understated ballad meanings; the value of India's ancient musical past; and techniques to coax my throat to open.

Taj sometimes checked in, sitting off to one side and voicing approval. Whenever he did this, I sat up straight, and my heart rate accelerated, grateful for the interest, for the support, as if I was in school and trying to please the teacher.

At the end of December, a big box arrived for Taj. When he saw it, he yelled, "Whoop!"

We all ran to the main music room. He opened his arms. "Special day for us. My family sent this for me, but I must share with—" he made a big circle with his arms, "—all of you. My other family." Ricardo hugged him, and the others embraced as well. They talked for a while in their native language.

I picked up a word or two, but often, I just waited, a familiar pattern. I didn't mind because I enjoyed watching Taj; the way he smoothed his hair back and tied it with a piece of cord, how he touched his friends, gentle and tender like a meticulous gardener tending his flowers.

The first things to be pulled out and shared amongst shrieks and shouts were a large bottle of something sweetly potent and a sealed container of olive oil. Krista ran to get fresh *chapattis*. Within minutes, we ate smothered flatbread in olive oil between sips of delicious liquor. My head felt like a floating piece of plastic.

"Oh, my God, this is so good!" I hugged Mani. "What's next?"

Fresh almonds, dried tomatoes and figs, soft caramel candies, and then another bottle of what Taj called "sweet wine." We got drunk on the luxury. Even though I couldn't understand half of what they said, I had never felt so connected to a group of people before. I cherished their easygoing style, their passion.

I tried to keep the reins on my feelings for Taj, afraid I might get hurt again. But I failed and let myself drown in a sea of wanting, like a boat in a deep fog, unable to see the beam of light from the lighthouse.

When we were alone, he placed his foot over mine. "This is for you." He put a journal in my lap. The cover was shiny and displayed a copy of the famous 1907 Klint painting of a man kissing a woman. "It reminds me of us," he said shyly.

> **What were you thinking? This was an incredible opportunity.**

A warmth spread from my belly to my toes, and I squeezed the journal tight to my chest. I kissed him twice on his cheeks. "It's beautiful. I love it."

We curled into each other like two kittens and talked about our dreams and thoughts. Taj wanted to learn everything he could from Indian masters. I hoped to find out more about Buddhism.

We both said, "Let's stay in India for a long time."

Every day the house filled with Taj's musical friends, comrades from home, colleagues at the university, or just pals he met at the chai shop that day. Music played at all hours. Some days, there was little time between the night jam session and daybreak.

Frequently we ate at home. The cook prepared pots of rice and stacks of *chapattis* wrapped in cloth. A giant container of chai, made fresh in the morning, kept us sustained all day.

Generally, I delighted in the gregarious lifestyle. The buzzing energy fired up my imagination and aroused something in me I had not felt before—community, a sense of belonging, promise.

Soon, word got out that Baba-ji visited our house, and more people came. They wanted to hear him sing. Baba-ji would stay after my lessons and perform for the small group that had gathered. Sometimes he did not leave until dark, Taj insisting on a taxi for his ride home.

One cooler-than-average evening, Taj mentioned, "Baba-ji said Ravi Shankar will be playing in Varanasi. We should all go. I'll get tickets tomorrow."

However, Baba-ji surprised me by asking if I would be his guest. He had been granted backstage access and a private audience with Ravi Shankar. He put his hands in the traditional prayer position and, in Hindi, asked, "Yes, please you come to meet the great master and my dear friend Mr. Shankar, yes?"

I felt self-conscious about being introduced to such an icon, and I was worried when I realized Taj was not invited. "Oh no, Baba-ji. Too great an honor for such a beginner as myself. Please, you go on without me."

I could tell by the way he looked at me that he felt jilted. I watched him get in a rickshaw alone. As soon as the cycle turned the corner, shards of self-doubt nipped at my psyche like tiny pinpricks.

When Taj found out, he shook his head back and forth. "Shanti. What were you thinking? This was an incredible opportunity."

I shrugged, my cheeks hot and splotched. "Yeah. I know," and quickly added, "I felt it should be you, not me."

Taj raised his eyebrows and glanced in Ricardo's direction. "Can you believe it?"

Ricardo narrowed his eyes. "No."

Taj and I did not speak much during the rickshaw ride to the theater, and when we got there, he chose to sit at the end of the aisle, placing several of his friends between us.

I hardly remember the show, wrapped up in guilt as profuse as a mist enveloping a mountain peak. I felt like such an idiot.

Later that night, I overheard Taj tell Krista about it. He said, "a defect in her character for sure."

I pinned the disappointment on my wall of regrets.

The children who trailed me down the street the next day, palms open for baksheesh and saying, "Ma'am Sahib, Ma'am

Sahib," felt taunting, as if they knew my imperfections, could see my Achilles' heel.

I don't know what hurt more, a missed opportunity or Taj's criticism.

Regardless, I felt small and embarrassed, a little less than everyone else.

36

Afghanistan – February 1977

*I was more than a little uneasy about
wandering into these regions by myself.*

The bus suddenly stopped about a hundred yards from the Afghani border. Native men in their turbans and women in their *burqas* began to murmur. The children's eyes grew wide with alarm. I looked at Johan.

A big, burly man got on the bus. He yelled, "Baksheesh. Baksheesh. BAKSHEESH!"

I whispered, "Are we supposed to give him money? Is this blackmail, or are we being robbed?" I shrunk into my sweatshirt, trying not to stand out.

The man walked down the aisle and paused at each passenger, demanding some sort of payout. I can't remember now if he had a gun. I kept my eyes on the ground.

Johan gave him a few dollars.

The man grabbed the money and snorted. "You more, no?"

Johan stood up, easily a foot higher than the man, and said, "No, I don't have any more money right now."

The man grunted a few times and left. Then, the bus driver got back on and drove to the border as if nothing had happened.

Once through Afghani customs, I asked one of the local men, "What was that back there? Why did that man demand money? Does this happen all the time?"

Two bus mates replied, speaking simultaneously, "Oh yes, every day—same thing. Bus driver and man make extra money. Drive to border or leave you in desert. You pick." They both grinned, revealing tobacco-stained teeth.

I shared this bit of news with Johan. "Gives new meaning to highway robbery, doesn't it? It's like something out of the old American West—cowboys and Indians. Except, it's Muslims and Muslims."

Johan wrinkled his forehead. "I don't think I know what you mean."

"Never mind."

We found the lodge Larry had recommended, just outside Herat. One word to describe the place: beautiful. The hotel's several rooms formed a rectangle around a large, enclosed courtyard. In the center of the square, a fountain splashed water into a blue-tiled pool. The bushes were in bloom: effervescent pinks, dazzling scarlet, oranges, and yellows next to spring greenery.

> **This is paradise after Iran.**

I let out a long sigh. "This is wonderful. I think we should stay here for a week at least. I could use the time to wash, write, tour this illustrious little town. What do you think?"

Johan sat on the smooth tile. "This is paradise after Iran, that's for sure. Why not? Let's stay. Maybe Larry will make it."

I noticed that although I had been in Muslim countries for several weeks now, each nation practiced the Islamic faith differently, and the subtle discrepancies made it seem as if they were dissimilar religions altogether.

Outwardly, they appeared to be similar. Women wore *burqas* and were primarily homebound. Men dominated society and heeded the call to prayer at mosques. They didn't drink alcohol. But it felt different—Afghanistan impressed me with her easygoing style, grandiose architecture, visible pride in the eyes of her people, and miles and miles of rugged terrain steeped in timeless history.

"It's really something how unique it feels here in comparison to Iran and Turkey," I told Johan. "Poles apart, don't you think? It seems special somehow. I saw a nomadic tribe in town today. Did you see them?"

Johan nodded. "Yeah. All bundled up in this heat."

"Someone told me they keep covered to avoid the sun's intensity. Not like us Westerners who strip down and expose ourselves when it gets above eighty degrees." I chuckled. "They had herds of sheep and goats with them. So, they just go from pasture to pasture, then? What do they do? Trade?"

Johan smirked. "What do you think was in your *pulao* today?"

"What? Goat meat? Really?"

Johan laughed. "Sometimes, you are so naïve."

I felt my cheeks warm. "Not the first time someone has told me that."

We discussed Afghanistan's pre-Islamic past with other travelers in the courtyard: Buddhism; Zoroastrianism; Alexander the Great; and some of the country's infamous artifacts, such as the Bamiyan Buddhas.

I asked a fellow trekker, "How far out of the way is it to go and see the Bamiyan Valley?"

"Hmm. Bamyan Province is not on your direct route to Pakistan, which is south to Kandahar, north to Kabul, then east up over the Khyber Pass. If you want to see more of Afghanistan, you might want to reconsider your route."

I mulled it over and asked Johan about it. He did not want to go, and I was more than a little uneasy about wandering into these regions by myself.

The travel thus far had been relatively safe, but the incidents in Tehran made me realize the precarious stability in this part of the world.

I found solace in dreams of hiking in the Himalayas.

37

Varanasi – January-March 1979

*I struggled to sound cheerful, pretending
that everything would work out.*

The two fifty-dollar traveler's checks sat on the bed next to each other like identical twins. These two checks were the last of the money I had brought with me. Not enough to stay in India, and not enough to buy a return ticket to Canada or America.

Not enough to do anything, really, except live cheaply for a few more months.

Krista poked her head into my room. "So, that's it."

I puffed out my cheeks and blew out some air. "Yep. I should have paid more attention. What am I going to do?"

Krista shrugged. "I heard they are looking for white women to teach Indian women English and Western customs. Maybe you could try there?"

"Who? Where? What?" I chewed on the inside of my cheek.

"At the university. You could ask Taj. He might know."

I loathed having to tell Taj I was out of money, but I didn't know what else to do. "Yeah, all right."

Taj nodded. "Okay. Will ask tomorrow."

He didn't appear bothered by the fact I had run out of money, and he seemed genuinely helpful, similar to the way he approached most things—taking the most complicated things in life and wrapping them up so small they'd fit right in my skirt pocket. "Everything will work out, Shanti. Don't worry." He lay back on the pillow and pulled me toward him.

"Uh. Thanks." I shivered a little in my nightclothes, but not from the cold.

Three well-dressed Indian women sat on cushions, their backs straight, eyes shining. They smiled and said in unison, "Morning, Ma'am Sahib. Thank you for teaching us English."

Oh, this is going to be nice. It seemed such an easy opportunity to make money.

Taj had inquired at the university and then had nonchalantly handed me a slip of paper with a contact. Things fell into place quickly and without problems.

Two Brahmin families had recently married their daughters to Indian men living abroad. The wives would be joining them in a few months. The families, especially the fathers of the households, wanted their offspring to be educated in American and European customs and improve their conversational English. All three were arranged marriages with heavy religious and familial implications, including a bride-price and dowry.

> They raised their hands like obedient first graders.

I guessed the women to be around my age or younger. Aalia, extraordinarily beautiful, tied her black hair neatly in a soft bun at the base of her slender neck. Chaaru sported a short, modern haircut. Esha, quiet and shy, let Aalia and Chaaru do most of the talking. She had big round eyes and held my gaze when I talked to her, smiling ever so slightly.

37 Varanasi – January-March 1979

The mothers greeted me first—apparently to approve. I was told by the contact to wear traditional Indian dress, preferably a light color, to be especially clean, and comply with all the Brahmin customs. I wore my white sari with pink needlework around the edges, and I took extra care with my hair, nails, and teeth.

At the door, I placed my shoes on the mat, bowed to the matriarchs, and thanked them, "Namaste, namaste."

They led the way to the main living area, a spacious great room with abundant throw cushions and plush rugs. In the center, a polished table with three notebooks and pencils. The writing materials were the same supplies I once used in elementary school, thick cardboard covers with lined paper pages bound by string.

I looked at those three stunning women sitting zazen-style on the floor, with their devoted families around them, so purely Indian in all the ways that are good and thought, *how in the world are they ever going to be ready to be immersed in Western society?*

And then I remembered... *Oh, yeah, that's my job.*

I asked each of them to share a smidgen about themselves and what they most wanted to learn. They raised their hands like obedient first graders. Their wholesome attitude endeared me to them immediately, and we began a two-hour English conversation.

Aalia talked first. "I was born in Varanasi and have lived here my whole life with my wonderful family. My new husband lives in Switzerland and works for an engineering company. His family organized our marriage." She fidgeted with an end piece of her sari. "I can speak and write English well, but I do not know much about Western customs." Aalia chatted about her life in Varanasi: washing clothes and hanging them out to dry; shopping in the marketplace with her girlfriends; braiding her hair; and making *puri*.

I wanted to say, "Aalia, Aalia, you are going to miss your family," but I knew I could not. Instead, I offered, "That's nice."

Chaaru proudly joined in. "My husband lives in Boston, where he works at a college there. I plan on decorating our apartment with the things I'm bringing from home, including a Hindu altar and lots of woven blankets." She went on for about fifteen minutes about her dream.

I twisted my mouth to keep from saying, "Chaaru, have you heard about the season called winter? Do you know people in America eat their food on a flat plate with a fork and knife, and you will sit in a chair next to a dining room table, not on the ground with bowls of steaming rice and your right hand to scoop up the vegetables? Chaaru, what homework have you done about Western society? Chaaru, your dream is just that, a dream." I simply listened.

Chaaru and Aalia coaxed Esha to talk. "Come, Esha. Tell Ms. Shanti about where you will be going. Come on."

Esha lowered her eyes. "I'm to be married soon to a distant relative of my father's family. He is older and lives in England. He may join Aalia's husband in Switzerland." She lifted her gaze, and her lip trembled a little. "I'm scared."

"Esha, I think that's brave of you to admit because there are a lot of things about Western society you may not know." I looked at the girls. "In fact, I think that might be where we start—learning about the differences between the two cultures. Write down any questions you may have, and we'll talk about them tomorrow. Yes?"

They moved their heads up and down several times.

Those winter months in Varanasi were some of my happiest memories. Up early to meditate, yoga, followed by music studies with Baba-ji.

After lunch, I'd take a bicycle rickshaw to Aalia's home to teach the three girls. Evenings were full of music and friends, eating late, and loving. I enjoyed every moment of those months, which felt full of promise—I had even thought of becoming an Indian citizen.

I appreciated any time I had with Taj. He sometimes waited for my return from Aalia's to share dinner and talk about our day before the evening music festivities. On occasion, we'd meet for chai or shop in the nearby bazaar.

> I cherished the silence and camaraderie of like-minded people.

Ricardo and Krista teased us. One time, Ricardo said, "I think he's in love with you." He pinched Taj's side and winked.

I also went to Sarnath to experience a ten-day residential Vipassana retreat, with a former Theravada Buddhist monk and insight meditation teacher at the Thai Buddhist Center, which further ignited my passion for Buddhism. Each day began with an early morning meditation, followed by breakfast, morning meditations, lunch, afternoon meditations, light dinner, evening meditation, and the Dharma talk—inspirational lectures to encourage one to practice mindfulness.

I cherished the silence and camaraderie of like-minded people, the *sangha*, and was intrigued by the Buddhist attitude of mind—that I was my own master and that universal truths were not the monopoly of anyone. I listened attentively to the sermons on Buddhist principles such as the Four Noble Truths (suffering, the origin of suffering, the end of suffering, and the truth of the path that leads to the end of suffering); the Noble Eightfold Path; and the doctrine of No-Soul, or *anatta*. I paid attention to my breathing. And I bought several books at the end of the retreat, eager to learn more.

Back in Varanasi, Taj's following grew, and it felt as if half of the Western population of Varanasi ended up at our house at one time or another. I joked, "That swinging door will let the monkeys in." I started to wish for quiet days.

One time I retreated to the roof to meditate. When I opened my eyes, a big fat lizard sat watching me. Thankfully, it wasn't a snake.

Aalia, Chaaru, and Esha matured in their awareness of Western culture. They asked lots of questions: "Is it true you clean your own toilets? How do you sit in a chair for so long? Why do you not have a nap in the afternoon? Why do you not haggle over prices? Why are there no open marketplaces? Do I have to wear closed-toe shoes? Will I have to wear a coat? Where are the Hindu temples?"

The answers were almost always difficult to explain. "There is no caste system in America, and usually everyone tidies their own homes or if you are wealthy enough, pay for a cleaning service. Sitting in chairs is common practice; you'll get used to it. Prices are mostly fixed for convenience and economic common sense. In the winter, you'll want to keep your feet warm. Let me tell you about winter."

Besides teaching cultural dissimilarities, we also conversed about possible social gatherings such as cocktail parties, after-work drinks at a bar, work-related picnics, the-boss-over-for-dinner kind of thing.

Perplexed, they replied, "Why do people drink alcohol? Don't they know it's bad? Why would anyone want to go to a place that serves alcoholic beverages? Those places are immoral."

I'd respond, "Many people do not believe that alcohol is evil. How are you going to engage in a conversation if your new husband takes you to his supervisor's home for dinner and they serve wine?"

At first, they all wanted to leave the house, or at the very least, tell their hosts about the wickedness of alcohol. Over time, they developed some comprehension, but they adamantly stood by their strong Brahmin faith, and I gave up trying.

"Okay. I get it. It's all right. Don't worry. Let's talk about how to set the table." I feared their upcoming immersion would be as toxic as the train toilet holes that emptied directly onto the tracks below.

At the end of each week, an envelope with my name on it contained a generous wage of several rupee notes. I'd splurge with lunch at one of my favorite street vendors or buy a bar of white soap. Life was good.

The music lessons continued, and I made some progress, especially with an awareness of *ragas,* which helped every time Taj's band played with any local performers. During this time, I made several new friends: Maggie and Rachel from England studying the Indian culture; Julia from New York completing her master's degree in social work; and Michael from California, a former Rajneesh follower. These friends had no connection to Taj, and as the lovely winter season ended and the hot temperatures returned, those friendships became even more precious to me.

As spring approached, the house was often full of people—day and night. The main living room reeked of pot. Dirty dishes were left piled up in the small kitchen area. Grubby travelers slept in the courtyard. The floor had sticky spots from spilled drinks, which attracted a line of ants. My home began to feel like a fleabag hotel.

> **It all began to ruin my sense of harmony.**

Taj craved the big crowds and joined them in smoking a lot of pot and other drugs, too. When I kissed him, his mouth smelled of tobacco, betel, or the thick, heavy scent of cannabis. When he came to bed, his feet were dirty, reeking of sweat.

It all began to ruin my sense of harmony. I started to long for solitude and quiet moments.

I still cared for Taj, probably too much, but our times together were becoming unpredictable because of his obsession with his music. He spent more and more time with his band and studied at the university, delving deeper into music composition. He stayed up late, sometimes until the gray light of dawn, climbing into bed as I awoke to practice early morning meditation.

Our rhythm changed.

One late afternoon, I returned from my teaching lesson at Aalia's and heard Taj's laugh in the main living area. I smiled, amazed his laugh still had the power to make my stomach do that somersault thing. I opened the door, eager to maybe have some alone time with him.

An attractive brunette sat close to him, smoking a joint. Their knees touched.

An unsettling heaviness crept into my chest. "Really, Taj?"

He didn't say a word.

I closed the door and went to my room.

Later that evening, he said, "No big deal."

But it *was* a big deal. I couldn't trust him, and I began to think he would always want a lot of women in his life—unlike me, who just wanted a single partner.

I talked to my friends.

Maggie retorted, "Geez, I don't know what you see in him. Ditch him. You deserve someone better. You should find your own place. Get out of that dump."

Her words stung. It was hard to convince my heart. I thought she might persuade me to stay. "Probably finding a new place to live would be a good idea, for now at least. Got any leads?"

I tried to muster some courage to leave. I told myself I'd find a home but still stay connected to Taj and the band.

Rachel chimed in. "I bet you could ask Bondi. He knows everybody around here and is well connected. He helped me find my apartment on the outskirts, about a quarter-mile after the last *ghat*."

37 Varanasi – January-March 1979

Bondi—American by birth but now thoroughly Indian—bobbled his head from side to side and chewed on his *betel*. I knew he was probably making a killing buying up cheap Indian land and building these recent housing developments.

But he had just the place. A one-bedroom concrete duplex-of-sorts just became vacant. A couple from France rented the adjacent space, and two Indian families lived in the north and south apartments.

Not far from the last *ghat*, a narrow alley led to a labyrinth of muddy streets, intersections, marigold fields, and water buffalo pastures. The concrete duplex apartment and the walls surrounding the place had metal spikes on top. The big front door opened into a small courtyard with a central water faucet.

> I zipped my heart back up and pushed thoughts of Taj into the Ganges River.

Two rooms in the back had glass-less windows with shutters to let in the morning sun and a tiny latrine. Everything had been white-washed and cleaned.

I looked at the big, open sky overhead. "This will be great, Bondi. Thanks."

"Taj, I'm moving out. Bondi found me a place about a mile from here." I crossed my arms. "I need different things right now."

I struggled to sound cheerful, pretending that everything would work out.

Taj shrugged and turned away, feigning interest in a book. He tapped his foot and clenched his jaw. I could tell he felt slighted, but he didn't say anything.

When he looked up, his eyes glistened with emotion, and I almost lost my resolve. My heart hammered, and I dug my nails into my palms to help keep my face from trembling. Taj put the book down and left without looking back.

He wasn't around when my friends helped move my sparse belongings: a bed platform, a few blankets, a straw mat, cushions, cooking utensils, the tanpura and harmonium, and two canvas traveling bags holding my clothes and books.

I set up house again, laughed, and joked with my friends. The French couple came over. They did not speak any English, so I reverted to my Quebecois French. We struck up a casual friendship.

I zipped my heart back up and pushed thoughts of Taj into the Ganges River.

But memories visited me in the middle of the night, much the same way gnats might buzz around my head. I calmed my heart by foolishly pretending that everything would work out—that Taj would come to his senses and choose me over anything else: his music, his growing fan base, himself.

Whether from the effort of moving or stowing my emotions into never-never land, I woke up often nauseous and feverish. My appetite vanished like a pickpocket on the Varanasi streets.

The doctor at the community clinic, a round Indian man with a wide grin, said in a big, booming voice, "Congratulations! You're pregnant!"

I stared at him for a long time, not saying a word, and then left.

I gawked at the orange and ruby horizon while I walked back to my haven, numb to the begging children and the street vendors trying to catch my attention, as if everything was just a dream.

38

Afghanistan – March 1977

It seemed surreal I would travel up and over this larger-than-life representation of world travel.

After a long bus ride, we arrived in Kabul late in the day and found a flea-infested hovel near the bus depot with bedbugs the size of a dime. I had several large, red welts from the bites.

Disgusted, we left early the next morning to find better lodging. A traveler recommended an inn closer to the city's marketplace, clean and well-kept. We deposited our bags and left to explore the city.

Raisins, apricots, and pistachios sold in paper cones lined a street vendor's cart. Johan and I bought two and munched the yummy treats on our way to the Kabul River, through a maze of crooked alleys: above, the vast sky and a pale moon; below, houses made of mud, tottering donkey carts, bicyclists, women cloaked in *burqas*, and men in Bedouin Arab scarves. In between passageways, I noticed homes built into the terra cotta hills creating a craggy splendor.

> I soaked up the rich, loamy pulse of a way of life so different from my past.

The warm spring sun beat down on my back, and my jeans clung to my thighs like a python. I turned to Johan. "I'm going to the open bazaar and see if I can find some different clothing. Want to come?"

Johan shrugged his shoulders. "Sure."

He gave me that puppy-dog look again. Our platonic relationship suited me just fine. I had no romantic feelings for him. I more than appreciated the camaraderie, but that was it. Earlier I had told him, "Once we get to India, I'll be heading to Nepal—on my own."

Besides, Johan had no interest in hiking the Himalayas and wanted to "get somewhere warm to paint." Looking at him, though, I began to wonder if I needed to have another talk with him.

A tangled web of slender streets led us to the Kabul open market—a network of shops selling exquisite rugs, finely woven clothing, embroidered shawls, and mouth-watering fried foods. I talked with shop owners, tried on embellished dresses, sipped on the ever-refillable cup of tea, and politely refused puffs from the hookah—soaking up the rich, loamy pulse of a way of life so different from my past.

I bought a coffee-colored shirt with stunning needlecraft on the front yoke. It felt as soft as a bunny's fur. Later, I found pants made from the same material, slightly long in the leg, as comfy as pajama bottoms, relishing wearing something loose and light. Feeling fresh and new, I convinced Johan to go out at night, searching for food and company.

On the way back to our much-improved inn, I mentioned to Johan, "I love this place. This land and her people are wonderful."

It did not take long to get a visa for Pakistan, and we booked tickets for the bus ride over the Khyber Pass into Lahore, Pakistan.

> **Tinges of regret surfaced.**

I heard many stories about the Khyber Pass: a massive project taking years to complete; an unforgettable zigzag ride up the mountain; so steep it'll make you sick; a titanic achievement; and "a picture cannot do it justice."

38 Afghanistan – March 1977

It seemed surreal I would travel up and over this larger-than-life representation of world travel—at least it felt that way.

When we got off the vehicle to take in the view at the pass, disappointment tugged at my heart. The distant Hindu Kush mountain range was far more moving than the colossal human road construction separating Afghanistan and Pakistan.

Tinges of regret surfaced. I wished I could've traveled back to Kabul and up into those beautiful mountains.

A few years later, I learned of the Soviet invasion and felt such profound tenderness for this country it hurt.

More years later, in a quaint coffee shop, I overheard someone discuss the Taliban blowing up the Bamiyan Buddha statues, and my insides collapsed. After 9/11, I wondered if anyone would see the Afghanistan of my youth, a magnificently proud and beautiful country—a powerful, energetic force not easily tamed or conquered.

That is the Afghanistan I remember.

The pendulum swung in the opposite direction in Lahore. The congested streets and unbearable smell of garbage, shit, fried oil, and human sweat clogged my nostrils; people everywhere, a bedlam of motion and hurry. Pools of sweat dripped off my forehead.

"Let's get out of here. I'd rather sleep on the train than stay here."

Johan did not seem as bothered. Perhaps I just missed Afghanistan.

On the train, I watched the Pakistani scenery: trees, villages, gray rivers, a farmer using oxen to till a field.

India loomed ahead.

39

Varanasi – April-May 1979

Worry knocked at my door, and I let her in.

Taj's crease in the middle of his forehead tightened. He looked at the ground. "What do you mean?" He pulled his hair back from his face and looked for a piece of cord.

"I'm not going to keep it if that's what you are worried about. I'll have an abortion right away." My breath quickened, waiting for the uncomfortable moment to pass.

Taj kept his gaze on the floor. "Abortion? Are you sure?"

"Do we have any choice?'

He exhaled noisily. "Shanti, there are always choices."

"What, you think you are ready for a child? I don't think so."

Taj nodded. He took a minute or more and said, "Okay. I'll go with you. When did this happen?"

"I don't know, Taj. The doctor said the IUD slipped, but I think he never put it in correctly. I'm sorry."

Why did I say I was sorry?

My thoughts kept jumbling into one another like a car crash. I wanted this to be over. The late afternoon sun was as hot as the underground pit ovens. I felt like one of those *chapattis* stuck against the blazing walls.

I came back in the evening to listen to the band and talk with friends, trying to quiet my overactive mind. Worry knocked at my door, and I let her in, along with a dozen other friends: undecided, awkward, concerned, distressed, apprehensive, restless, fearful.

I chewed on my fingernails and couldn't eat.

"Shanti, what's up with you and Taj?" Ricardo gazed at Taj.

I clutched my hands. "What do you mean?"

Ricardo put down his cup. "Well, Taj seemed troubled at dinner. He didn't eat much. I think he wasn't happy that you moved out." He turned to face me. "You know Taj has a hard time expressing his *amour* sometimes."

> You don't look good.

I looked over at Taj, who appeared so aloof, relaxed, distant. His skill at avoiding me was close to genius.

Amour? Love? Really?

I watched him interact with the people gathered to play and compose. He laughed lightly, and when he turned his head, the candlelight created a soft halo around his face. He appeared to have an easy enough time sharing his *amour* with everyone else.

I swallowed my words and let the comebacks dance on my tongue.

The next day, Aalia noticed. "Ms. Shanti, everything all right? You don't look good."

I lied. "Oh, yes, everything is okay. I'm just sad that our time together will be ending soon. You will be leaving for Switzerland, yes?"

Aalia brightened. "Yes. Very soon."

She believed me. I fibbed to everyone and devoured any thought of keeping the child.

During my music lessons, I fidgeted with my sari instead of listening to Baba-ji. He detected something was wrong.

"No learn, Ms. Shanti?" He struggled with his meager English, the words slow and accentuated.

My cheeks felt hot. "I don't know. Maybe it's time for a break?"

39 Varanasi – April-May 1979

His quiet eyes gazed into mine, but I could not hold his stare and dropped my eyes to the ground. Baba-ji talked for a few minutes in his own language. I didn't try to offer any other excuse. I had let him down. My heart felt like lead.

When Baba-ji left, he looked over his shoulder, opened his mouth for a moment, and then closed it. I watched him leave, his silhouette and the wide, trackless sky behind him blurring in a never-ending blue.

I never studied with him again.

Taj arrived late at the community health clinic. He kept pushing his hair back behind his ears and swallowing and squeezed my hand as the nurse led me into a sterilized room, the walls pea-green and bare. He seemed distracted—as if he'd rather be somewhere else.

I wanted to shout, "Somebody help me. I don't know what to do. I'm scared." Instead, I stuffed those words deep down in my guts. Everything was moving too quickly for me to process. Images of what-could-be flashed through my mind. My heartbeat raced so fast I got dizzy.

While Taj stayed in the waiting room, the doctor explained the procedure. "I will insert an instrument through your cervix to remove the fetus by using a suction device. This will not take long. Just relax."

Relax...how can I relax?

I feigned bravery, hoping it would turn real. I concentrated on my breathing and wrestled a thousand thoughts. Buddhists did not kill any living thing. Abortion was frowned upon.

I was a bad person...

Did Taj really love me? Did he ever love me?

I felt so alone. Would I always be alone? Was this my fault?

More than anything, I did not want to bring a child into the world without a mother and father who would truly be there for him or her. It felt I was only a breath away from that myself.

I wanted a real marriage. I did not want to raise a child on my own. I did not have any money.

What was I doing? Was I making a mistake?

I drove myself crazy with self-doubt, my breathing shallow one minute, fast the next. The cold metal against my insides hurt. A sting spread through my chest, like glass smashing against the hard concrete.

Letting out a deep moan, I counted my breaths, breathing in, breathing out.

The doctor rubbed my arm. "It's no good. Your cervix opening is too small for any of our instruments. I used the smallest one we have. I will give you the name of a specialist. She can help you, yes?" He bobbled his head from side to side as if to assure me everything would be okay.

A nurse pointed to a small dressing room. Tears flowed down my face like a waterfall.

I didn't believe everything would be okay—in fact, just the opposite.

Misery clung to my guts, black as tar.

When I saw Taj sitting on that hard chair waiting for me, I felt the dam of trying so hard to be brave explode, and I burst into a torrent of sobs.

Taj's foot moved up and down, and he kept crossing and uncrossing his arms, tugging at his hair and twisting his mouth. The other women in the room, waiting their turn to be emptied into the void, stared.

Taj jumped up and began to shush me. "Shanti. Stop. Just sit here." He took my arm and led me to a firm chair. "Sit down. What are you doing?" Looking around the room, he smiled at the Hindi women as if to reassure them he would take care of this hysterical woman.

The women's eyes followed us. They continued to gawk, waiting to see what might happen. Good Indian women do not show their emotions in public. It's disgraceful.

But I couldn't stop. I lowered my head into my lap and cried, soaking my sari.

I wanted to scream, "This is wrong! Something's not right! What's wrong with me?" Instead, I muffled my howls into my wet sari. My throat throbbed and swelled like an ocean eddy whooshing against the gray rocks.

Taj went outside the clinic to hang around until I "felt better." When I went out later, I found him chatting with a few people. He was laughing.

Laughing? Really?

He spun around when he saw me. "Ready?"

The indifference burned. "I think I want to walk home." Suddenly, I hated his laugh. I didn't want to be around him. I didn't want him to touch me. "Alone."

He smoothed a fresh growth of hair on his face with his fingers and tried to take my arm. I moved out of his reach and turned away. Silence, thorny like an unruly rose vine, followed.

"Okay," he said.

Even though I hated him at that moment, I also hoped he would suddenly morph into a knight in shining armor, pick me up, and whisper that everything would be all right, that he'd take care of me and save me from my mounting despair.

But he didn't.

I watched him hail a rickshaw and leave. He did not look back.

I don't know how I made it through the overcrowded Varanasi streets. My heart seemed to be disintegrating into a million pieces. Everything appeared vague and faraway, as if I was sleepwalking.

A small pocket of relief swept over me when I unlocked the gate and walked into my small, concrete apartment. I lay on my bed and curled around a silky blanket, rocking back and forth like a child until I fell asleep.

I woke in the middle of the night, my mouth dry and bitter. A hundred questions snapped at my ankles.

What am I going to do now? Go to the specialist?

Time was important here. I could not wait.

Should I return to Canada? How? I did not have any money.

Should I tell anyone?

I wore myself out thinking, thinking, thinking—my thoughts heavy, weighted down with uncertainty.

Late in the morning, I felt as if someone had cut out my tongue. The sea between Taj and me had grown into mythical proportions. My head, fuzzy as cotton candy, floated in a river of no return. A few foggy days passed. I mostly slept, unable to find the energy to get out of bed.

Maggie banged on the door. "Shanti, Shanti. Where have you been? What's up with you? Lunch? C'mon, open up."

I unbolted the door and collected my thoughts. "Hey, Maggie. Nice to see you. I haven't been feeling very good."

She plopped herself down on my bed and looked around—clothes in a heap, dirty dishes. "You must be not feeling well. Your place is a mess." She knew I preferred order and cleanliness.

> **I lay on my concrete bedroom floor and felt only days hemorrhage out of me.**

I changed the subject. "Maggie, do you know of any herb doctors, Indian folk medicine women around here?"

She suffered from a skin condition and had sought out natural remedies that had apparently worked. "Sure. What do you need?" Her smile was innocent and unsuspecting.

"Having some stomach issues." Another untruth.

"Come, we'll take a rickshaw. I'll take you to his shop."

Once there, Maggie waited in the street.

I went in and talked to the witch doctor. "I need medicine to get rid of this pregnancy."

He gave me a small bottle of a rank-smelling liquid, dark and murky. "This will do it, Ma'am Sahib, for sure."

I hoped he was right. He wasn't. The potion made me vomit, vomit, vomit until nothing was left inside except the unborn. I lay on my concrete bedroom floor and felt only days hemorrhage out of me.

Two weeks went by.

I received a letter from Mudita.

> *"I am not returning to India. I met someone! We get along fabulously. He works as a carpenter, and guess what? He's going to build a house for us! Yes, a house. I want to add an outside shower and plant grapes around the perimeter, maybe some stained glass on our front door. Oh, Shanti, everything is wonderful..."*

She wrote five pages about her newfound happiness. I let the sheets of paper float to the floor like leaves in autumn.

I continued to teach Aalia, Esha, and Chaaru, but my enthusiasm waned. I was glad the teaching assignment neared its natural close. The girls were leaving for the West. They were giddy with excitement.

"Best wishes for everything good to unfold for each of you." I clasped their hands. "Namaste. Namaste. Write a postcard when you get there."

Esha hugged me tightly. "Thank you."

It was as if she knew.

The specialist, a tender middle-aged woman, listened while I explained my predicament. She urged me to keep the child. "Your pregnancy is far along now. Abortion would be painful and possibly harmful to you."

I let out a long sigh. "Thank you for your concern, but I know what I must do. When can you schedule me in?"

She looked at her calendar. "Next week. Here." She positioned her finger on the date.

"Okay, I'll be there."

I didn't tell Taj. I didn't speak to anyone. I barricaded myself in my small apartment and watched the clock.

Misery took on a new dimension; lonely as an island, dark blue turning black, the color of the ocean before a drop-off—a mixture of repugnance and fear freezing my ability to think clearly. I lost track of time while uncontrolled tears slid down my cheeks and onto my trembling lips.

A nurse led the way toward a small cubicle where I changed into a hospital gown for the procedure. Afterward, she escorted me to the operating room. The kind doctor grasped my hand and said, "Don't worry. Everything will be fine now."

> **Everything went dark.**

I counted my breaths as she performed the procedure, explaining as she went along.

"...dilation of the cervix, you'll feel something cold, hmmm, okay, relax, dilating the cervix again, hmmm, okay, relax, take some deep breaths, dilating the cervix..."

Each time I felt my internal organs shrivel and complain, the pain like a severe paper cut or banging my elbow against a steel edge.

The doctor stopped and looked over at me. "We're going to put you out, okay. Your cervix will not open, and I'll have to use force which will be very painful. Relax. Everything will be all right."

I started to cry. "Okay."

Everything went dark.

When I woke, the nurse said, "The doctor will speak with you shortly."

I dropped my shoulders, releasing tight knots of tension I did not know I was carrying. *Okay, it's over.*

But it wasn't.

"Your cervix would not dilate, and we have no other tools here in India to help you. You must go back to your country now or have a hysterotomy. You are too far along now to consider anything else."

Her words sounded nonsensical, as if she might be speaking a foreign language.

She continued, "If you choose the hysterotomy, you will have to wait until there is an opening in my schedule, and you will need time to get ready. You understand?"

I nodded. I did not understand at all.

I wished I could time-travel, like Spock, in *Star Trek*.

A hysterotomy abortion was comparable to a cesarean section performed under general anesthesia. The doctor cautioned against such a procedure. "We have limited tools here in India, and I worry about you being without your family. You must have someone, surely?"

Family...what is family?

I lied; a common practice, it seemed. "Yes, I can find someone to help me."

An eerie calm spidered into my heart, the web bushy and noxious.

What did she mean by someone to help? Help with what?

I mulled over her words and realized she was right. Even if I could return to the West, it would be too late. I had to do this. Now. We scheduled the operation.

After leaving the clinic, I walked to Taj's place. I wanted to let him know and ask if he could be there for me. The unlocked front gate probably meant Taj was home. I climbed the stairs and heard a door open.

Taj and a lovely young woman ambled toward the top of the stairs. He stopped.

"Shanti."

His eyes darted back and forth between the lady in question and me. He opened his mouth as if to say something but furrowed his brow instead.

The woman's sweet eyes followed Taj's every move. She reminded me of someone.

"Taj. Sorry to interrupt. Can we talk?"

"Not now, Shanti. We're meeting Ricardo and Krista for a recital. Later?" He began to meander down the stairs. The woman trailed behind, identical to a well-trained dog.

I let them pass and watched as they left through the gateway. The voice inside me went still. I couldn't even muster a whisper. An eerie calm spidered into my heart, the web bushy and noxious.

I went to the hospital alone. Floated would be a better word. I hadn't talked to anyone since I went mute, hushed like the early morning quiet on the Ganges.

The cotton gown, stiff from airing in the sun, brushed against my skin, and a chlorine smell burned the inside of my nose. I willed myself to take deep breaths, counting to ten and back again.

The operating room had bright lights and although antiquated in comparison to Western hospitals, it was clean and uncluttered. That reassured me somehow.

The gentle-voiced doctor held my hand. "Close your eyes and go somewhere peaceful in your mind." She smiled. "You have someone, yes, for after?"

I nodded and conjured up the beach in Goa, the soothing sounds of the ocean waves splashing on the white sand.

I woke in a room with a dozen other beds occupied by Indian women. Families filled the empty spaces. A fan swirled above, circulating the sour air. My bed, next to a barred window, allowed a view of an outside patio. A few people sat on the ground and chatted.

I did not recognize anyone. The people spoke in hushed Hindi. Deep, resonant moans escaped my lips. I felt glued to the plastic mattress. The fire of hurt increased with each breath, torturing my capacity for endurance.

Once, when I worked for the national parks and spent the night out in a ranger cabin, I woke in the middle of the night to the sound of whimpering and shone a flashlight on a little mouse caught in a spring trap. Compassion flooded my heart, and I released her from her agony.

The next morning, my fellow workers chided my foolishness. One of the workers said, "What's one mouse? God, do you want mouse poop in your oatmeal?"

But that mouse's eyes looking back at me touched the spongy center of my being, and for a moment, I thought we were the same, that mouse and me. I couldn't explain it then.

In those first moments, waking up to my inferno, I remembered that mouse and wished someone could release me from my torment.

WHERE IS HER HELP?

My tongue lay swollen in my parched mouth. My insides smoldered. My hot, blistered nerves pounded and stung. I had to pee so bad and couldn't. I tried to call out to someone, but no words left my lips, only little, spontaneous sobs.

I wanted to move. Nothing worked. My head hammered. Nausea overtook my senses. My body stung with the sensation of pins and needles. The pain pulsated and throbbed. A thunderclap of dizziness left my neck stiff. Flashes of light came and went. Swallowing took great effort.

My skin became clammy, and I still could not pee. I just wanted to pee.

In the middle of the night, somewhere close to dawn, my bladder let loose, and I urinated all over myself. The momentary respite from the constant pain sent a wave of happiness through me.

And then the burning started again.

I moaned and fainted.

"What's this? WHAT?" The mellow doctor was not using her inside voice. "WHERE IS HER HELP?" She yelled a series of commands in Hindi.

I tried to open my mouth, but nothing came out.

Two hospital aides took off my clothes and wrapped me in a warm sheet. The doctor took my hand, "Shanti, where is your help?"

I tried to tell her I didn't really have anyone, but the best I could do was sigh. Tears collected in the corners of my eyes, then trickled over like miniature streams.

She shouted to a young woman, possibly a medical student, standing next to her. "Go to the pharmacy and get these medicines. Tell the pharmacist I need these things immediately! Now go."

A short time later, someone raised my head and made me swallow two pills. They had a hard time going down. I had to chew them; the taste was as bitter as juniper berries.

A few moments later, I fell blissfully asleep.

I must have slept for a full day because it was the next morning when I opened my eyes.

Liza, the French woman from the apartment next door, sat next to my bed. She spoke in French.

"Shanti, someone came to your apartment to see if anyone could help you. I volunteered. Can you pick up your head? The doctor wants you to swallow these tablets."

39 Varanasi – April-May 1979

I nodded, and she put her small hand under my neck, her other arm beneath my back for support. I swallowed the tablets and a full glass of water. The cool liquid soothed my dry, cracked lips.

In the afternoon, I heard the doctor's confident voice. "Liza, time to get her up on her feet."

I opened my eyes. "No, no. Too much pain."

The doctor shook her head. "Yes, your abdomen is tender and sore. But best practice is to get up and walk. Liza will help you."

She gave Liza instructions. "She must move. Get her up and going, first in the room and then in the courtyard. Several times a day. Up and down. She will get well quickly. Make sure she takes her medicine."

I thought I'd pass out, trying to get my legs to the floor. The doctor would not leave until I had stood up. I held on to Liza with one hand and clutched the bed frame with the other, breathing in and out, ten times and then back again.

The doctor smiled. "Yes, good, good. Now, take small steps and straighten your back."

I winced and took long inhalations with each attempt to go from a slouched position to being upright. It hurt a lot, but not as much as the night before.

With Liza's help, I walked and went outside for a bit and looked at the sky.

A soft breeze loosened the matted hairs on my neck. An early morning rain had fallen. Sugar pink roses released a sweet, delicate scent. Several families sat on woven mats visiting their loved ones. A young girl ate a ripe golden mango, the thick juice dribbling down her chin.

I looked over at Liza. "Thank you."

I wanted to say more, but my words got stuck in my eyes.

40

India – April 1977

*At that moment, though,
my whole life lay in front of me...*

A group of about fifteen western travelers waited in line to go through Indian customs in Wagah, the border crossing between Lahore, Pakistan, and Amritsar, India. I could tell it would take a long time.

The chief officer, a woman in a bright crimson sari, showed no evidence of weakening to the flirtation from the men or cute smiles from the women. She took her job seriously, painstakingly going through each and every luggage item.

The American man in front of me started to complain. "What are you doing? You don't have to unwrap that. It's a gift. Oh, for God's sake. This is gonna take all afternoon. I need to catch a train from Amritsar."

His comments only seemed to fuel the official's need to be scrupulous in her search. I took mental notes. When my turn came, I did not smile and only talked when asked a question. I willed myself to breathe long, full inhalations and exhalations. I didn't have anything to hide.

She asked, "Where are you going? Why are you here? When will you go home? Do you have any drugs? How will you return to your country?"

I answered, "I'm going to Nepal to trek in the Himalayas. I need to go to New Delhi first to get a Nepalese visa. After that, I plan on touring India for a bit. I'll most likely fly out of India. I'm not sure yet if I'll continue through southeast Asia. It will depend on my time in Nepal. Right now, I should only be in India for a few weeks, and I hope to take a train and then a bus into Nepal."

I bit the inside of my cheek to keep my smile in check.

She took my passport and stamped it.

I could stay in India as long as I needed to.

I waited for Johan under a huge hibiscus tree, the blooms bright red and fresh from a recent rain. Underneath, the newly mowed grass released a clean, green scent. Several monkeys swung in the branches, screeching and chattering. I lay down on the smooth earth and listened to the sounds of India: a bicycle bell, the coo of pigeons, a bus horn.

How long had I dreamed of being here? A rigidity in my chest loosened, and I sighed. A light wind touched my damp skin, the air pleasantly humid and warm.

I dozed and let Mother India into my heart.

After an awfully long time, Johan came out. "Now that was an ordeal."

> **It all looked and smelled distinctly different from the Middle East.**

Some American travelers joined us under the tree. They embellished each other's stories.

"Ah, that was terrible. I thought she was going to strip-search me. I'm not coming through that border again. What did she think we were? Drug dealers? Did we miss the bus to Amritsar?

Where are you staying? It's hot here. I need some new clothes. Man, I could use a joint. Let's get out of here."

A man with dark curly hair said to me, "Hey, I admire your patience. Wish I could've been more like you in there. It would've helped."

"Thanks," I whispered.

We walked to the transport depot and boarded a badly-maintained bus to Amritsar's city center searching for lodging and food.

Amritsar, the capital city of Punjab State and home to Sikhs, bustled with activity. We passed several gold-domed mosques.

Someone on the bus pointed. "Look. That's the Harmandir Sahib—the Golden Temple. Spectacular, no?"

I strained my neck to get a better view. "Should we spend a day here and tour the city?"

Johan leaned on his pack. "Good idea. Yes, let's do that before we head to Delhi."

The bus snaked past men in white turbans, women wearing long, flowing tunics over pajama pants, maimed beggars in the street, bicycle rickshaws, cows, camels, outdoor street vendors selling fried foods. It all looked and smelled distinctly different from the Middle East.

I was anxious to be on my own again.

"This is so cool. I can't believe I'm here—what a journey. I don't think I'd ever do the overland trip again. You?" I peered over at Johan.

He let out a long exhale. "I dunno. Right now, I'm hot, thirsty, and tired. Let's stay at the same hotel these Americans are going to. It'll be easier than trying to find something on our own."

I shrugged. "That's fine. Do you think the water is okay to drink?"

"No. We'll have to be careful about that. Otherwise, you'll end up with a bad case of dysentery—which is no fun." He laughed.

I suddenly felt a tenderness for Johan and gratitude for all he had done for me. "Hey, I'll miss you when we have to part ways in New Delhi. You've been a good friend. Thanks." I squeezed his shoulder.

He looked me in the eye. "What do you mean?"

"Well, you are headed to South India, right? And I'm off to Nepal. Aren't you on contract to paint for the museum?" I wanted to be polite, but the truth be told, I was anxious to be on my own again. I hoped to discover things for myself. I thought our travels together were for convenience, security, shelter from the Middle East.

Now that we were in India, I did not feel I needed any protection. I added, "I'm looking forward to being on my own."

Johan's mouth formed a thin line, and he stared out the window.

We walked the crowded streets and admired the unique architecture.

It was hot. Really hot. The sickly air threatened to glue my jeans to my legs. Even the thick cotton bottoms I bought in Kabul seemed too warm.

"I've got to find much cooler clothing. This sucks." I wiped the sweat off my face. "And it's only April." I spotted a road merchant selling cold sodas in glass bottles. "Oh, yes. That's what I need."

The soda seller asked, "Ma'am Sahib, ice?"

I gladly accepted some ice and drank up. The chill was sweet and pleasant.

40 India – April 1977

I talked to Johan. "You know, I'm ready to leave for Delhi whenever you are. I know there are probably a lot of things to see here, but I'm itching to get to Nepal."

He agreed, and we traveled back to our hotel via the train station to secure tickets for the next day.

The first morning in New Delhi, I bought new clothes—similar to what I had seen the women wear in Amritsar—at a large open market near the city's center and close to our inn.

In the afternoon, I slipped on the fresh, super-light cotton Indian clothes, sapphire plastic flip-flops, and braided my hair.

The walk to the Nepal Embassy took me through a novelty of narrow streets; wholesale bazaars promoting bright-colored saris, bins of plastic shoes, baskets of beads, and cloth. Men sewed at old-fashioned black sewing machines, the needle going up and down. Women fried chilies and flatbread in hot oil, the smell of curry and cinnamon heavy in the air.

I bought a *samosa*—it was delicious. The spice made me thirsty, and I paid a few pennies for a cold drink with ice.

At the embassy, a Nepali woman said, "Your visa will be ready in two days." She spoke English accentuating the "o" and raising the pitch at the end of her sentences as if asking a question.

I almost skipped back to the hotel, excited about everything. I felt confident things would only get better and better.

I'd be rich. I'd be famous. I'd be happy. *Que sera, sera.*

The next day I had a visitor—dysentery.

I picked up my Nepalese visa but still had the runs and stomach trouble. "I'm taking the train to Rishikesh for a few days. Maybe the cooler weather will help. I think I can catch a train from there to Gorakhpur."

Quieter than usual, Johan replied, "Mind if I head up there with you? I want to see Rishikesh, too. Maybe I'll stay there. Who knows?"

I tilted my head a little. "You sure? I'll be fine if you want to get going to Kerala."

"No, no. It's all good." He lifted his eyes and blew the hair off his forehead.

We stayed at a more modern lodge near the ashram area. I spent a few days recovering: boiled water for everything, peeled the fruits and vegetables we bought in the market, walked, and did a lazy man's version of yoga.

Johan became needy. I resented his questions. "How are you feeling? When are you leaving? What can I get you?"

> **It's not you; it's me.**
> **I just want to be friends.**

"Johan, I'm leaving for Nepal tomorrow." I paused. "By myself."

He sighed. "Are you sure? I can come with you—just until you get your trek visa and are feeling better. It'd be nice to see Katmandu."

"No. I'm good. You've done a lot for me already."

His eyes drooped, and he curled his upper lip.

"It's better this way, Johan. Thanks for everything. It's not you; it's me. I just want to be friends." I wanted to take the words back immediately. They sounded so trite.

Johan stared down at his empty hands.

At the train station, Johan bought a ticket returning to New Delhi. "Not sure where I'll end up. Maybe I'll go south. Maybe back to Holland."

"What about your painting?" I asked.

"Oh, I can do that anywhere." He lifted his bags.

"Well...goodbye. Best of luck." I didn't want to offer hope that we'd meet up again or get together in the way he had wished for, so I left it at that, put on my pack, and walked to my train car without looking back.

I never did see him again.

At that moment, though, my whole life lay in front of me, and I wanted to devour everything in my path: adventure; cultural immersion; ethnic foods; to be wild and crazy sometimes; to leap at the unexpected; to experience the surreal and the mystical; and of course, to fall in love.

For all of it to pierce my world deeply and profoundly.

To wake up to each and every possibility.

To be alive.

To live.

41

India – June-July 1979

*And then, in a moment of painful clarity,
I knew it was over, just as if a door had swung
open and I could see the outside for the first
time, the full blue sky shocking my senses.*

"In India, family care for family when they are in hospital or need medical attention. They go to pharmacy and pay for medicines the doctor orders. We do not have the kind of nursing you have in your country. I did my doctor residency in England, so I know first-hand. When I asked you if you had help and you said yes, I thought you knew. Besides, didn't you say you have lived in this country for over two years, yes? Your recovery was too painful. Sorry for that."

The doctor examined my stitches and felt my abdomen. "Everything is healing up nicely. How are you feeling?"

I sat up and adjusted my sari. "It's been okay. For the past week, I have just stayed at home. Liza has been going to the market and buying what I need. I'm feeling better and not as sore. I'm bleeding a lot, though."

"Yes, this is normal. Keep that bandage on your scar and rub this ointment on it twice a day, once in the morning and before bed. This will protect you from infection, especially this time of year. The days are getting very hot." She handed me a jar of gooey yellow cream.

"Thank you for all you have done. I'm sorry I did not understand."

She shrugged. "Shanti, I suggest you consider going back to your country. Follow up with the good medical care you have there."

Home? Where was home?

"Do you not think I'll get well here?"

My bruised insides kept time with my breath.

"You are far away from your family, and you have been through quite a bit, both physically and emotionally. Think about it."

I nodded. "Okay, I will. Thanks."

I did think about it. And the more I thought about it, the more it felt right.

But I wasn't going to go home to my biological family in Quebec. That was not home.

I did not know where home was anymore.

I sat on my bed and wrote a long letter to a friend in Vancouver, asking for monies to help with an airline ticket and a little more. Nothing moved fast in India, and I calculated that I would be in India at least a month or two until the money arrived.

Many of the people I knew in Varanasi were leaving for cooler climates. Maggie and Rachel had rented a house in Mussoorie, a northern Himalayan hill station. Mussoorie was colonized in the eighteen-hundreds as a summer vacation spot for military personnel stationed at British armed forces forts and bases.

Maggie said, "The houses resemble Western bungalows with an indoor kitchen and bathroom. I'm renting a two-story on the ridge overlooking the Doon Valley. You should come."

> **I did not know where home was anymore.**

I told her, "I have to wait for my money to arrive by mail. But I would love to visit before I head back to Canada. Thanks. Generous of you, really."

She squeezed my hand. "Great. We'll wait for you."

I hadn't seen or been in touch with Taj or his band since that ominous day he stood at the top of the stairs and left with that young woman.

Feeling slightly better, I thought I should at least go to see him and let him know I'd be returning to Canada—maybe even patch up our differences, be friends at least.

When I got to his house, the door was locked, and no one answered when I shouted, "Hello! Taj! Anybody home?"

I walked to Carlos's place and found his wife, Stephanie, playing with their four-year-old daughter.

"Stephanie, hi. How have you been?"

Stephanie nodded. "Good. Good. Carlos and I leave for Paris next week. Haven't seen you around. Heard you and Taj had a falling-out. Nothing too serious, I hope. He gets quiet whenever Carlos or I ask about you."

I paused for a moment. "Well...it's complicated."

I replayed the last time I saw Taj over and over in my head, his silky new beard matching his ebony hair, the intensity of his gaze, his long legs and slender waist, the tender glimmer in his eyes. My eyes welled up.

Stephanie raised her eyebrows. "Heard a rumor you were in the hospital?"

How did she hear that?

"Yes, female issues. You know." I didn't want to talk about it. "So, Stephanie, where is Taj anyway? I went by his house, and the door had a padlock on it. Nobody seemed to be around."

"Everyone has gone to Mussoorie before they head back to Europe. Didn't he tell you?" Her eyebrows lifted slightly. "Would you care for some tea?"

The hot summer sunlight peeked through the trees. "No."

Suddenly, I wanted the chitchat with Stephanie to be over. I felt like someone had kicked me in the ribs. "Thanks for the tea invite. Maybe next time. Just remembered an appointment." I tried to construct a barrier of polite indifference. "Safe journey to Paris. Give my best to Carlos." I smiled at her daughter, who had stopped playing with her doll to look at me.

After Carlos and Stephanie left for Paris, Julia flew back home, and so did Michael. Maggie sent a postcard from Mussoorie.

The house is great and the view—wow! You'll love it here. Flowers in bloom. Quite a hike up the hill from town, but it's getting me in shape. Lost five pounds already. Hope you get your money soon. Rachel is leaving at the end of the month, but I'm staying. Might get a new roommate named Ella from Australia. See ya soon.

Liza and her boyfriend came to say goodbye. They were going home to southern France.

I held Liza in my arms for a while longer than she was comfortable with. "Thanks for everything. Hope to see you again." Although I sensed the chances were slim of that happening, I was still grateful for their kindness. *"Bonne chance."*

The chai shops emptied of Western tourists. The heat intensified. And still, the money did not come. The days were hot, oppressive—akin to being underwater and struggling for a breath.

An acquaintance, someone I met through the university, asked if I would check on her apartment while she, too, fled the heat. "Shanti, could you make sure everything is all right. I don't want anyone breaking in. I haven't left anything too valuable there, just books, clothes, furniture, those kinds of things. Here's the key. Feel free to spend time there."

The apartment, closer to shops and markets, became a pleasant stopping place for a shower in her full-size bathroom and to read under a big overhead fan. She had a comfy chair, too—all things I did not have.

One day the temperature reached 120 degrees. I poured water on her tiled living-room floor and lay in a tepid two-inch pool. The fan above spun around and around, providing some relief. Later, I opened one of her books, and maggots filled the center. They seemed to hate the light and scurried into the corners.

I, too, felt as if I was disintegrating, decomposing back into the earth. Each afternoon, I sought respite in that quaint little apartment, resting in a puddle of water, waiting until the sun went down. A dog bark or a rooster signified I'd survived another day.

The night filled with activity. Bazaars opened. People flooded the streets for food and to get things done. I spoke my pidgin Hindi with the locals, and I rarely saw another white face.

My abdominal scar was an angry red color. Only a tablespoonful of the healing ointment for my wound was left in the jar.

Hot daylight hours blended into one another. Time passed.

Late one afternoon, neighborhood children ran up to my door. "Ma'am Sahib live here. Ma'am Sahib here. HERE!" They yelled and pounded on the metal grate.

"What, what? I'm coming..." I opened the gate and saw a middle-aged man holding a registered letter.

In Hindi, he said, "Letter for you, Ms. Shanti?"

"Yes, yes." I wanted to jump up and down. "Thank you." I signed for the brown four-by-six envelope and thanked the youngsters.

Anne, my Vancouver friend, sent six hundred American dollars in a bank money order with a letter and a card: *Hope this is enough to buy an airline ticket. Look forward to seeing you soon. You can stay at my house for as long as you need to get on your feet.*

Her kindheartedness made my heart swell.

I told Bondi I'd be leaving and said goodbye to my Hindu friends. I stopped by Aalia's home. Her mother appeared sad to see me.

I mimed, "Mata-ji, are you okay?"

In Hindi, she replied, "You remind me of my daughter, and she is now gone. The pictures she sends, she looks miserable."

She showed me two pictures of Aalia. In one, she had a long dark coat over her sari, and her arms hung at her side. In the other, she stood next to her new husband, her face taut with hesitation.

Where was the joyful, high-spirited woman I had known just a few months ago? Maybe I could say the same for myself.

I handed the pictures back to her mother, wished her well, and left.

The air, cool and fresh, brushed my cheek. I got off the bus in Mussoorie's town center and admired the open market stalls. Vendors in their quaint hill station booths sold bright clothing, shawls, handcrafted sandals, jewelry, mementos, and Hindu tokens.

> **The breeze held a hint of iciness, luscious after the Varanasi inferno.**

I wanted to browse but decided to make the short hike up a precipitous hill to Maggie's place first. I hired a porter to bring my bags because I still felt weak.

Sweat poured into my eyes by the time we got to the top of the ridge. I checked the directions and found a path leading to a fine-looking home with a view of the snow ranges to the northeast and Siwalik ranges to the south. At over six thousand feet, the breeze held a hint of iciness, luscious after the Varanasi inferno.

Maggie ran out. "Woo-hoo! You made it!" She hugged me tight and introduced a group of friends gathered in the kitchen. "This is Traci. Sorry, you just missed Rachel. She left for England yesterday. This is Jake and Clarisse from next door."

"Hi. Nice to meet you. Beautiful place."

"We're just making a late lunch. Come, I'll show you the guest room."

On the far corner of the second floor, a mosquito net was carefully wrapped around a soft, downy bed. "Lovely, Mags. Thank you. Thank you."

The next day I told Maggie, "I want to go to town. There are some things I need." I purposefully left out that I planned to find out where Taj might be.

Maggie, a chess piece ahead, said, "Oh, Shanti, no need to look for Taj. He left for Haridwar. I saw him and his band at a tea shop several days back." She peered through her side bangs to catch my reaction.

Composed, I replied, "Oh yeah. I was going to see if he was here—you know, say goodbye, because I probably won't see him for a long time. No big deal. I'm going into town anyway." I wanted to find out for sure.

In town, I saw one of Taj's friends. "Hey, hi. Heard Taj and the band left for Haridwar."

"Yep. They left three days ago. Sorry you missed them. They are supposed to go back to Europe for the rest of summer and fall, I think." He shrugged. "See ya. Have a good time here."

On the way back, I sat on a stone bench and appreciated the view.

My heart dropped a little, knowing Taj was truly gone and not in Mussoorie. One minute I was trying to convince myself to stay in India and look for him, then chastising myself for such foolishness, determined to move on.

I found myself lost in memory.

India moments floated in and out: *Maharaja*'s eyes; Sonya sitting in Samadhi; Mudita's laugh; Swami Vibhodanada's Vedic teachings; Swami-ji pruning his roses; the Mount Everest trek; Baba-ji singing ragas; Goenka leading a meditation session; the beach in Goa; the Herat inn; Taj's sitar; Taj; days and weeks and months of new beginnings.

And then, in a moment of painful clarity, I knew it was over, just as if a door had swung open and I could see the outside for the first time, the full blue sky shocking my senses.

I would not go to Haridwar. What Taj and I had was not love, at least not the love I wanted or felt I deserved.

I don't know how long I sat on that rock. The sun dipped between the trees and formed long shadows until the sky turned into ribbons of pink and orange.

A lighthearted feeling swept through my body, and I made a promise to cherish and love my life.

42

England, Canada, and America
August 1979–March 1980

I'd only been gone for three years,
but it felt like three lifetimes.

The world seemed cold. Summer in England was not summer in India. People wore long pants and sweaters, not thin pajama pants and flip-flops.

I waited in a long line for a standby plane ticket to Seattle, Washington. Anne said she'd pick me up there and drive us back to Vancouver, British Columbia.

People appeared tense and agitated. A man nibbled at his fingernails. Another shuffled from foot to foot. A young woman crossed her arms and let out a loud sigh. A sense of urgency permeated the space around me. The man behind me tapped his foot impatiently.

The woman at the ticket booth did not look up at me. "Passport," was all she said.

The bathroom smelled of bleach, foreign and sterile. Nobody stopped to chat or barter. There were no open street vendors. No rickshaws. No smells of frying oil, shit, or mold. No blasting of Bollywood music. Everything looked closed in.

Seattle customs and immigration passed in a blurry fog. I went through the motions but was not truly present.

I kept waiting for my Indian friends: "Hey, Shanti, let's go for chai, yes?"

A swell of nausea engulfed me as if I were a tiny boat capsizing in the open ocean, immersed in the unknown.

I'd only been gone for three years, but it felt like three lifetimes.

> My goal was to buy a pair of shoes. I couldn't think past that.

I puzzled over strange smells such as antiseptic soap, laundry detergent, furniture polish, window cleaner, fast food. Overwhelmed by industrial noises, I plugged my ears. On the highway, cars and trucks whizzed past. It felt surreal.

Anne asked a thousand questions. I couldn't answer one.

At night, I lay awake in Anne's lovely home near the University of British Columbia, perplexed by the lights, blurred by my muddied feelings.

Home. Where was home?

Does a fish know it is in water?

Broke and bewildered about how to get on with my life, I found a job at a health food restaurant making salads for the lunch crowd. My goal was to buy a pair of shoes. I couldn't think past that.

When I made enough money to buy warmer clothing, I found another job at a pottery studio and rented a tiny apartment in West Vancouver. I worked five days a week and, on the weekends, hiked in the surrounding hills: Stanley Park, Capilano, Lighthouse, Whytecliff. I stayed in these places until the sky turned a bruised, inky color.

I bought a bicycle and rode everywhere. Vancouver was going through a growth spurt. Favorite hangouts, now too pricey and spotlessly clean, seemed out of reach. People talked about things to which I could not relate: *Star Wars*, Barry Manilow, *The Deer Hunter*, Margaret Thatcher, nuclear testing, The Police, *Midnight*

Express. It was comparable to trying on my best pair of jeans and realizing that they did not fit anymore...and were horribly outdated.

I made an appointment at the women's clinic and scheduled several subsequent visits. My reproductive system required laser surgery and a long cycle of antibiotics.

Remnants of an inner ear infection lingered. A fungus grew between my toes. Lice eggs remained in my hair and necessitated a series of treatments. Without the use of fluoride and dental hygiene, several cavities had flourished. A specialist remedied a few staph infection scars. *Giardia* hung around for months.

My life was centered on getting well. A nutritionist recommended vitamins. At the health food store, I bought organic foods: yoghurt, fruit, vegetables, nuts. I read cookbooks and exercised.

> My feelings opened and scabbed over similar to a lesion that would not heal.

I missed India terribly. And even though I had successfully reasoned that a relationship with Taj was not good for me, nor in my best interest, my heart had a hard time catching up.

I saw glimpses of him in the strangest of places: the smile of a stranger; the lead guitarist of a rock band at a Vancouver Festival; the gentle look in a child's eye; even a handsome gentleman who sat across from me at the library who had brown eyes and olive skin.

The difficulties of assimilation into my own culture mystified me, and I struggled with numerous unresolved issues: Taj, the abortion, *Maharaja* and Sonya, leaving India, my friends.

My feelings opened and scabbed over similar to a lesion that would not heal. I walked through my days numb, oblivious to the world, an actress portraying a happy woman. My cheeks felt thin and hollow. The nights were quieter than my yesterdays.

I discovered a meditation group in downtown Vancouver and found refuge in silent sittings. Books on Buddhism graced my nightstand. I talked to new friends, but they appeared more eager to give advice than listen.

I did not know how or where to ask for help and chose a veil of secrecy instead.

Winter came, and I longed for green, lush hills and sticky heat.

I did a Vipassana retreat on Gabriola Island. The teacher told me a meditation center in Barre, Massachusetts, had a job opening. I applied and got the post, packed everything I owned in my two canvas bags, and flew to Massachusetts.

I felt alone but not lonely—and although still confused by my feelings, realized I could decide for myself what I wanted or needed.

What was happiness? Where could it be found? Was it sitting still for three days? Was it climbing the tallest mountain? Was it perfecting yoga poses? Was it finding true love?

I had experienced the adventure of a lifetime: moments of joy, moments of sorrow, moments of pain. I thought about the abortion and played with the *mala* wrapped around the handles on one of my bags. I touched every single bead, pausing at each one to think about all that I had loved and lost.

> There is no past, no future, only this moment, this wonderful moment.

Could I forgive myself...my past... Taj?

I finally realized forgiveness was to free myself from memories, let go of the hurt, and move forward, not backward. Tears dripped down my cheeks and splashed onto my hands like little flash floods.

My heartbeat started to slow, and a fragile wildflower of love seeped into my canyon walls, tender as a newborn.

When I got off the bus in Worcester, Massachusetts, waiting for my ride to the facility, a slight breeze came over the hill and played with my hair, promising a new beginning. A bird flew overhead, and the light stretched and quilted. The air was still and quiet, my breath light, my thoughts flowing like a thin stream of water running through the sand.

A vision of the small village of Marpha in Nepal floated through my head: the golden sheaths of millet bending in the wind; the Tibetan monk, his gentle voice chanting an ancient prayer.

The image of him sitting cross-legged on his roof, motioning, "Come, come, sit for a moment." His face was turned upward. "Shanti, there is no past, no future, only this moment, this wonderful moment."

I picked up a dead thistle, thin and brittle with some wisps on top, and blew the down into the fresh air, watching them float and drift until the wind caught a few and lifted them up into the haze of the day.

Afterword

*I've learned how truly wonderful it is
to embrace the present, my heart free
and happy like a hundred Canadian geese
returning to their summer grounds.*

I stayed at the meditation center for almost two years.

During my time there, I had the privilege of studying with many world-renowned spiritual teachers whose support and guidance helped me emotionally, physically, and spiritually. It wasn't easy. It required a dedicated mindfulness practice and the courage to see things as they were and not as how I wished they could or should be.

After I left the center, I traveled to Australia to visit Mudita. We had a wonderful time together, laughing and talking late into the night, often reminiscing about our time in India.

When I returned from Australia, a letter from Taj, handwritten on an Indian aerogramme, was in a pile of accumulated mail at a post office box. In the letter, Taj professed his love and asked if I would, "please return to India. I miss you."

I agonized for weeks on what to do: go back or stay. It was tempting, but deep down, I knew I would never truly be happy with Taj.

So, I chose to stay and go back to school to make something of my life.

I've not been back to India, although I certainly believed I would when I first returned to North America. After I completed my undergraduate degree and then two graduate degrees, I kept telling myself, *maybe someday.*

But that someday has not yet come, and the truth is, the India of my youth no longer exists.

Taj dedicated his life to music and made several original recordings before he died in a car accident while on tour in Europe. We never saw each other again after that last encounter in India.

I found the love of my life in 1985 and settled into a wholesome lifestyle. My husband and my two beautiful children, now living their own lives, never cease to amaze me; our love for each other running so deep and wide it often takes my breath away.

It took the longest time for me to talk about my world travel experiences. I needed to wrap my head around many of the occurrences, and I felt uncomfortable talking about the abortion to anyone; the pain I went through, the humiliation. So, I wrote. I found comfort with other writers; I listened, read their stories, and realized we are more alike than different.

I view the lines on my face as a historical map of all that I've had the privilege to live through, equating the deeper lines to the intensity of each experience.

Now when I travel to foreign countries, I have my cell phone and anything I might need at my fingertips: how to find the nearest restaurant, historical facts, best hotels, museum listings, and so on. I laugh every time, recalling how difficult it was to maneuver the simplest of things in those travel years of my youth.

Today, the heat radiating through my chest and the swing in my step remind me how much I've learned and how truly wonderful it is to embrace the present, my heart free and happy like a hundred Canadian geese returning to their summer grounds.

Acknowledgments

I want to thank Judith Briles, for her wisdom and vision; Barb Wilson, editor, for her thoughtful edits on this book; Rebecca Finkel, for the book cover design and layout; to Peggie Ireland, editor, for her attentiveness on the final drafts; Natalie Kreider for the map illustrations; and to Janel Gion for the author photo.

I would also like to thank April Moore who read the first version of this book and encouraged me to never give up as well as the Northern Colorado Writers Association critique groups I worked with when I lived in Colorado.

A special thank you to my brother, Tony, who believed in this book even before I did. Here's to the memory of our mother, father, stepfather, grandmother, brother, sister, countless aunts and uncles and cousins and friends who have since passed.

Although it has been forty-five years since I lived in India and toured the Middle East, I wish to thank all the many amazing people I had the privilege of meeting while I toured those countries.

This book took me over a decade to bring to fruition and I could not have done so without the unconditional support from my family—my son, Peter, my daughter, Natalie, and especially to my husband, Rea, who read all the versions and drafts and kept telling me how much he "loved this book." I love you more.

About the Author

Bestselling author Sharon Kreider, a former mental health therapist turned writer, weaves the emotional and psychological fabric of the human condition into her writing and prose to help shed light on many relevant issues facing society today—its conflicts, its tragedies, and windows of hope.

Born and raised in a small northern Canadian town, she left home at an early age to travel the world, and eventually settled in Colorado where she penned her first book, *Sylvie*. The siren call of the Pacific Northwest lured her to a new writing home: several acres of wild, natural land to live a quieter life with her husband.

Sharon is currently working on her next book, titled **Maélie**, another women's fiction novel, about a young woman growing up during the Depression era in a remote northern Canadian village, bordering land reserved for the First Nation peoples, and the choices she has to make in order to survive.

Discover her blog at
www.SharonKreider.com

www.ingramcontent.com/pod-product-compliance
Lightning Source LLC
Chambersburg PA
CBHW021052080526
44587CB00010B/219